SAMUEL DANIEL

LIVERPOOL ENGLISH TEXTS AND STUDIES

GENERAL EDITOR: KENNETH MUIR

Titles in this Series

SAMUEL DANIEL,
one of the Groomes of his Majesties
most honorable Privie Chamber.

Published August 1.ˢᵗ 1798. by W. Richardson York-house N.ᵒ 31 Strand.

SAMUEL DANIEL

Samuel Daniel

A CRITICAL AND BIOGRAPHICAL STUDY BY

JOAN REES

Lecturer in English
in the University of Birmingham

LIVERPOOL UNIVERSITY PRESS
1964

PUBLISHED BY
LIVERPOOL UNIVERSITY PRESS
123 GROVE STREET LIVERPOOL 7

Printed in Great Britain by Hazell Watson & Viney Ltd
Aylesbury, Bucks

Acknowledgements

I am grateful to many people for help in many different ways and in particular to the present Borough Librarian at Taunton, Mr D. M. Laverick, and his predecessor, Mr K. D. Leach, for their kindness and generosity in answering questions and offering me the use of books and of the two portraits which are reproduced as a frontispiece and opposite page 168; also to Edinburgh University Library for permission to reproduce the facsimile opposite pages 158 and 159; and to Professors Douglas Bush and Mark Eccles for their courtesy in answering letters and giving me references which I might otherwise not have found.

I have acknowledged other specific debts at appropriate points in the text.

J. R.

Contents

List of Illustrations

Samuel Daniel   *Frontispiece*

This is the same picture of Daniel as that in the Cockson engraving made for
the 1609 edition of *The Civil Wars*. All known portraits of Daniel are basically
the same image, of which the Cockson engraving is the earliest and most
familiar version. The engraving reproduced here, and Plate 4, may be based
on Cockson or on the original portrait from which presumably all derive but
which has not been traced. The caption to this engraving describes Daniel,
incorrectly, as a Groom of the King's Privy Chamber whereas he was, in
fact, in the Queen's service. From an engraving in the possession of Taunton
Public Library.

Daniel's Memorial   *facing page* 82

The memorial bust and tablet in Beckington Church, Somerset, where Daniel
is buried. This was set up by the direction of Lady Anne Clifford in memory
of her former tutor, 'a long time after, when she was Countess Dowager of
Pembroke, Dorset, and Montgomery'. Photograph by Clifford L. Bennett,
Frome.

Facsimile of an addition in Daniel's hand to the Drummond MS of *Hymens Triumph*   *facing pages* 158–159

The song of the first chorus from *Hymens Triumph* in Daniel's autograph,
reproduced from the manuscript given by William Drummond to Edinburgh
University Library in 1627. The manuscript was probably a presentation
copy to Jean Drummond, the bride whose wedding *Hymens Triumph* was
written to celebrate, and it contains several additions in Daniel's own hand,
of which this song is one.

Samuel Daniel as an older man   *facing page* 168

The 'original picture' referred to in the caption cannot be traced but there is
evidently a common source for this, the Cockson engraving and Plate 1: the
outline of clothes, head and face is the same but in this version modifications
have been made to indicate an older man. This is the picture of Daniel
included in the big family triptych at Appleby and it has some special
interest since it was commissioned by Lady Anne Clifford and completed in
her lifetime so that it apparently satisfied her as a good likeness of her old
tutor as he was in later life. From an engraving in the possession of Taunton
Public Library.

Abbreviations used in the footnotes and bibliography

E.S. *English Studies* (Amsterdam)
J.E.G.P. *Journal of English and Germanic Philology*
M.L.N. *Modern Language Notes*
M.L.Q. *Modern Language Quarterly*
M.L.R. *Modern Language Review*
N.Q. *Notes and Queries*
P.Q. *Philological Quarterly*
R.E.S. *Review of English Studies*
S.P. *Studies in Philology*
S.Q. *Shakespeare Quarterly*
T.L.S. *Times Literary Supplement*

Introduction

Samuel Daniel, the contemporary of Shakespeare and Jonson, protégé of the famous Countess of Pembroke, a man important and respected in his day, at the centre of the activity of the greatest age in English literature, is one whom, nevertheless, critics, scholars and general readers have to a large extent neglected. The present study sets out to do what has not yet been done, to provide as complete an account as possible of his life and work, so that his importance in literary history and his qualities as a writer can be recognised and assessed on the basis of more information than has hitherto been available. How worthwhile such an undertaking is may be indicated by C. S. Lewis's description of Daniel as '. . . the most interesting man of letters whom that century produced in England'[1] and by Coleridge's praise of him in *Biographia Literaria*. He is, Coleridge writes,[2] 'one of the golden writers of our golden Elizabethan age, now most causelessly neglected', his diction bears no mark of time but remains always contemporary, and the sentiments which he expresses remain fresh after many readings because, 'though they are brought into the full daylight of every reader's comprehension; yet are they drawn up from depths which few in any age are privileged to visit, into which few in any age have courage or inclination to descend'.

C. S. Lewis's description of him provides an admirable introduction to a study of Daniel, for he was pre-eminently a man of letters. He combined a poet's gift of words and music with a scholar's care for culture and the things of the mind, and he had at all times a professional concern with the craft of writing and the status of literature. He wrote lyrics, narrative poetry, verse epistles, a verse treatise, tragedies, masques, pastorals, an historical poem, a prose history, and a critical essay: in some things he excelled, in none was he ever less than intelligent. As Coleridge recognised, respect for his mind and character and his accomplish-

1. C. S. Lewis, *English Literature in the Sixteenth Century* (Clarendon Press, 1954), p. 531.
2. S. T. Coleridge, *Biographia Literaria* (Everyman edn.), p. 253.

ment grows in proportion as one reads more of what he wrote and comes to know him better.

Yet in spite of all this and in spite also of some increased interest in him in recent years, Daniel's work and career have not yet received the attention they deserve, and the reasons why this should be so are not far to seek.

Daniel's voice, unlike those of some of his more famous contemporaries, does not reverberate through the centuries. His tone is quieter than theirs and what he has to say does not immediately grip the imagination. Though his choice and treatment of material reveal at every point an extensive, sympathetic and deeply thoughtful observation of human affairs in both their personal and political aspects, he does not seize attention by picturesque personality or by high astounding verse. His work as a whole needs the application of what Virginia Woolf called, in another connection, a 'cherishing and humanising process'.[3] Individual pieces, of course, stand firmly on their considerable and obvious merits: the sonnet sequence *Delia*, for example, ranks among the best of its time, the *Defence of Ryme* is one of the finest things in Elizabethan criticism and outstanding in any age, two or three of the verse epistles have been greatly and widely admired; but to savour and appreciate much of the rest it is necessary to make a voluntary offering of respect and to be willing, above all, to take things at Daniel's own speed without impatience at the lack of dramatic movement and exciting effects. The attempt to find the man in the poetry, to trace the impress of experience on what he wrote – all that is involved in the word 'humanising' – is also necessary, to warm and animate *The Civil Wars*, for example, or the neo-classical dramas.

Not everyone is prepared to love a writer in order that he may be found worthy to be loved, and the following study, besides bringing together widely scattered biographical material and providing the first comprehensive review of Daniel's work, aims also at justifying the patient process of cherishing and humanising by pointing to the rewards which Daniel offers to a sympathetic reader.

> I know I shalbe read, among the rest
> So long as men speake english . . .[4]

3. In her essay on Addison in *The Common Reader* First Series (Hogarth Press, 1945), p. 135.
4. *To the Reader* ll. 59–60 (*Poems and A Defence of Ryme*, ed. A. C. Sprague, Harvard University Press, 1930).

he wrote, and he was not deceived in thinking that his was a genuine contribution to his country's literature and that to disregard it would be a real impoverishment. He is an important figure in the literary history of his period, but to recognise this only is not enough: he is also a poet and a prose writer to be read with enjoyment and considerable satisfaction.

I have hoped to bring out his special qualities and strengths and to clear the way to a fuller understanding of him by telling as fully as possible the story of his life and by tracing the development of his mind and art through the chronological study of his works. I have made use of all reliable sources of biographical information but I have not thought it necessary to record the guesses or assumptions of unreliable records. Close study of the texts has on a number of occasions provided supplementary biographical evidence which previous biographers have overlooked and the story of his life appears, consequently, in a more complete form than it has ever done before. In discussing the individual works I have quoted fairly extensively, since copies of Daniel are not yet easy to come by and there is no danger that his lines will be over-familiar.

In the absence of a satisfactory complete edition, the following texts have been used:

Poems and A Defence of Ryme, ed. A. C. Sprague (Cambridge, Harvard University Press, 1930). This edition includes *To the Reader* (1607), *Delia*, *The Complaint of Rosamond*, *Musophilus*, *Epistles*, *A Defence of Ryme*, *Ulisses and the Syren*. It is referred to throughout as 'Sprague'.

The Civil Wars, ed. Laurence Michel (Yale University Press, 1958). Referred to as 'Michel'.

The Tragedy of Philotas, ed. Laurence Michel (Yale University Press, 1949). Referred to as 'Michel's *Philotas*'.

The Tragedie of Cleopatra nach dem Drucke von 1611, ed. M. Lederer (Louvain, 1911). Referred to as 'Lederer'.

For the rest of Daniel's works the five-volume edition by A. B. Grosart (1885–96) has been used. This is referred to as 'Grosart'.

Quotations have been checked against the 1623 text or appropriate early editions but modernised punctuation has been allowed to stand. All occasions on which an early reading not retained in the 1623 text is used are recorded in the footnotes. v is printed instead of u where modern use requires it, s for long ſ, w for vv, and j for i.

I

Early Years: The Translation
of Paulus Jovius

Daniel's early life is scantily documented as is only to be expected, but we know that he was born in Somerset, that he studied at Oxford, that he served for a time with Sir Edward Dymoke, the Queen's Champion, and that afterwards he entered the household of the famous Countess of Pembroke, 'Sydney's sister, Pembroke's mother', at Wilton. In addition to this, we catch some glimpses of the kind of young man he was in the pages of his translation of Paolo Giovio's *Dialogo dell'Imprese* and the documents printed with it. On the basis of the available information this chapter will trace his career as far as 1592, the date of the first authorised edition of his sonnet sequence, *Delia*, and the narrative poem, *Rosamond*.

Daniel was born in Somerset in the year 1562 or 1563. The exact place and date are unknown. Fuller says[1] that his birth-place was 'not far from Taunton' but no record has been discovered in that area. Wood says[2] that he was born 'at or near to' Philips Norton or Beckington. Which of these places he means is not quite clear but the parishes are within a few miles of each other, in North Somerset between Bath and Frome. There is no record of his birth at either place but the parish register of Philips Norton (nowadays Norton St. Philip) contains an entry for the marriage of one Thomas Daniel and Magdalyn Denman on June 30th, 1558, and there were Daniels there in the eighteenth century. A Thomas Daniel was baptised at Beckington in 1567 and an Editha Daniell in 1574. Daniel retired to Beckington towards the end of his life and the burial of a 'Mrs. Daniell' (she may perhaps have

1. T. Fuller, *History of the Worthies of England* (London, 1662), Somerset, p. 28.
2. A. à Wood, *Athenae Oxonienses* (London, 1815), ii, pp. 267-74.

been his wife) is recorded in the Parish Register on March 25th, 1619. He himself was buried there on October 4th, 1619. In the *Apology* for his play *Philotas*, Daniel says that he wrote the first three acts of his tragedy while he was 'living in the Country' and that he intended 'to have had it presented in Bath by certaine Gentlemens sonnes, as a private recreation for the Christmas'. At this time (late summer, 1600) Daniel was employed as tutor to Lady Anne Clifford and 'living in the Country' may refer either to his place of residence with the Cliffords or to a visit home to Somerset, but, in either case, the reference to Bath, taken together with the other evidence, suggests that the Beckington-Bath area is more likely than Taunton as the place of his birth.[3]

Wood says that he was born of a wealthy family, but if so, little of the wealth passed to him for he was continually in financial difficulties, sometimes acute. Fuller vouchsafes the equally unsubstantiated information that his father was a master of music. This seems to be the result of confusion with his brother, John, who took the degree of Bachelor of Music at Christ Church College, Oxford, on July 14th, 1604, published a collection of songs in 1606 and was a member of the royal company of 'the musicians for the lutes and voices' in December 1625.[4]

The first positive fact we have about Samuel Daniel himself is that in 1581 he was nineteen and that on November 17th of that year he matriculated at Magdalen Hall, Oxford.[5] If Wood is to be trusted (and he gets the date of matriculation wrong), Daniel stayed there about three years and had an excellent tutor: 'But his geny being more prone to easier and smoother studies, than in pecking and hewing at logic, he left the university without the honor of a degree . . .' Fortunately we have also some first-hand evidence about Daniel at this period, the fruit, probably, of the 'easier and smoother studies', in the shape of a translation of Bishop Paolo Giovio's *Dialogo dell'Imprese* (first published in Rome in 1555) with a preface, Daniel's own composition, 'contayning the Arte of composing them [i.e. imprese], with many

---

3. I have made fairly extensive enquiries in this area but so far without success.
4. Sir John Hawkins, *History of Music* (London, 1875), ii, p. 570. I have found the baptismal entry for a John Daniell at Wellow, near Bath. The date is November 6th, 1564. At Combe Hay in the same district the marriage of a John Daniel to Edith Bridges is recorded on September 6th, 1607. Unfortunately neither register throws any light on Samuel Daniel.
5. *Alumni Oxonienses*, 1500–1714, ed. J. Foster (Oxford, 1891).

other notable devices'.[6] The book was published in 1585 and Daniel is described on the title-page as 'late student in Oxenforde'. In addition to the translation and Daniel's preface, it also contains a letter signed by one N. W. and dated 'From Oxenforde the xx of November' (the book was entered on the Stationers' Register on November 26th, 1584). A number of personal touches in this letter make it a particularly valuable document, for through them we gain some genuine, if brief, acquaintance with the young Daniel.

N. W. is apparently a few years older than Daniel and he feels half protective towards his junior whom he seeks 'to animate and encourage'. His young friend shrinks from publicity but N. W. exhorts him to be more ambitious and not over-modest: 'I knowe not', N. W. begins, taking his function as mentor very seriously, 'whether to excuse your nature (good M. Daniel) or blame your shamefastnesse, which so much laboreth (as the utter enemy of your good name) to defraude your labors of their deserved Lawrell, & in despight of arte to deprive us of so delicate inventions, which the best wits in *Europe* have dedicated to posteritie: wherein surely, you injure your countreymen publikely, unnaturally your frends, and unadvisedly your selfe'.[7] His work is well able to face the judgement of competent critics, N. W. argues, and he turns to another scruple of his 'good frend': 'There is another point in your last letter, wherein you seeme to marre al that you have made, and dash that which so cunningly was devised. For sooth you blush to open another mans shop, and sell *Italian* wares as though you were a Bankerupte in philosophie, and could not afforde any pritie conceipt without borowing or embeselling.'[8] Characteristics of the later Daniel are plainly to be recognised in the objections which N. W. is trying to overcome for they speak of that diffidence and modesty, mingled with a consciousness of worth, which is revealed again and again in personal statements of later years. N. W. deals here with the second objection fairly briskly and in the course of his reply makes an interesting remark: 'You cannot forget', he writes to Daniel, 'that which *Nolanus* (that man of infinite titles among other phantasticall toyes) truely noted

6. Mario Praz makes frequent reference to Giovio's book in his *Studies in Seventeenth Century Imagery* (London, 1939). He notes (ii, pp. 69–70) that there were a number of editions between 1555 and 1574 but that Daniel's translation is from one of the earliest of these.

7. Grosart iv, p. 5. 8. Grosart iv, pp. 6–7.

by chaunce in our Schooles, that by the helpe of translations, al Sciences had their offspring . . .'[9] Here we have a momentary glimpse of Daniel listening to Giordano Bruno during his visit to Oxford in 1583 when, probably in a lecture, he used the striking phrase quoted by N. W., one which was remembered also by Florio, years later, in his address to the reader before his translation of Montaigne.[10]

Daniel was also worried, we learn from N. W., about 'the nakedness' of his style. It is shamefully deficient, he believes, because it is 'without the colours or florish of Rhetorique'. N. W. attempts to convince him that this bareness is a merit, and that even if it were not, the subject is so good it would scarcely matter. But Daniel was not quite persuaded, for the text offers interesting evidence of a straining after effects which were evidently always uncharacteristic and which contrast sharply with his later mastery of strong, supple, unaffected prose. Here is Daniel, in his early twenties, excusing himself for this very sparsity of colour and flourish and drawing heavily, in the process, on Euphuistic figures and devices. He relies, he says, on the wisdom of his readers: 'who had rather gather a pleasant flower springing amongst the sharpe thornes, for the sweet savour, then a gay colored weede for all the fayre semblance: esteeming the value of the precious treasure not by the outward shewe, but the inward substance, sith often we finde by triall *meliora latere*, and faire shewes to prove often fond shadowes. The tree *Caliestephenon* in Palestine, hath a corrupt barke, but a pure body: And well may a gallant blossome fit the humour of a delicate eye, when the gaynfull fruite shall satisfie the savour of a discreet taste. But the Diamant hath ingendred a naturall forme, so that it neede no artificiall frame, a gay glosse may better beseeme a course Kersey, then a fine Skarlet.'[11]

The dedication is similarly highly wrought and stands alone in Daniel's work for its devious elaboration.

Having disposed of Daniel's hesitations, N. W. plunges with obvious delight into an orgy of references, definitions and descriptions, from which he emerges at last with a final plea to his friend to publish. 'Therefore now to conclude', he writes, 'seeing

9. Grosart iv, p. 7.

10. The reference to Bruno was pointed out by Frances A. Yates in *John Florio* (Cambridge University Press, 1934), pp. 88-9.   11. Grosart iv, p. 15.

your argument is plausible, the arte a noveltie, your first fruites ripe, what reason is there, why you should privately bestowe them of [sic] some one gentleman . . .'[12] The reference here is to Sir Edward Dymoke, the Queen's Champion, to whom the printed book is dedicated, a young man five years older than Daniel, who travelled abroad a great deal and had a special interest in Italy. He had probably been to Rome before 1584,[13] and it was he who had urged Daniel to compile his book of emblems. Dymoke was thus Daniel's first patron, and the association, however it began, lasted over a number of years.

Daniel at this time was himself a good Italian scholar. In the original part of the book he names Petrarch, 'Devine Ariosto', Dante and Bembo, and he had read copiously in the Italian authorities on imprese.[14] It is very likely that Daniel had learnt his Italian from John Florio who was teaching Italian at Oxford from 1580, or a little earlier, until 1583. Daniel was certainly on friendly terms with Florio in 1582[15] and sometime before 1585 (when a child of the marriage was baptised) Florio married Daniel's sister.[16] Her name may have been Rose and she *may* have been the Rosa-linde of Spenser's *Shepheardes Calender*. Perhaps Florio helped Daniel to collect material for the original part of his work since all the examples in his own collection of devices are Italian and it is not easy to find the sources. It is unlikely that Daniel had gathered them himself on the spot for, if he had been to Italy by this early date, there would surely be some reference to the visit in the dedication or N. W.'s letter or the text itself, and in the year following publication, Daniel was describing himself as 'a raw traveler' in a context which suggests that he was then on his first visit abroad.

12. Grosart iv, p. 13.

13. See Mark Eccles, 'Samuel Daniel in France and Italy', *S.P.*, xxxiv, 1937, pp. 148–67.

14. See G. R. Redgrave, 'Daniel and the Emblem Literature', *Transactions of the Bibliographical Society*, xi, 1909–11, pp. 39–58. Giovio's book had been translated into French in 1561 but there is no evidence that Daniel based his translation on the French version rather than the Italian original.

15. See H. Sellers, 'Samuel Daniel: Additions to the Text', *M.L.R.*, xi, 1916, pp. 28–32. Sellers prints from a manuscript dated 1582 of Florio's *Giardino di recreatione* a tetrastichon by Daniel in commendation of Florio.

16. Wood says that Florio married Daniel's sister and the statement has been doubted. No record of the marriage has been found but on the whole it seems more likely than not that Wood was right. See Yates, *op cit.*, pp. 49–50 and p. 54, and Longworth Chambrun, *Giovanni Florio* (Paris, 1921), pp. 28–32.

Daniel concludes his address to the reader with a promise of more to follow on the same subject and he has evidently not exhausted either his knowledge or his enthusiasm. 'There is no doubt that interest in emblems was widespread in the 1580's,' writes Rosemary Freeman in her study of *English Emblem Books*, 'and even though the direct literary expressions of it were still few the taste was well established in other fields. A sense of the emblematic was so much a part of the disposition of the age that it asserted itself on every side.'[17] Daniel's, in fact, was the first English emblem book, and in choosing to translate Paulus Jovius he was introducing English readers to a typical example of the many collections and expositions of devices which were common in France and Italy in the sixteenth century. Daniel does not scruple in his preface 'To the friendly Reader' to correct his author on some points and he speaks with the authority of one who knows his subject very well. If we are not disappointed by his failure to pursue it further, we must nevertheless be grateful for *Paulus Jovius* and what it enables us to see of Daniel as a young man. N. W.'s letter offers an early view of traits familiar in the later Daniel, and we catch sight, also, of some things which we might less have expected, for *Paulus Jovius* reveals a young man fully sharing in the age's taste for visual excitement. Emblems were taken seriously in their day as notable contributions to culture and learning and Daniel's treatment of them is by no means lacking in seriousness; but there is, besides, a truly Elizabethan love for the show of things to be found in, for example, his considerable satisfaction with the story of the gentleman who 'having ill successe in his amorous service, and spending his time in dolor and griefe' dressed himself in three degrees of black when he heard of the death of a friend's wife: 'which mourning habite was no soner seene of such as knewe the historie of his love, but they perceived what it signified, as well as if he himselfe had declared it: and greatly did they commend the invention. For with the uppermost blacke he represented sorowe for the dead: with that underneath he mourned for his freend, but his owne blacke appeared more and signified some greater griefe, and that of his frend seemed lesse, and represented lesse in effect. For in his opinion lesse griefe was it to bee deprived of a wife, sith she is called to the heavens, then to stand secluded from the favour of a

17. Rosemary Freeman, *English Emblem Books* (London, 1948), pp. 48-9.

proude disdainefull dame, whilst an other enjoyes the fruite of his deserved affections.'[18] The passage presents us with a perhaps unexpected but by no means altogether displeasing glimpse into the youthful preoccupations of a future ethical verse-writer and prose historian.

The translation of *Paulus Jovius* may possibly have brought Daniel to the notice of the Earl of Pembroke, husband of Sidney's famous sister, Mary, for the Earl was interested in heraldry and related subjects, but Daniel's connection with the Pembrokes did not begin at once, as it has often been assumed to have done. Two letters written by Daniel early in 1586 and sent by him from Paris to Sir Francis Walsingham, make it clear that he left England sometime towards the end of 1585 and that he had employment for a few months between March and August 1586 under the English ambassador in Paris, Sir Edward Stafford.[19] The letters to Walsingham are reports, not very accurate, on current affairs in Paris, offered in the hope of persuading Walsingham to employ him further. '. . . my intent is to Studie', writes the young Daniel, 'to thend to render my self fit for the service of my countrie; to whom I am bounde by nature, and of yor Honor, to whom I am vowed by inclination to be always at yor Honors co'maund, yf my slender abillitie might be thought worthy the least place about yor Honor after I have heare spent some time in Paris, the Theater of *Europe* . . .' The letters show an ingenuous pride and pleasure in being at the hub of affairs, though Daniel is far from having attained the happy combination of brevity and clearness for which Fuller, justly, praised his latest study of men and nations, the prose *History*. Their principal interest is their revelation of a young man who is eager to participate in the management of things – not by any means a scholarly recluse willing to retire from the pressures of active life. They add some slight substantiation to Wood's account of Daniel's Oxford career, for they are marked more by enthusiasm than by care in the collecting and presenting of information. Nevertheless, Daniel's interest in the study of history as a preparation for judging rightly of the present may first have been stirred during these months in Paris, for, as he notes in the dedication of the early editions of the prose *History*, to Robert Carr, it was 'in forraine countries' especially that he

18. Grosart iv, pp. 20–1.
19. See Eccles, op. cit., from which the letters are quoted.

picked up most of his ideas about the writing of history.[20] However this may be, Daniel's ambitions in 1586 clearly lay in the direction of making history rather than writing it: the career he seeks is in government service, and not, so far as appears, in literature.

Daniel came back to England in early September 1586, carrying despatches from Stafford to Walsingham which he delivered at Windsor Castle and for which he was rewarded.

Sometime after this first excursion abroad and before 1592, when, among his *Delia* sonnets, he included a poem written in Italy,[21] Daniel went abroad again, and this time with the Italophile, Dymoke, the patron and instigator of the translation of *Paulus Jovius*. Daniel refers to this visit in a sonnet written in 1602,[22] when a translation of Guarini's *Pastor Fido* was published and dedicated to Dymoke, and he recalls that he and Dymoke met Guarini in person when they were together in Italy. The most likely date for the journey during which the meeting or meetings took place is 1590 or 1591. Guarini was then living in Padua, or in the summer of 1591, at his villa between Padua and Venice,[23] and possibly Daniel was there when, in 1591, his first verse was published, twenty-eight of his sonnets included, without his permission, in a pirated edition by Thomas Newman of Sidney's *Astrophel and Stella*.

Certainly he was back in England early in 1592, still with Dymoke, and attached to his household in Lincoln: a remarkable series of events produces the scrap of evidence which establishes this.[24] It appears that Sir Edward Dymoke and his brother were at daggers drawn with their uncle, the Earl of Lincoln, and in 1596 Lord Lincoln brought an action against Sir Edward in the Court of Queen's Bench, in respect of events which had taken place four years previously, i.e. 1592. The charge was that on March 1st, 1592, Dymoke had written a letter to Lincoln's son saying in effect that the Earl's villainies deserved the punishment of death. In his defence in Court, Dymoke said that on February 20th, 1592, he had made a move towards reconciliation with his uncle but the Earl had replied only by a personal assault upon him. He then

20. Grosart iv, p. 75. 21. Sprague, no. 44.
22. Grosart i, p. 280. 23. Eccles, op. cit.
24. They are described by Leslie Hotson in 'Marigold of the Poets', *Essays by Divers hands being the Transactions of the Royal Society of Literature of the U.K.*, n.s. XVII, 1938, pp. 47–68.

wrote the letter, but his friends dissuaded him from sending it and he gave it to 'his servant Samuel Daniel' to be burnt. Daniel, however, instead of burning it, put it into a hole in the wall of Dymoke's house in Lincoln. Four years later Dymoke sold this house to his uncle and in the course of some alterations the wall was pulled down and the letter discovered among the stones.

The fact that Daniel was at Lincoln in 1592 helps to establish another date in his career, for although it cannot be claimed that the revelations of the lawsuit prove that he was in the service of Sir Edward Dymoke continuously from 1585 to 1592, they strongly suggest that he was, and if so the date of his entering the Pembroke household must be pushed forward from 1585, the commonly accepted date, as far as 1592. That this is in fact the right date is confirmed by the evidence of Daniel's early dedications to the Countess of Pembroke.

The first of these is prefaced to the earliest authorised edition of *Delia*, Daniel's sonnet sequence. *Delia* was entered on the Stationers' Register on February 4th, 1592, and in the prose dedication to the Countess of Pembroke Daniel writes: 'I desire onely to bee graced by the countenance of your protection . . . And if my lines heereafter better laboured, shall purchase grace in the world, they must remaine the monuments of your honourable favour, and recorde the zealous duetie of mee, who am vowed to your honour in all observancy for ever.'[25] This sounds very much as though the patron-poet relationship between Lady Pembroke and Daniel was a new one. The fact that his name has been coupled with Sidney's in Newman's pirated edition serves as an introduction which Daniel makes use of in asking for the Countess's 'protection'. If he writes better and more successfully in future, it will be because of her 'honourable favour', but the poetry he has already written, it appears, owes nothing to her. The sonnet which replaced the prose dedication in the third edition of *Delia* in 1594[26] is, by contrast, altogether different in tone. It suggests closer and more familiar acquaintance, and Daniel does not now merely hope for the Countess's protection, but he confidently enjoys it. By right of her patronage and her encouragement of him, the early poems become retrospectively hers – 'Vouchsafe *now* to accept them as thine owne' – and the glory of future achievement will likewise be laid at her feet.

25. Sprague, p. 9.   26. Ibid., pp. 170–1.

A comparison of these dedications makes a strong prima facie case for believing that Daniel did not come under the Countess of Pembroke's patronage until after the publication of some of the *Delia* sonnets in Newman's edition of 1591, at the earliest. Some remarks in the *Defence of Ryme* (1603) seem to offer conflicting evidence, but on examination it is plain that they do not necessarily do so. The *Defence* is dedicated to the Countess of Pembroke's elder son, William Herbert, and at the beginning of it, addressing the young man, Daniel writes of his first steps in poetry: 'Having beene first incourag'd or fram'd thereunto by your most Worthy and Honourable Mother, receiving the first notion for the formall ordering of those compositions at *Wilton*, which I must ever acknowledge to have beene my best Schoole, and thereof alwayes am to hold a feeling and gratefull Memory.'[27] This has usually been taken to indicate that Daniel went to Wilton soon after leaving Oxford, but the phrasing which suggests this ('first incourag'd . . .', 'the first notion . . .', 'my best Schoole') is probably misleading, for although Daniel had written *Delia* and *Rosamond* before 1592, he still regarded himself, two years later, as a novice in poetry. This is made quite clear by the dedication to the Countess of Pembroke of the verse-drama *Cleopatra* which was first published with the 1594 edition of *Delia*.

> Loe heere the worke the which she did impose,
> Who onely doth predominate my Muse,[28]

it begins, and it goes on to tell how the Countess inspired him with strength and confidence to become more ambitious and 'To sing of State, and tragicke notes to frame'. He has been – and the inference is that he refers to a time before he came under her influence – 'contented with an humble song' and would never have aspired beyond his love plaints had not Lady Pembroke urged him to attempt a 'higher straine'; but now he is fully enrolled in the lists of those who are sworn to emulate and even to 'out-go' the culture of the south. In the light of this there is nothing strained in supposing that the *Defence of Ryme* passage refers, not to the first poetry Daniel ever wrote, but to the time, after the publication of *Delia* and *Rosamond* in 1592, when it

27. Ibid., p. 129.
28. Grosart iii, p. 23, prints the 1623 text. His version of the lines first appeared in 1601.

seemed to him that he began his poetic career proper under the tutelage of the Countess of Pembroke.

Thus there is no evidence of any connection before 1591, but undoubtedly between 1592 and 1594 Daniel came deeply under the influence of the Pembroke circle including Spenser, 'our Spenser', as he calls him in the dedication of *Cleopatra*. *Colin Clouts Come Home Again* is eloquent in praise of the Countess of Pembroke and contains also a well-known comment on Daniel, which must have been written after the publication of *Delia* (1591–2) and before that of *Cleopatra*:

> ... there is a new shepheard late up sprong,
> The which doth all afore him far surpasse;
> Appearing well in that well tuned song,
> Which late he sung unto a scornful lasse.
> Yet doth his trembling Muse but lowly flie,
> As daring not too rashly mount on hight,
> And doth her tender plumes as yet but trie
> In loves soft laies and looser thoughts delight.
> Then rouze thy feathers quickly, Daniell,
> And to what course thou please they selfe advance:
> But most, me seemes, thy accent will excell
> In tragick plaints and passionate mischance.

The gist of the admonitions offered by Spenser and Lady Pembroke to their new protégé is evidently the same: that Daniel should deepen his notes and assume greater literary responsibility. The encouragement and exhortation of these powerful voices, together with the cultural and intellectual interests of Wilton, helped him to discover his métier as poet and man of letters. From then on his course is established and his literary character begins to set. It is no wonder that he speaks of Wilton as his 'best Schoole', even if he did not come to it till he was thirty.

The probabilities point then to Daniel's association with the Pembroke family beginning in 1591–2 following the illicit publication of some of his sonnets alongside Sidney's. Once at Wilton he may have assisted with the education of the young William Herbert, for Hugh Sanford, who had been the boy's tutor since about 1586,[29] also acted as the Earl of Pembroke's secretary and

29. Ashmole MSS. 174 f. 149. Quoted Yates, p. 196.

probably delegated some of his tutoring duties to Daniel.[30] Certainly during the next few years the patron-poet relationship between Daniel and the Countess of Pembroke ripened on his side into a whole-hearted admiration and discipleship, of which *Cleopatra*, written at her wish as a companion-piece to her translation of Garnier's *Marc-Antoine*, was the first and most obvious evidence.[31]

30. Sanford was 'a good scholar and poet' (see J. Aubrey, *Brief Lives*, ed. A. Clark, Oxford, 1898, i, p. 311). He helped the Countess of Pembroke with the 1593 edition of the *Arcadia* and Daniel, who described him as 'my kinde friend and countriman', discussed poetry with him. (See *Defence of Ryme*, Sprague, p. 156).

31. A poem *To the Angell Spirit of the most excellent, Sir Phillip Sidney* is printed in the posthumous edition of Daniel's poems in 1623 but it is plainly not his. It refers to the translation of the Psalms undertaken by Sidney and his sister, the Countess of Pembroke, and was evidently written by her after his death. The manuscript, perhaps a copy made by Daniel during his Wilton years, was presumably among his papers and was taken to be his work though in tone and substance it is quite inappropriate to him and the style is too rough and unskilful to be his.

In the edition of *The Poems of Sir Philip Sidney* (Clarendon Press, 1962) which has appeared since this note was written, W. A. Ringler confirms the Countess of Pembroke's authorship of this poem (p. 551) and offers the same explanation of its appearance among Daniel's works.

II

'Delia' and 'Rosamond'

Precise information is lacking about Daniel's activities from 1586 to 1592, between the ages, that is, of twenty-four and thirty, and this is probably the most serious gap in his biography for they are likely to have been important years with a determining influence on his future. His comment in the prose *History* that he had picked up most of his ideas about the writing of history in 'forraine countries' seems to point to a considerable period of travel abroad at some time and Daniel may have gone to Italy with Dymoke or on his business on more than the one occasion which is referred to in the 1602 sonnet. Apart from this and the glimpse of the turbulent household in Lincoln, there appears to be no clue to his activities, unless his earliest published poetry, the sonnet sequence *Delia* and the narrative poem *Rosamond*, embodies some genuine autobiographical information.

Delia is Daniel's most completely perfect achievement, and although the first dedication to the Countess of Pembroke asserts quite categorically that the poems derive at least some of their impulse from experience,[1] their lyrical beauty does not invite analysis in terms of biography. The beauty and resource of Petrarchan rhetoric are exploited in these sonnets by a poet with an exquisite sense of poetic decorum and a fine ear for the subtleties of assonance and alliteration. The music is lovely and unfailing, but *Delia* is not a dramatic sequence like *Astrophel and Stella* and personal tensions, if there ever were any, seem to have dissolved away in melody and lucid imagery. As far as the implied situation of an unfulfilled love is concerned, for the most part Bembo's words and Bembo's attitudes seem appropriate: *fingo*

1. '... although I rather desired to keep in the private passions of my youth, from the multitude, as things utterd to my selfe, and consecrated to silence: yet ... I was betraide by the indiscretion of a greedie Printer, and had some of my secrets bewraide to the world ...' Sprague, p. 9.

SAMUEL DANIEL

per aver da rimare. Even so, there are one or two points at which
personal experience seems to leave its impress on the poems and,
though the sonnets in which this happens are not the best, they
are worth examining because they offer a view of Daniel such as
we do not have elsewhere and shed a gleam of light on his
experiences in the obscure years before 1592. The sonnets concerned are: number 48; the group of four which followed number
26 in the second edition of 1592; and the two poems connected
with Italy, number 44 and '*At the Authors going into Italie*' which
was first published in 1594.

Sonnet 48 provides one small piece of factual information for it
refers to Delia's home being near the Avon. The Wiltshire Avon
runs through Bath and the surrounding country where Daniel's
own home probably was and the detail gives Delia some authen-
ticity and also suggests an explanation of one of Daniel's revisions.
In 1592 he describes the river as 'rich in fame, though poore in
waters' but in 1594 he changes this to 'poore in fame and poore in
waters': this is a very natural change supposing that the poems
were written in the first place for a local girl, for the river would
be famous enough in north Somerset, but the original phrasing
was obviously extravagant when the poems were published and
began to circulate more widely.

A richer source of biographical information seems to be offered
by the four sonnets which follow number 26 in the second edition
of 1592.[2] (This edition contains 54 sonnets in all.). Number 26
itself is an account of how the poet has appealed finally to the
lady's love and kindness and she has cruelly rejected him although
he has served her well and faithfully for a number of years (three
in 1592, five in 1601 and subsequently, an alteration of no
recognisable significance). He is rejected where most he expected
to find favour, and against ladies, as against tyrants, there is no
appeal. After this follows the sonnet beginning:

> Still in the trace of my tormented thought,
> My ceaselesse cares must martch on to my death:
> Thy least regarde too deerely have I bought,
> Who to my comfort never deign'st a breath.

2. Sprague, pp. 180–1. Sprague prints from the first 1592 edition of *Delia* and
gives variants and poems added in later editions at the end of the volume. This
accounts for the awkwardness of some of the references.

14

The tone is stronger and bitterer than in the preceding sonnet and
the sestet too opens strongly:

> Injurious *Delia*, yet Ile love thee still,
> Whilst that I breath in sorrow of my smart:

and the idea is introduced that he will take blame upon himself in
order to excuse her to the world. Following this comes a not
particularly distinguished poem on the familiar theme that her
eyes are like stars, but this is immediately followed by the startling,
even grim, poem headed 'To M. P.' This sonnet is not necessarily
about a love situation at all and if it includes frustration in love
that would seem to be only one element in a whole bitter and
gloomy state. Like the ermine, itself pure but surrounded by
'filth and lothsome mud', which cannot break free and improve
her lot, so the poet is hemmed in by 'a hatefull want'. Neither
heaven nor earth offers him any help and he himself is wretched
and powerless to remedy this 'want' and by so doing release
himself from the misery which oppresses him; so there is nothing
for him to do but grieve and even that he cannot do freely and
openly for what he feels must not be known to others. His life is
dark so long as these 'wants' last.

This is a far cry from:

> Oft doe I muse whether my *Delia's* eyes
> Are eyes, or els two faire bright starres that shine

but the mood is very similar to:

> Still in the trace of my tormented thought,
> My ceaselesse cares must martch on to my death.

It is tempting to construct a situation on the evidence of these
two sonnets: that he has loved and been disdainfully rejected: the
world may justly accuse her of a hard heart but he will shield her
by belittling his own merits. She has disdained him because he has
neither rank nor wealth – the 'hatefull want' – and these sordid
considerations offend the purity and beauty of his love. He has
not even a sufficiently independent status to be able to grieve
openly the crushing of his ambitions but he must conceal his
feelings, and the anguish of frustrated love blends with a sense of

social injustice and a bitter awareness of his powerlessness to help himself either in love or in society.

The M. P. to whom the 'ermine' sonnet is addressed has sometimes been identified with the Countess of Pembroke – Mary Pembroke – herself but there is another and much more likely candidate for the dedication of this poem. The same initials, M. P., occur in N. W.'s epistle prefaced to *Paulus Jovius* and the person whom they designate is evidently a mutual acquaintance of Daniel and N. W.[3] 'A frend of mine', writes N. W., 'whom you know, M. P. climing for an *Egles* nest, but defeated by the *mallalent* of fortune, limned in his studie a *Pine* tree striken with lightning, carying this mot, *Il mio sperar*, which was borowed also from Petrarch. *Allor che fulminato e morto giaacque il mio sperar che tropp'-alto mintana.*' Whatever form the 'egles nest' may have taken for him, it looks as though the M. P. who was N. W.'s friend had been in much the same situation as that described by Daniel in '*To M. P.*' and '*Still in the trace of my tormented thought*'. He had aspired high and his hopes had been blasted. Daniel had known this M. P., had perhaps been in his study and seen his emblem, and To M. P. at the top of his poem may simply be a recognition of the similarity of their fate. The word 'pine', which N. W. emphasises, occurs three times in the sonnet, twice in one line, and the play on the word would be full of significance to anyone acquainted with M. P.'s emblem. The evidence suggests fairly strongly that this poem is a confidence addressed to someone who will sympathise because he has personal knowledge of the same kind of situation and someone, moreover, who will be able to fill in from his own experience the details which are not explicitly stated but only hinted.[4]

3. Grosart pointed out N. W.'s reference to M.P. (i, p. xviii) but did not identify him. He does identify N. W. (v, p. 326), I think wrongly. The following quotation is in Grosart iv, p. 13.

4. A search of the Oxford matriculation registers reveals that the N. W. most likely to have been Daniel's friend is one Nathaniel Webbe who entered Magdalen College on December 20th, 1577, at the age of eighteen, was a demy from 1577–80, and took his B.A. from Magdalen Hall on May 2nd, 1583. He had contacts, consequently, with both the Hall and the College. Up at Magdalen College at the same time as Webbe was Robert Parker, who was a chorister in 1575, proceeded B.A. November 1582 and M.A. 1587, and who was a fellow from 1585–93. Robert Parker held from 1591 a number of livings in Wiltshire, including that of Wilton, he was a protégé of the Earl of Pembroke and a friend of Hugh Sanford, the Earl's secretary, young William Herbert's tutor, and Daniel's friend. In 1607 because of his uncompromising Puritan views Parker was forced to leave the country and in

Following the sonnet to M. P. comes the one beginning:

> My cares draw on mine everlasting night,
> In horrors sable clowdes sets my lives sunne:
> My lives sweet sunne, my deerest comforts light,
> Will rise no more to me, whose day is dunne.

He is about to die, he says, and in the other world:

> If any aske me why so soone I came,
> Ile hide her sinne, and say it was my lot,
> In life and death Ile tender her good name,
> My life nor death shall never be her blot.
> Although this world may seeme her deede to blame:
> Th' *Elisean* ghosts shall never know the same.

This must mean that in some way she has become quite unattainable to him beyond any possibility of hope. Perhaps she has married someone else. However she has rejected him, her conduct is liable to censure by the world and he will shield her as well as he can. (This is the idea of the sestet of *'Still in the trace of my tormented thought'*.)

The history of the publication of these four sonnets is interesting. *'Still in the trace of my tormented thought'* appears in all editions from 1592 onwards but in and after 1601 with some major alterations. The second line:

> My ceaselesse cares must martch on to my death

is modified to:

> My ceaselesse cares continually run on

1611 he completed and published in Amsterdam a theological treatise by his friend Sanford which Sanford had left uncompleted at his death in 1607. This was *De Descensu Domini Nostri Jesu Christi ad Inferos* and in the introductory epistle 'Candido Lectori' Parker speaks of his admiration for the Herberts, father and son, and his association with the family. Parker's connections with Magdalen and with Wiltshire and the Pembrokes suggest that M. P. stands for M. Parker, M. being a common Elizabethan abbreviation for Master. The case for the identification is strengthened by a note in Bloxam's *Register of the members of Magdalen College, Oxford*, under the date May 30th, 1591: 'Concessa est licentia Magistro Parker ad contemplationem literarum nobilissimi herois, Comitis Pembruchiae, ut absit a Collegio usque ad Festum Nativitatis Christi.' Thus Daniel could have met Parker through Nathaniel Webbe in their college days and seen the pine emblem in his study. In 1591 the pirated edition of Sidney's and Daniel's sonnets was published and brought Daniel into contact with the Wilton household at exactly the time when Parker was working in the library there. His memory of Parker's emblem was revived and he connected it with his own situation in 1591 and wrote the poem to unburden his feelings to M. P., an old acquaintance who was particularly qualified to understand it.

and the next seven lines are rewritten altogether to read:

> Seeking in vaine what I have ever sought,
> One in my love, and her hard hart still one.
> I who did never joy in other Sun,
> And have no stars but those, that must fulfill
> The worke of rigor, fatally begun
> Upon this hart, whom cruelty will kill.

This compares with the original version:

> Thy least regarde too deerely have I bought,
> Who to my comfort never deign'st a breath.
> Who should'st thou stop thine eares now to my cryes,
> Whose eyes were open ready to oppresse me?
> Why shutt'st thou not the cause whence all did rise,
> Or heare me now, and seeke how to redresse me.

It is obvious that the revision provides a very much watered down version of the original. The later text is smoother and more graceful, but it is entirely conventional and without bite. The original version is much more dramatic, much more immediate, as, for example, in the forceful 'now' of line 5 and the future tense in line 9 – 'Injurious *Delia*, yet Ile love thee still' which reinforces the impression of something just happened and a course for the future being decided at the moment of writing. In 1601 and after, 'Ile love' becomes 'I love' which is much calmer, all passionate reaction being spent. Daniel's ear became too fine for 'should'st' and 'shutt'st' and he came to disapprove of rhymes like 'oppresse me' and 'redresse me', but it is arguable that such roughnesses were permissible in the context of the original lines. The force of 'injurious *Delia*' in line 9 is very much weakened by the alteration of the preceding six lines and line 10 is also altered to substitute a nerveless expression for a strong one. Originally it reads:

'Whilst that I breath in sorrow of my smart' but from 1601 onwards it becomes:

'And will whilst I shall draw this breath of mine.'
The companion phrase in line 11 is consequently altered from 'for to excuse thy hart' to 't'excuse that hart of thine' which is weak in every way. Line 13 is also altered, from: 'Then judge who sinnes the greater of us twaine' to 'See then who sinnes the greater of us twaine', a less striking line.

The unavoidable conclusion is that Daniel deliberately went

through this sonnet, sometime after 1598, and systematically altered its character: from a passionate outburst which seems to have one particular person and a recent incident in mind to a conventional and unexciting 'cruel fair' sonnet.

Some minor variants appear in later editions of the second of this group of sonnets, the eyes-stars one, but they do not affect the mood or the substance. Neither the third sonnet (*To M. P.*) nor the fourth '*My cares draw on mine everlasting night*' appears again, however, after 1592. It may be relevant that 'I say no more, I feare I saide too much', is the last line of the whole sequence as Daniel brings *Delia* to a close on a note of hopelessness and with a shade of retrospective bitterness.

This study of the material, the manner and the fate of '*Still in the trace of my tormented thought*', *To M. P.*, and '*My cares draw on mine everlasting night*' suggests the strong probability of some acute crisis in Daniel's experience which it became prudent to allow to drop out of sight. References to a saddening and chastening experience occur elsewhere in Daniel's poetry: in the dedication of *A Letter from Octavia to Marcus Antonius*[5] (1599) to the Countess of Cumberland, Daniel writes that he has

> ... adventur'd to bestow
> Words upon griefe, as my griefes comprehend;
> And made this great afflicted Lady show,
> Out of my feelings, what she might have pend

and in the verse epistle to the Countess of Bedford (1603) he writes:

> How oft are we constrained to appeare
> With other countenance then that we owe,
> And be our selves farre off, when we are neere!
> How oft are we forc't on a cloudie hart
> To set a shining face, and make it cleere ...

These are general comments, but they are significant when taken in conjunction with the rest. All in all, there seems to be some grounds for believing that the tone of lofty stoicism which pervades the epistle to the Countess of Bedford and also that to the Countess of Cumberland may have been attained by Daniel not quite easily by right of that quiet and placid nature which is commonly ascribed to him, but only after some passionate and

5. Grosart i, p. 117.

searing experience of his youth of which the traces are to be found in *Delia*.

Some detail may be added to this story by a comparison of the two poems specially connected with Italy. Sonnet 44 appeared first in 1592, and in 1594, 1595 and 1598 was given the heading 'This Sonnet was made at the Authors beeing in Italie'. In 1594 there appeared for the first time a preceding sonnet labelled in 1594, 1595 and 1598 'At the Authors going into Italie'. If both poems refer to Daniel's visit to Italy with Dymoke in 1590–1, it should presumably have been possible for Daniel to publish them at the same time, in 1592. What is more surprising than the separate publication, however, is the great difference in tone between the two poems. *Being in Italie* is a pleasant, relaxed and hopeful poem but whereas 'happy', 'joyfull', 'hopes' are key-words in this sonnet, in *Going into Italie* 'forsaken' is repeated with heavy emphasis and 'sorrow', 'woe', 'forlorn' and similar words occur in almost every line. He is forsaken and disgraced. She scorns him and his love and 'of both, wrongfull deemes, and ill conceaves'. He cannot escape from his bitter knowledge of all this no matter where he may go. It is a sonnet in the mood of '*Still in the trace of my tormented thought*' and *To M. P.* and 44 pairs oddly with it, just as the eyes-stars sonnet comes strangely between the other two. It looks very much as if the two poems relate to two different occasions, *Going into Italie* belonging to the same time of emotional crisis as *To M. P.* and the poems associated with it, and *Beeing in Italie* belonging to an earlier and sunnier time. If this is so, the *Delia* crisis must have taken place about 1590[6] and Daniel must have been in Italy on some occasion between 1586, when he was a 'raw traveler' in Paris, and 1590–1 when he went with Dymoke.

A close examination of the early editions of the sonnets, then, offers this information to fill out our knowledge of Daniel's life up to 1592: parts at least of *Delia* are based on a genuine love-affair – the lady at first encouraged him but finally rejected him – there was some social inequality between them and he was bitterly conscious of his own lack of independent means – the crisis in this affair occurred in 1590–1 just before he travelled to Italy with Dymoke on what seems to have been a second visit. The most interesting and important result of looking in the son-

6. This is supported by the date, 1591, suggested for *To M. P.*

nets for biographical material is that we gain a fresh insight into Daniel's character. As the years passed he took some pains to cover over the traces of this early love-affair and strove, on the whole successfully, to be self-contained and disciplined, to damp down, both in his life and his work, the indiscreet ardours and over-ambitious 'wants' of his youth; but in some of the *Delia* poems we may see him, as we never quite do again, moved to deep and painful personal feeling, thwarted in his desires, and unresigned.

Daniel worked over his sonnets time and again between 1592 and 1601. In successive editions new poems were added and old ones dropped and some sonnets passed through three or four versions. An obvious principle in the revisions is the elimination of feminine endings which Daniel came to consider a blemish in his work (see *Defence of Ryme*, Sprague, pp. 156–7, and pp. 87–8 below), but although between 1594 and 1601 he altered 37 feminine endings, even so more than half the original weak rhymes remained unchanged. The revisions after 1592 are not usually an improvement but tend to reduce the fervour of the early statements of love or despair and to retreat from what is striking to the more conventional and trite. Daniel's whole development is towards sober, restrained and meditated utterance and away from the impulsive and extravagant and it would have been wiser, from the point of view of their poetic effectiveness, to leave the early poems to speak for his youth without trying to bring them into line with maturer standards of smooth versification and qualified statement. Yet although it is no doubt partly true, as E. H. Miller concludes in his study of the revisions,[7] that an increased and sometimes pedantic scrupulosity concerning rhyme and diction is responsible for many of the revisions, Daniel's motives in recasting his sonnets may not have been altogether aesthetic. As the fate of the M. P. group suggests, prudence and self-protection may also have played their parts in the process of what Mr Miller calls 'transforming agonised frustration into sober acceptance of the lot of the rejected lover'.

Because of the mite which they contribute to our understanding of Daniel – and in attempting to establish contact with the Elizabethans, remote as they are and in many ways so alien, every

7. E. H. Miller, 'Samuel Daniel's Revisions in *Delia*', *J.E.G.P.*, 53, 1954, pp. 58–68.

fragment of fact has to be cherished – these apparently biographical sonnets deserve to have attention drawn to them, but it would be folly to overstress the impact of urgent personal experience on the sequence as a whole. Like every other Elizabethan sonneteer Daniel drew freely on French and Italian models and though he is far from being slavishly dependent on them it is clear that in the main he is writing a deliberately traditional poetry and that his own pleasure in it derives not from the indulgence of laying bare his heart but from the exercise of his skill in modulations of traditional themes and traditional verse patterns.

His most important creditor is Desportes, whose sonnets to *Diane* were published in 1573, and he also draws upon du Bellay's *L'Olive*. Among the Italians, he makes use of Petrarch, Tansillo, Tasso, Guarini, with reminiscences possibly of Cariteo, della Casa and Angelo di Costanza.[8] With so much freedom of traffic in ideas, themes and phrases during the cult of the sonnet, the minute genealogy of each indebtedness becomes tedious and unprofitable but some examples of Daniel's use of his models will serve to put the old charge of over-much borrowing in proper perspective and to draw attention also to aspects of his sonnet-writing technique.

> Sweete hony-dropping *Daniell* may wage
> Warre with the proudest big Italian
> That melts his heart in sugred sonetting:
> Onely let him more sparingly make use
> Of others wit, and use his owne the more:
> That well may scorn base imitation.[9]

Compliment and reproof are nicely blended in this contemporary comment, but the lines produce on the whole a misleading impression of excessive dependence on models. In fact, Daniel shows considerable independence in his use of other poets as may be seen by a comparison of some of his sonnets with their French originals. One of the most obvious examples of 'imitation' on the face of it is provided by sonnet 9 which is clearly closely related to Desportes' *Diane*, Book 1, sonnet XXIX, but putting the two side by side makes it plain that there is little servility in the imitation.

8. For identification of Daniel's sources, see Janet G. Scott, *Les sonnets élisabethains*, (Paris, 1929).

9. The Second Part of *The Return from Parnassus* (Act 1, sc. ii, ll. 235-40).

Si c'est aimer que porter bas la vue,
Que parler bas, que soupirer souvant,
Que s'égarer solitaire en rêvant,
Brûlé d'un feu qui point ne diminue;
Si c'est aimer que de peindre en la nue,
Semer sur l'eau, jetter ses cris au vant,
Chercher la nuict par le soleil levant,
Et le soleil quand la nuict est venue;
Si c'est aimer que de ne s'aimer pas,
Haïr sa vie, embrasser son trespas,
Tous les amours sont campez en mon ame;
Mais nonobstant, si me puis-je louer
Qu'il n'est prison, ny torture, ny flame,
Qui mes desirs me sçeust faire avouer.

If this be love, to drawe a weary breath,
Painte on flowdes, till the shore, crye to th'ayre:
With downward lookes, still reading on the earth;
The sad memorials of my loves despaire.
If this be love, to warre against my soule,
Lye downe to waile, rise up to sigh and grieve me:
The never-resting stone of care to roule,
Still to complaine my greifes, and none releive me.
If this be love, to cloath me with darke thoughts,
Haunting untroden pathes to waile apart;
My pleasures horror, Musique tragicke notes,
Teares in my eyes, and sorrowe at my hart.
If this be love, to live a living death;
O then love I, and drawe this weary breath.

Daniel has picked up the general movement of the French
sonnet and also some of its single features but his sonnet as a
whole is fresher and more forceful than the original. 'Peindre en
la nue Semer sur l'eau, jetter ses cris au vant' becomes much more
strikingly 'Painte on flowdes, till the shore, crye to th'ayre'.
'Porter bas la vue' expands in Daniel to:

> With downward lookes, still reading on the earth;
> The sad memorials of my loves despaire

the second and beautiful line of which replaces the trite image of
unquenchable fire in Desportes. The second quatrain of Daniel's
sonnet includes the material of Desportes' ll. 7–11 in its first two
lines and the second two are original and contain a striking image.

Daniel's third quatrain transforms 's'égarer solitaire en rêvant', into 'Haunting untroden pathes to waile apart', a fine, imaginative line, while the other three lines of Daniel's quatrain are original workings of the theme of unhappiness. The final couplet sums up syntactically and emotionally, whereas the equivalent conclusion of the Desportes poem comes in l. 11 and the final tercet is a 'turn' of idea, that nothing will make him, in spite of all his miseries, confess his love. It would be impossible to deny Desportes's service in the composition of Daniel's poem and yet nothing could be further from 'base imitation'. The Daniel poem has considerable and original merits.

Sonnet 15 of *Delia* and number VIII of Book 1 of *Diane* are likewise very closely related.

Si la foy plus certaine en une ame non feinte,
Un desir temeraire, un doux languissement,
Une erreur volontaire, et sentir vivement,
Avec peur d'en guarir, une profonde atteinte;
Si voir une pensée au front toute dépeinte,
Une voix empeschée, un morne estonnement,
De honte ou de frayeur naissans soudainement,
Une pasle couleur, de lis at d'amour teinte;
Bref, si se mespriser pour une autre adorer,
Si verser mille pleurs, si toujours soupirer,
Faisant de sa douleur nourriture et breuvage;
Si, loin estre de flamme et de pres tout transi,
Sont cause que je meurs par defaut de mercy,
L'offense en est sur vous, et sur moy le dommage.

If that a loyall hart and faith unfained,
If a sweete languish with a chast desire:
If hunger-starven thoughts so long retayned,
Fed but with smoake, and cherisht but with fire.
And if a brow with cares caracters painted,
Bewraies my love, with broken words halfe spoken,
To her that sits in my thoughts Temple sainted,
And layes to view my Vultur-gnawne hart open.
If I have doone due homage to her eyes,
And had my sighes styll tending on her name:
If on her love my life and honour lyes;
And she th'unkindest maide still scornes the same
Let this suffice, the world yet may see;
The fault is hers, though mine the hurt must bee.

24

The pattern is the same as that of the two poems just considered, composed of a series of 'if' clauses leading to an emotional and syntactical conclusion. The poem has come to Desportes from Petrarch, so that Daniel had two possible models, though he appears to have had Desportes immediately in mind. He does not rearrange the ideas which he chooses from Desportes in the same way as he does in number 9 but he makes some complete and interesting departures from the French. The syntax of Desportes' first quatrain is awkward, with its change in line 3 from noun to verb. Daniel tightens the structure by the three times repeated 'if' and writes completely new lines 3 and 4 which introduce verbs more naturally and more vigorously than the French. The Desportes sonnet continues with its list of 'symptoms' to the end of the poem, but Daniel's sonnet introduces a new motif in line 7, the idea of the lady herself. He has, in fact, two sequences of 'if' clauses, the first culminating in ll. 7–8. The third quatrain develops a second series which centre on the lady and which prepare for the couplet and the conclusion. These modifications make the structure of the poem firmer, and the introduction of the lady at an earlier point and with greater distinctness than in the Desportes sonnet very much heightens the drama in Daniel's version.

Sonnet number 30 also derives from Desportes (*Cléonice*, number LXII) and there is again an Italian model in the background, this time Tasso.

Je verray par les ans, vengeurs de mon martire,
Que l'or de vos cheveux argenté deviendra,
Que de vos deux soleils la splendeur s'esteindra,
Et qu'il faudra qu'Amour tout confus s'en retire.
La beauté qui, si douce, à présent vous inspire,
Cedant aux lois du tans, ses faveurs reprendra;
L'hyver de vostre teint les fleurettes perdra,
Et ne laissera rien des thresors que j'admire.
Cet orgueil desdaigneux qui vous fait ne m'aimer,
En regret et chagrin se verra transformer,
Avec le changement d'une image si belle.
Et peut estre qu'alors vous n'aurez déplaisir
De revivre en mes vers, chauds d'amoureux desir,
Ainsi que le phénix au feu se renouvelle.

I once may see when yeeres shall wrecke my wronge,
When golden haires shall chaunge to silver wyer:

25

And those bright rayes, that kindle all this fyer
Shall faile in force, their working not so stronge.
Then beautie, now the burthen of my song,
Whose glorious blaze the world dooth so admire;
Must yeelde up all to tyrant Times desire:
Then fade those flowres which deckt her pride so long.
When if she grieve to gaze her in her glas,
Which then presents her winter-withered hew;
Goe you my verse, goe tell her what she was;
For what she was she best shall finde in you.
Your firie heate lets not her glorie passe,
But Phenix-like shall make her live anew.

The most interesting alteration which Daniel has made here is in the last six lines and it is less a matter of technique than of personal tone. Desportes himself is very much in the picture which he paints of the coming of age to his lady and the loss of her beauty. He writes of the disdainful pride which causes her to refuse him the love he seeks, and of how this will change to regret and chagrin when she finds herself no longer lovely. Daniel allows no malice to enter the poem but he thinks tenderly of his lady's feelings and offers her the consolation of his verse which will enshrine her as she was. He makes a delicate point in his reference to his lady looking into her glass for this picks up the motif of the preceding sonnet, that Delia might see her beauty mirrored better in the effect it has on him than in her looking-glass. The first of these two sonnets is about Delia in the pride of her beauty and the second anticipates the decline of it all: the glass idea links them and gently underlines the inexorable harshness of 'Tyrant Time'. (Sonnet 29 itself is based very closely on Desportes's *Les Amours d'Hippolyte*, number 18.)

Daniel used these sonnets of Desportes as a kind of springboard for his own imagination, but he seems to have been much less at ease when he was drawing on du Bellay. Three of his sonnets have been traced to du Bellay and they are all fairly close renderings of the French. A comparison of *L'Olive* 91 and *Delia* 18 provides one or two points of some interest:

Rendez à l'or cete couleur, qui dore
Ces blonds cheveux, rendez mil'autres choses:
A l'orient tant de perles encloses,
Et au Soleil ces beaux yeulx, que j'adore.

Rendez ces mains au blanc yvoire encore,
Ce seing au marbre et ces levres aux roses,
Ces doulx soupirs aux fleurettes decloses,
Et ce beau tein à la vermeille Aurore.
Rendez aussi à l'Amour tous ses traictz,
Et à Venus ses graces et attraictz:
Rendez aux cieulx leur celeste harmonie.
Rendez encor'ce doulx nom à son arbre,
Ou aux rochers rendez ce cœur de marbre,
Et aux lions cet' humble felonnie.

Restore thy tresses to the golden Ore,
Yeelde *Cithereas* sonne those Arkes of love;
Bequeath the heavens the starres that I adore,
And to th'Orient do thy Pearles remove.
Yeelde thy hands pride unto th'yvory whight,
T'*Arabian* odors give thy breathing sweete:
Restore thy blush unto *Aurora* bright,
To *Thetis* give the honour of thy feete.
Let *Venus* have thy graces, her resign'd,
And thy sweete voyce give backe unto the Spheares:
But yet restore thy fearce and cruell minde,
To *Hyrcan* Tygers, and to ruthles Beares.
Yeelde to the Marble thy hard hart againe;
So shalt thou cease to plague, and I to paine.

Daniel has taken the general pattern of du Bellay's sonnet but
enriched it in details. His first quatrain, for example, is more
gorgeous and more specific than the equivalent lines in *L'Olive* and
the strong placing of the verbs is characteristically employed to
increase the force of the lyric impulse. The desire to be prodigal
of beauty and to work the French up to a higher pitch is demon-
strated again in the second quatrain: 'ces mains' becomes 'thy
hands pride' and the rather weak 6th and 7th lines of the French
are replaced by:
    'T'*Arabian* odors give thy breathing sweete:' (l. 6)
and   'To *Thetis* give the honour of thy feete' (l. 8)
There is no suggestion for these in *L'Olive* 91 but Daniel may have
been remembering *L'Olive* 7, ll. 5–6:

    ... ceste bouche, ou souspire une halaine
    Qui les odeurs des Arabes excelle

27

and *L'Olive* 15, an extravagant poem in praise of the lady's feet, which contains also, like 91, a reference to Orient pearls:

> Pié, que Thétis pour sien eust avoué,
> Pié, qui au bout monstres cinq pierres telles,
> Que l'Orient seroit enrichi d'elles,
> Cil Orient en perles tant loué.

Daniel heightens the luxury of the original, but his ending is weak whereas the French finishes strongly. He gets in the idea of his mistress's 'fearce and cruell minde' in contrast to the beauty of her body and still has one line to spare whereas du Bellay achieves a more dramatic finale by reducing the idea of her harshness to the last two lines and reinforcing the unexpectedness by his striking 'humble felonnie'.

A similar failure to reproduce the dramatic succinctness of the French is noticeable in *Delia* 22 which begins by translating *L'Olive* 92 fairly closely, but du Bellay's treatment of the last six lines is altogether more effective. The theme is delusive hope:

> Ce bref espoir, qui ma tristesse alonge,
> Traitre à moy seul et fidele à Madame,
> Bien mile fois a promis à mon ame
> L'heureuse fin du soucy qui la ronge.
> Mais quand je voy' sa promesse estre un songe,
> Je le maudy', je le hay', je le blâme:
> Puis tout soudain je l'invoque et reclame,
> Me repaissant de sa doulce mensonge.
> Plus d'une fois de moy je l'ay chassé:
> Mais ce cruel, qui n'est jamais lassé
> De mon malheur, à vos yeulx se va rendre.
> La faict sa plainte: et vous, qui jours et nuitz
> Avecques luy riez de mes ennuiz,
> D'un seul regard le me faictes reprendre.

> False hope prolongs my ever certaine griefe;
> Traytrous to me and faithfull to my love:
> A thousand times it promis'd me reliefe,
> Yet never any true effect I prove.
> Oft when I finde in her no trueth at all,
> I banish her, and blame her trechery:
> Yet soone againe I must her backe recall,
> As one that dyes without her company.

Thus often as I chase my hope from mee,
Straight way she hastes her unto *Delias* eyes:
Fed with some pleasing looke there shall she bee,
And so sent backe, and thus my fortune lyes.
Lookes feede my Hope, Hope fosters me in vaine;
Hopes are unsure, when certaine is my paine.

The relative weakness of Daniel's handling of du Bellay seems to be due to the difference in verse form between the octave-sestet division which du Bellay uses and Daniel's four quatrains and a couplet. Daniel's technique of condensing the sestet into four lines and adding a couplet worked well with Desportes and gave tension and bite where the original was slack; but a dramatic movement runs right to the end of the du Bellay sestets and Daniel's condensation of the sense loses the finer points while his couplets add nothing but are mere anticlimax. It sometimes seems odd to modern readers that the Elizabethan poets, when they translated or imitated, should have paid so much attention to weaker poets or weaker poems, but the Elizabethans were concerned primarily with creating, not with transplanting, and weaker poems may provide stimulus while at the same time they offer less resistance to individual rehandling than better poems do. Daniel's relations to Desportes and to du Bellay provide an illustration of this. He is much closer to the text when he translates the more formidable du Bellay and he is not able to make successful new poems out of his models as he does out of the malleable Desportes sonnets. Moreover, his own conception of the sonnet form conflicts with du Bellay's, which is carefully constructed on a different principle, so that Daniel's treatment spoils the delicate organisation of the sestet in each of the poems he translates.

Daniel's treatment of his Italian models follows much the same lines as his treatment of the French. His recreation of the ideas of a poem could be illustrated from number 31, which is a rendering of Tasso's *Gerusalemme Liberata* XVI, 14–15 (Spenser's version in *The Faerie Queene*, book II, canto xii, is much closer to the original), and his eclecticism could be illustrated from his treatment in number 16 of Petrarch's *Beato in sogno*, where Petrarch's 'd'abbraciar l'ombre e seguir l'aura estiva' provides two images in Daniel: 'imbracing cloudes by night' (l. 2) and the very nice 'Still must I goe the Summer windes pursuing' (l. 11). But the French examples chosen are enough to demonstrate that Daniel was by no means bound to close translation and to draw attention to some features of his technique as a sonneteer.

For the form of his sonnets he favours overwhelmingly the so-called Shakespearean pattern which suggests that the love for alternate rhyme, which is constant throughout his career, developed early. The discussion of his adaptations of Desportes and du Bellay has illustrated the use he liked to make of the final couplet for a full rounding off and summing up of the preceding twelve lines. Sometimes he has a trick of echoing the last line of one sonnet in the opening lines of the next, giving the effect of picking up, after a pause, a continuing line of song. The group on the passing of youth and beauty are all linked in this way (numbers 31–5) and as a consequence they acquire special emphasis within the whole sequence. There are altogether five examples of the Spenserian sonnet form,[10] none of which appeared before 1594. Sonnet 46, with its reference to 'others' who '... sing of Knights and Palladines in aged accents and untimely words', indicates that Daniel had read part of *The Faerie Queene* by 1592 and he may have seen a manuscript version of some of the *Amoretti* sonnets between 1592 and 1594 and been sufficiently attracted by Spenser's rhyme scheme to want to try it for himself. In the 1592 edition only numbers 28 and 30 vary from the basic pattern.[11] These sonnets had already appeared in Newman's pirated edition which also contains a second example of the form of number 30 (not reprinted by Daniel).[12] In 1601 appeared a sonnet to follow number 20[13] with a rhyme scheme which experiments with an even closer linking of the first twelve lines than the Spenserian scheme provides and retains the couplet at ll. 8–9.

These few experiments apart, it is evident that Daniel settled early on the form which suited him best. Within this chosen pattern he could achieve considerable variety of effect, the careful artificiality of sonnets 11 and 14, for example, with their structure of triplets, the sad and tender beauty of 42, the harsh tone of the

10. They are: the dedicatory sonnet to the Countess of Pembroke, the sonnet following number 18 'What it is to breathe and live without life' (Sprague, p. 175), the version of number 20 which was first printed in 1601 (Sprague, pp. 176–7), and the sonnet following number 46 (Sprague, pp. 188–9).

11. 28 runs abba abba cdcdcc, and 30 abba abba cdcdcd.

12. Number 30 is a translation of Desportes (see above pp. 25–6) but it does not reproduce the rhyme pattern of the French nor of Tasso's Italian.

13. 'Tyme, cruel tyme, come and subdue that Brow' (Sprague, p. 177).

sonnet *To M. P.* and the tightly knit '*Care-charmer sleepe*' (number 45). This last, a famous anthology piece on a familiar theme, marks a climax in the sequence, a point of passionate intensity. It is a sombre and impressive poem with a heavy rhythm and strong alliterative effects, reaching its climax in the third quatrain and ending on a note of weary disillusion. The description of dreams as 'th'ymagery of our day desires' which 'modell foorth the passions of the morrow' suggests effectively and economically a state of acute emotional frustration, and the whole poem is too highly charged and taut to be adequately described in terms of the delicate and rather languid beauty often ascribed to Daniel's sonnets. It is more perfectly executed than *To M. P.* or *At the Authors going into Italie* but it shares with them the same characteristics of concentrated feeling and forceful language. These qualities add some tougher strands to the beautiful texture of Daniel's sonnets, but there is another kind of strong material in *Delia* also, of an unusual and striking kind. This is Daniel's highly characteristic use of mythological images to express psychological states. The final couplet of number 45 provides an example of this:

> Still let me sleepe, imbracing clowdes in vaine;
> And never wake, to feele the dayes disdayne.

'Imbracing clowdes in vaine' is, of course, a reference to the myth of Ixion, and similar mythological references are frequent. Sonnet 27 and the sonnet which followed it in 1594[14] both have as their motif the story of Daedalus and number 28 makes use of the fable of the giants' war against the gods in which they attempt to scale the heavens by heaping mountains one on top of the other. In sonnet 9, which is based on Desportes, occurs the striking original line:

> The never-resting stone of care to roule

with its implicit reference to the story of Sisyphus.

The use of mythology which these examples illustrate is very different from that of Sidney. Sidney, as J. W. Lever has pointed out,[15] tends to make little dramatised fabliaux of the myths he uses, and Greville, part of whose *Caelica* was written in friendly rivalry with Sidney, does the same sort of thing. In both there is humour,

14. Sprague, p. 183.
15. J. W. Lever, *The Elizabethan Love Sonnet* (London, 1956).

31

or irony, and a sense of drama. Daniel's treatment is quite different, for he uses the myths which he takes, not for their narrative, but for their metaphorical qualities, and for the purpose of describing an inward or psychological situation. Thus, often, he does not give names, but the mythological background is drawn upon to give a range of associations to the metaphor so as to make it a particularly evocative and meaningful description. Bush notes that the Elizabethan attitude to classical myth was 'mainly ethical and humanistic'[16] but Daniel's psychological interpretations are distinguished among the rest by their seriousness and subtlety. This inwardness in the use of mythology is characteristic of his poetry generally, for his concern is always less with outward event than with character. It is typical of him that even in his earliest, lyrical work he should use the rich potential of myth to articulate more clearly the inmost feelings of the lover in this unfulfilled love relationship.

An important example of his use of mythology occurs in sonnet 5, in which Daniel gives an account of the beginning of his love for Delia in terms of the Diana-Actaeon myth, a favourite story with writers of the time.[17] The poem opens with the idea that before he met Delia he was young and without any settled aims. The word 'wandering' is used, and his thoughts, he says, ranged in 'heedeles waies'. It soon becomes clear that the implied spatial image is not being used merely perfunctorily for it is in these 'wanderings' that he comes across his Diana. She disdains to see him 'in that place' and because of her scorn, his sport is changed into 'a Harts dispaire'. The action of the Diana-Actaeon story interweaves at this point with the personal experience of unrequited love and Daniel plays subtly on the two levels of meaning.

16. D. Bush, *Mythology and the Renaissance Tradition* (University of Minnesota Press, 1932), p. 71.

17. Drayton uses it in his *Epistle of Rosamond to King Henry the Second* and is probably imitating Daniel when he does so. This is his version:

> Here, in the garden, wrought by curious hands,
> Naked Diana in the fountaine stands,
> With all her nymphes got round about to hide her,
> As when Acteon had by chance espy'd her:
> This sacred image I no sooner view'd,
> But as that metamorphos'd man, pursu'd
> By his owne hounds; so by my thoughts am I,
> Which chase me still, which way soe'r I flye.

The use of the myth in Daniel's sonnet is much more complex and fine-drawn than this.

Thus it is 'water-cold disdaine' which the lady throws in his face and the pun on hart is not merely a verbal quibble but a point at which the two meanings of the story interlock. There is a progressive deepening throughout the poem of the idea that the 'place' where all this occurs is some region of inner experience, and the literal and figurative meanings coalesce with brilliant effect in the line:

My thoughts like houndes, pursue me to my death,

with its implications well outside the range of the conventional love situation.

A similar use of spatial metaphor to describe inward experience occurs elsewhere in these sonnets, not always related to mythology but always with specially striking imaginative effect. The clearest examples are:

A modest maide, deckt with a blush of honour
Whose feet doe treade greene pathes of youth and love

(number 6) and

If this be love, to cloath me with darke thoughts,
Haunting untroden pathes to waile apart

(original – i.e. not translated – lines in number 9).

Such images are reminiscent of the line which Shelley quoted from Sophocles:

Coming to many ways in the wanderings of careful thought,

and of which he said, 'What a picture does this line suggest of the mind as a wilderness of intricate paths, wide as the universe, which is here made its symbol . . .'[18] The idea of 'a world within a world', which especially appealed to Shelley, is firmly rooted also in Daniel's imagination, and it produces some fine moments in *Delia* of a rare kind.

Beauty of sound and image, occasional bursts of strong feeling, and a notable psychological subtlety, combine to make *Delia* one of the finest and most pleasing of the Elizabethan sonnet sequences. By 1592 Daniel had taken to himself, at one step, as it seems, all the wealth of new material and new expressive power which came into English literature in the golden decades of the Elizabethan

18. Mrs Shelley's 'Note on *Prometheus Unbound*' in Shelley's *Poetical Works* (Oxford, 1904), p. 269.

heyday. Out of them he made an instrument for his own playing which he handled with superb and easy mastery. There was little more for him to do in this line and *Delia* itself contains the seeds of future development. Henceforth Daniel will develop the intellectual power already adumbrated in the handling of the tightly woven patterns of imagery and he will enlarge the interest in the reading of character which is foreshadowed in his treatment of emotional states in *Delia*.

The Complaint of Rosamond, which was first published in 1592 together with the first authorised edition of *Delia*, is a transition poem, linked on the one hand to the sonnets by its style and much of its material, and on the other to later work by the seriousness of its tone and the increasing pressure of thought on the lyrical material. It tells the story of Rosamond Clifford, mistress of Henry II, and it contains several references to Delia. The ghost of Rosamond, pleading with Daniel to undertake the recital of her story, apologises for intruding on his private griefs but suggests that Delia's heart may be moved by such evidence of sympathy for her sex; and at the end, before she vanishes, she appeals to Delia to sigh for her and so help her to pass to 'The sweet Elisean rest beyond the Styx.' Daniel is left alone to return to his own woes:

> But ah the worlde hath heard too much of those,
> My youth such errors must no more disclose.
> Ile hide the rest, and greeve for what hath beene,
> Who made me knowne, must make me live unseene.

This recalls *To M. P.*:

> But I must pine, and in my pining lurke,
> Least my sad lookes bewray me how I fare

and *Delia* 50:

> I say no more, I feare I saide too much.

Delia is remembered also, rather unexpectedly, in the body of the poem when Rosamond is reflecting on the cruelty of shutting beauty away from the admiration of the world. See, she says, how the most beautiful women flock to town to display their loveliness, except, she adds, Delia, who is 'left to adorne the West' (i.e. north Somerset?).

Rosamond is closely linked also with *The Mirror for Magistrates*. The form is the seven-lined stanza of the *Mirror* stories and the

opening provides an introduction equivalent to those supplied
by the prose links in the *Mirror*. Rosamond asks Daniel to hear
and record her complaint in the same way as the figures in the
Mirror choose an auditor and spokesman for their woes. And the
fall from high estate to misery and the drawing of a moral form,
of course, the ever-recurrent pattern of the *Mirror* stories. These
are general affinities but there is a special link between *The
Complaint of Rosamond* and one of the *Mirror* tales, Churchyard's
tragedy of Jane Shore, and both Daniel and Churchyard recognised the connection. Daniel's Rosamond is aggrieved that no one
remembers her, while, as she says,

> *Shores* wife is grac'd, and passes for a Saint.

'Her well-told tale' has won compassion while the griefs of Rosamond remain unsung and consequently unlamented. This is one
of the arguments with which she persuades Daniel to write her
history. Churchyard, for his part, was encouraged by the success
of *Rosamond* to reprint *Shore's Wife* in 1593, thirty years after the
original publication, and to add new verses to it. The similarity
between the two stories is obvious. Both women became king's
mistresses, both had a tragic end, and both conclude with
a warning to other women to 'fall not to follie so'. But the resem-
blances extend further than to the outline of the stories. Both
Daniel and Churchyard are sympathetic towards their heroines.
Like Criseyde, Rosamond and Jane Shore are 'sliding of corage'
and like Chaucer, Daniel and Churchyard give all the weight they
can to excuses. Churchyard even goes so far as to suppress any
reference to Jane Shore's liaison with Hastings, though in the tale
of Hastings himself, told by Sackville, it is plainly enough
described. Jane Shore blames the friends who forced her at a
tender age into an uncongenial marriage and, by making her a
prey to temptation, 'bent the wand that might have growen ful
streight'. Daniel makes a great deal of the corrupting effects upon
a young and inexperienced girl of court life and the adulation paid
to beauty, and he stresses the particular temptations and dangers
involved in the fact that it was no less than a king who wooed her;
and for good measure he introduces an older woman who is
deliberately employed by the king to corrupt her by argument and
advice. The unhappiness of forced marriages which Churchyard
makes an excuse for Jane Shore, is also noted by Daniel, and in

one of the two additions which he made to his poem in 1594 he takes up the point again and makes Rosamond feelingly advise young women to wait for a lawful and mutual love and not to sell themselves for wealth or for honours.

Churchyard's story of Jane Shore is, on the face of it, remarkable among the *Mirror* stories for its personal rather than political emphasis. Her unchastity is a private fault, and as far as her position brought her into contact with public affairs, her influence, Churchyard seems to say, was wholly good and her conduct unselfish and generous. There is, in fact, some ambiguity in Churchyard's approach to the story. Lines 169–217 read like an account of the ideal royal favourite and to that extent are political. The fall of Jane Shore, moreover, is brought about not as a necessary consequence of her sin but rather through the perfidy of Richard III. Lines 292–357 are largely concerned with the wickedness of Richard and ll. 336–50 are direct exhortation to 'Ye Princes all, and Rulers everychone' to judge with equity and punish without spite. This also is political and is only rather awkwardly applied by Jane Shore to her own story. On the other hand the final moral of the whole tale is:

> Example take by me both maide and wyfe,
> Beware, take heede, fall not to follie so,
> A myrrour make of my great overthrowe:
> Defye this world, and all his wanton wayes,
> Beware by me, that spent so yll her dayes.[19]

This scarcely seems to comprehend all the motifs of the story for Jane has been more sinned against than sinning and is less an example of the just punishment that awaits the wrongdoer than of the fickleness of fortune which turns prosperity to penury and pride to penance, and which exposes the shallowness of fair-weather friends.

There is thus some confusion of political and personal interests in Churchyard's poem, with the theme of the world's vanity also included. The various sets of ideas are not well integrated but there is something to be said for a multiplicity of interests at any level in a *Mirror* story, whatever judgement might be passed by more exacting standards. No doubt this contributed to the feeling

19. *The Mirror for Magistrates*, ed. Lily B. Campbell (Cambridge University Press, 1938), p. 386, ll. 388–92.

of the original hearers that here were riches indeed and, as Baldwin records, they 'all together exhorted me instantly, to procure Maister Churchyarde to undertake and to penne as manye moe of the remaynder [of the stories in the collection] as myght by any meanes be attaynted at his handes.'[20]

In *Rosamond* Daniel allows no such confusion of interests, for he ignores any possible political aspect of his story and concentrates exclusively on the personal tragedy and the contrast, which Churchyard too draws, between exaltation and misery, the change of fortune which may be brought about in a brief space of time. It is characteristic of him to treat the subject like this, for later on, in dealing with more obviously political material he will be always deeply and even primarily concerned with the study of character. In the sort of emphasis he gives to *Rosamond*, he may also have been influenced by John Higgins's additions to the original *Mirror for Magistrates*, for when Higgins compiled his *First parte of the Mirour for Magistrates* his view of the functions of his stories was altogether less political than that of Baldwin and his associates had been. 'I have here', he writes, in his dedication[21] '. . . only reproved foly in those which are heedelesse: injurie in extortioners, rashnes in venterers, and excesse, in such as suppresse not unruly affections'. Clearly his emphasis is on personal morals. Higgins's *First Parte* was first published in 1574, and both parts (i.e. Higgins's and the original *Mirror for Magistrates* now called *The last Part of the Mirror for Magistrates*) were combined in 1587 in one volume. Daniel may have taken to heart Higgins's words at the end of the dedication: '. . . I doubt not', Higgins wrote of his work, 'but it maye pleasure some, if not, yet give occasion to others which can do farre better, either with eloquence to amende that is amisse in mine, or else when they see these so rudely pende, to publishe their own.'[22]

Perhaps this seemed a challenge to Daniel. At least, he may justly have felt, he could give more subtlety and more poetry to such a theme as Higgins took when he wrote of 'Elstride the concubine of Locrinus myserably drowned by Gwendoline his wyfe' who 'declares her presumption, lewde life and infortunate

---

20. Ibid., p. 387, ll. 1–4.
21. *Parts Added to the Mirror for Magistrates*, ed. Lily B. Campbell (Cambridge University Press, 1946), p. 34, ll. 73–6.
22. Ibid., p. 34, ll. 78–81.

fall', a story very similar in its essentials to *Rosamond* and treated by Higgins with all the heavy-handedness which the title suggests.

Daniel, in fact, infuses considerable lyric warmth into his *Rosamond*. Churchyard's favourite method of emphasising points in his story of Shore's wife is to pile up a series of exempla:

> Compel the hawke to syt that is unmande,
> Or make the hound untaught to drawe the dere,
> Or bryng the free agaynst his wil in band,
> Or move the sad a pleasaunt tale to heare,
> Your time is lost and you are never the nere:
> So love ne learnes of force the knot to knyt,
> She serves but those that feele sweete fancies fyt.

This does not compare with Daniel's capacity for increasing the pressure when he wants to. He celebrates, for example, the power of beauty in a stanza which was certainly extravagant enough to evoke parody,[23] but which uses musical imagery to produce beautiful music of its own:

> Ah beauty Syren, fayre enchaunting good,
> Sweet silent rethorique of perswading eyes:
> Dombe eloquence, whose powre doth move the blood,
> More then the words, or wisedome of the wise,
> Still harmonie, whose diapason lyes
> Within a brow, the key which passions move,
> To ravish sense, and play a world in love.

This is one of the passages whose rich texture, produced by closely woven imagery, is reminiscent of the sonnets. The language and tone of the following stanza likewise recall the sonnets though the sentiments here are in the mouth of the 'sinfull monster' suborned to corrupt Rosamond's morals:

> Thou must not thinke thy flowre can alwayes florish,
> And that thy beautie will be stil admired:
> But that those rayes which all these flames doe nourish,
> Canceld with Time, will have their date expyred,
> And men will scorne what now is so desired:
> Our frailtyes doom is written in the flowers,
> Which florish now and fade ere many howers.

It is amusing to notice the effect of *Rosamond* on old Churchyard

23. See Jonson's *Every Man Out of His Humour*, Act III, sc. i.

when he reissued in 1593 his *Tragedie of Shore's Wife Much aug-mented, with divers new Additions*. In the dedication he writes: '... because Rosimond is so excellently sette forth (the actor whereof I honour) I have somewhat beautified my Shore's wife, not in any kind of emulation, but to make the world knowe my device in age is as rife and reddie, as my disposition and know-ledge was in youth.' Churchyard may deny 'emulation' but it is plain that he had in fact been struck by the lyric quality of *Rosa-mond* and wanted to show that he could do the same sort of thing. The two passages just quoted from Daniel seem to have challenged him especially. To compete with Daniel's lines on beauty he added three stanzas to his own poem, in one of which Mistress Shore makes direct reference to Rosamond who, she says,

> For beauties boast could scarce compare with me.
> The kindly buds and blossomes of brave tree
> With white and red had deckt my cheekes so fine,
> There stood two balles like drops of claret wine,

and he tries a passage on the beauty-fades-like-a-flower theme to pair with Daniel's:

> Of flowers a while men doe gay poses make:
> The sent once past, adue dry withered leaves.
> Love lasts not long prickt up for pleasures sake,
> Straw little worth when corne forsakes the sheaves;
> A painted post the gazers eie deceives,
> But when foule fauts are found that bleard the sight,
> The account is gon of girlls and gugawes light.[24]

These passages are old enough now to have some charm but in 1593 Churchyard's Muse was merely old-fashioned and stiff in the joints whereas Daniel was revelling in newly discovered sources of inspiration and a new facility. He can produce the set-piece of ornamental near-allegory describing the engraving on the casket which the king sent to Rosamond, and, by contrast with all the elaboration of sentiment and description in the poem, he can create also a miniature pastoral for 'a happy Country mayde':

> She's deckt with trueth, the River where she drinks
> Doth serve her for her glasse, her counsell giver:
> She loves sincerely, and is loved ever.

24. The revised version of Churchyard's poem is printed in Collier's Reprints, Green Series, ii, London, 1866. When Daniel 'augmented' *Rosamond* in 1594 he did not in his turn reflect the 1593 *Shore's Wife*.

> Her dayes are peace, and so she ends her breath,
> True life that knowes not what's to die till death.

As for imaginative entry into the subject, there is nothing in
Churchyard to compare with the pathetic reflection of the dying
Rosamond as she considers the tragedy of women who let love
slip by them:

> And o what are we, if we be not lov'd?

Daniel's poem ends with Rosamond returning to the 'Stygian
flood' and Daniel to his thoughts of Delia, but immediately before
these final stanzas, Daniel picks up another of the themes of the
sonnets and speaks of the ravages of time and the greater strength
of poetry than either marble or brass or the monuments of the
past. Lines 708–14 seem to refer to Stonehenge, as does sonnet 37,
but the *Rosamond* stanzas do not conclude with a statement that
poetry can immortalise: poetry may prolong memory for 'some
further date' but, says Rosamond to the poet, there will come
other ages which 'shall neglect thy rime' and she goes on to a
curiously gloomy prophecy of the future:

> Then when confusion in her course shall bring,
> Sad desolation on the times to come:
> When myrth-lesse Thames shall have no Swan to sing,
> All Musique silent, and the Muses dombe.
> And yet even then it must be known to some,
> That once they florisht, though not cherisht so,
> And Thames had Swannes as well as ever Po.

As they stand in *Rosamond*, these stanzas seem to introduce a note
of more universal melancholy, to set the individual story in a vast
diminishing perspective of time and to include the poet himself,
and it seems, a whole civilisation, in a final Sic transit. The stanzas
anticipate verbally the dedicatory poem to *Cleopatra*, first published
in 1594, although in mood they contradict it. In 1594 Daniel
speaks with excitement and enthusiasm of rivalling and surpassing
the poets of Italy and longs for a wider audience so that all the
world in future ages may know the 'eternall Songs' of Sidney and
Spenser and see 'what great Elizaes raigne hath bred' and in
Musophilus also, five years later, he looks forward to the future
triumphs of English 'eloquence', not to its extinction. A sombre

tone, of course, befits a *Complaint*, and Daniel is certainly appropriately dejected.

It seems beyond question that Shakespeare learnt something from Daniel's mastery of language and melody and his skilful handling of images in *Delia* and *Rosamond*. He found suggestions of another kind also in Daniel's early work, for Romeo's words over the apparently dead Juliet (*Romeo and Juliet*, Act V, sc. iii, ll. 92–115) derive from Henry's lament over the dead Rosamond, a touching passage in the context of Daniel's poem and one that is even dramatic in the sense that it seeks to realise a sharply-felt emotion.

Overcome with grief, Henry embraces the body:

> And as he in hys carefull armes doth hold it,
> Viewing the face that even death commends,
> On sencelesse lips, millions of kysses spends.
>
> Pitifull mouth (quoth he) that living gavest
> The sweetest comfort that my soule could wish:
> O be it lawfull now, that dead thou havest,
> Thys sorrowing farewell of a dying kisse.
> And you fayre eyes, containers of my blisse,
> Motives of love, borne to be matched never:
> Entomb'd in your sweet circles sleepe for ever.
>
> Ah how me thinks I see death dallying seekes,
> To entertaine it selfe in loves sweet place:
> Decayed Roses of discoloured cheekes,
> Doe yet retaine deere notes of former grace:
> And ougly death sits faire within her face;
> Sweet remnants resting of vermilion red,
> That death it selfe, doubts whether she be dead.
>
> Wonder of beautie, oh receive these plaints,
> The obsequies, the last that I shall make thee:
> For loe my soule that now already faints,
> (That lov'd thee lyving, dead will not forsake thee,)
> Hastens her speedy course to over-take thee.
> Ile meete my death, and free my selfe thereby,
> For ah what can he doe that cannot die?[25]

What Shakespeare made of this is, of course, of quite a different

25. *Rosamond*, ll. 663–86.

order but the stimulus and the imaginative suggestion were nevertheless there in Daniel.[26]

Daniel works a great deal into his *Rosamond*, not only the lyric themes, but an attack on cosmetics, an account of the worldling's view of honour, a passage on jealousy, and in the second passage added in 1594, the celebration of mutual love, already mentioned, and a lengthy and bitter attack on 'Bed-brokers uncleane' who corrupt the innocent of their own sex. Thought, as well as feeling, has gone into the composition of the poem and the serious comments on the story which emerge reflect the developing moral attitudes as well as the maturing character of the man who wrote. 'Daniel is the first to appreciate fully the psychological possibilities of the *Mirror* form',[27] Drayton's editors comment in reference to *Rosamond*. Daniel's recognition of these possibilities and his response to them paves the way for the next step in his career, the composition of *Cleopatra*.

26. For a summary of work on the relation between Shakespeare's non-dramatic poetry and Daniel's sonnets and *Rosamond* see the volumes of *Poems* and *Sonnets* in the *Variorum Shakespeare*, ed. H. Rollins (Philadelphia and London, 1938 and 1944). See also R. A. Law '*Rosamond* and Shakespeare', *University of Texas Studies in English*, xxvi, 1947, pp. 42–8, and a recent study of the relations between *Delia* and Shakespeare's sonnets: *An Elizabethan Sonnet Problem* by C. Schaar (Lund, 1960).

27. *Works of Michael Drayton*, ed. Hebel, Tillotson and Newdigate (Oxford, 1931–41), v, p. 23.

III

Pembroke Patronage and 'Cleopatra'

Delia and *Rosamond* were dedicated to the Countess of Pembroke in 1592 but her patronage extends only to the finished work. She did not produce the seminal ideas for the poems and the evidence considered earlier suggests that she did not even know Daniel during the years when he was composing them. By 1594, however, Daniel was deeply immersed in the Wilton atmosphere and *Cleopatra* is Pembroke work in a much fuller sense than *Delia* and *Rosamond* are. Daniel is keenly aware that this verse drama marks a new and probably decisive stage in his literary career and the pressure of the influences surrounding him is apparent in the verse dedication of the early editions to the Countess of Pembroke. The shade of Sidney accompanies him as he enters the lists under the Pembroke banner to fight against 'this tyrant of the North; *Grosse Barbarisme*', 'our Spenser' has already encouraged him in verse, and the Countess herself is urging him on at every step. He feels it a great honour to have been chosen as champion but he is not altogether at his ease. He is not sure that this piece of work suits his particular vein, and he is a little oppressed by the splendour of his company:

> Alas, what honour can a voyce so low
> As this of mine, expect hereby to find?
> But, (Madam,) this doth animate my mind,
> That yet I shall be read among the rest,
> And though I doe not to perfection grow,
> Yet something shall I be, though not the best.[1]

1. This is the text of 1601 and 1623 (Grosart iii, p. 27). In 1594 and 1599 the last four lines were more tentative:

> But, (Madam,) this doth animate my mind,
> That favored by the Worthyes of our Land,
> My lynes are lik'd; the which may make me grow,
> In time to take a greater taske in hand.

The background to the composition of *Cleopatra* can be filled in with considerably more certainty than the background to *Delia* and *Rosamond* because it belongs to literary rather than to personal history. *Cleopatra*, in fact, owed its origin to the Countess of Pembroke's intention to strike a blow in a literary crusade, a crusade which had been initiated by her brother in the *Apologie for Poetry* and which she had been prosecuting as best she could, since his death. The advent of Daniel, whose name had been linked with Sidney's in Newman's publication, whose first volume had been received with acclaim as contemporary tributes show,[2] and who not only had true poetic power but was also content to take up residence under the Pembroke roof and be educated by the Countess herself (Wilton was his 'best Schoole' we remember), must have seemed to her something of a godsend. To find not only a good poet but one amenable to instruction was the very thing she needed if her campaign was to make any ground at all.

Sidney had written the *Apologie for Poetry* in 1580 or 1581, probably while he was at Wilton. It is a plea, in general, that imaginative literature should be restored to the high esteem which, he argues, it enjoyed in ancient times, but at the end it turns to a special theme, and Sidney urges the creation of a modern English literature to compare with the work which has been done on the continent. He reviews briefly but cogently the existing state of English writing and exposes its deficiencies, and he declares his faith that, in spite of the small harvest since Chaucer, 'our tongue is most fit to honor Poesie, and to bee honored by Poesie'. When, after his death, his sister took upon herself his function as literary patron, she seems to have felt that it also devolved on her to do what she could to bring about the literary resurgence that Sidney's *Apologie* called for. Sidney had singled out Spenser for praise on the showing of *The Shepheardes Calender* and since Sidney's death, Spenser's poetic career had gone from strength to strength. Spenser might be counted on to champion a high ideal of poetry in the field of non-dramatic verse but there was no comparable defender of Sidney's ideals in drama and the ground seemed to be giving way all round his position. It is to shore up this weak point that Daniel and his talents are seized

2. Tannenbaum (*Concise Bibliography*, pp. 17–18) makes a full list of contemporary allusions. Grosart collects critical comments from the sixteenth century to his own day in iv, pp. vii–xxxi.

upon and *Cleopatra* is 'the labour' imposed upon him by the Countess, whose influence 'predominated', as he says, his Muse. What she expected of *Cleopatra* may be best seen by going back a little to look at what Sidney had praised and what the Countess herself had done in the years between the *Apologie* and *Cleopatra*.

Sidney looking round on the drama of his day found that tragedies and comedies alike observed 'rules neyther of honest civilitie nor of skilfull Poetrie', but he made an exception of *Gorboduc* which he praised for being 'full of stately speeches and well sounding Phrases, clyming to the height of *Seneca* his stile, and as full of notable moralitie, which it doth most delightfully teach, and so obtayne the very end of Poesie'. All the same, he adds, 'it is very defectious in the circumstances, which greeveth mee, because it might not remaine as an exact model of all Tragedies'. The cause of Sidney's disappointment was the violation of the unities of place and time. *Gorboduc* was first acted in 1561-2, published surreptitiously in 1565 and in an authorised edition in 1570-1. As a piece of theatre it has long been utterly extinct and the dead matter has been freely anatomised. Its use of dumb-shows, its sources, its treatment of the chorus, its political themes, its metre and its style have all contributed their quota to literary history and it is difficult now to put the play together again and to try to see it in something like the light in which it appeared to Sidney when he found it the only sign of health in the English theatre. To us it appears undramatic and wordy, but Sidney would not have shared our sense of drama. The essential activity of the play for him, with a different scale of dramatic values in mind, lay in the intellectual working out of the situation proposed in the first act and the bloodshed and disaster which are involved by the way were merely the incidental accompaniment of the intellectual process. The argument moreover was a very real and important one and in the last act the theme of the dangers of an uncertain succession, one of the major preoccupations of Elizabeth's courtiers and counsellors, implicit throughout the play, becomes dominant and insistent. A passage of impassioned verse stands out, even today, in Eubulus's speech which closes the play, that in which (Act v, sc. ii, ll. 201-33) he describes the miseries of civil war and anticipates the scene in *Henry VI*, part 3, where the tragedy and futility of civil war are epitomised in the father-son episode (Act II, sc. v). For all its defects, both those which are apparent to us and those different ones which Sidney deplored, we ought to recognise that *Gorboduc* must once have appeared a promising play. It has shape, not perfect by neo-classical standards, but at least some degree of formality, and in 1580 that was a specially welcome merit; it has substance, and within the more or less antique mould it treats a subject of contemporary importance; and, moreover, in the last two acts of the play, Sackville's contribution, both the human interest of the story and the immediate implications of the political themes are realised with some vividness and presented not without effect.

Gorboduc helps us, then, to some conclusions about what Sidney admired and the lines on which he would have liked to see English drama develop. He believes in strict observance of the unities; he believes in Seneca, French Seneca that is to say, with his high style and 'notable moralitie' – not Italian Seneca with an interest in sensation and theatrical effect [3] – but a toughened French Seneca who by no means eschews contemporary affairs but on the contrary comments in virile and forthright terms, and he does not disapprove of the purely native ingredient added to *Gorboduc*, the dumb-shows which derived from the allegorical tableaux or 'stands' which were a feature of pageants and masques. In other words, he would have neo-classical form wedded to native vigour and seriousness and the compound, he thinks, will produce edification and delightfulness in full measure.

The new dramatists who had sprung up since Sidney's death disregarded all this and threatened to sweep the cherished ideals of cultivated neo-classicism before them on a great wave of popular and 'barbaric' drama. It was evidently with some idea of stemming the tide that the Countess of Pembroke translated in 1590 the *Marc-Antoine* of Robert Garnier and published her translation in 1592.

Garnier's *Marc-Antoine* first appeared in 1578 and the first complete edition of his works was published in 1585. It is thus possible that Sidney had read the *Marc-Antoine* and other plays before his death in October 1586 and discussed them with his sister. At any rate, she presumably believed that her brother would have approved of her attempt to use Garnier to give a

3. For an excellent account of the main streams of Senecan influence see the introduction to the *Works of Sir William Alexander*, ed. Kastner and Charlton (Edinburgh and London, 1921).

new impulse to the cause of English classical drama since it was now clear that *Gorboduc* alone would never be enough to win the day.

Marc-Antoine certainly opens up themes, and possibilities of treatment far beyond the scope of *Gorboduc*. Garnier's outstanding characteristic is his lyrical gift. The lyrical choruses of his tragedies became more and more important in the course of his career, and his plays throughout sound an elegiac note. His care is devoted to decorating the static rather than motivating the dynamic and his plays are meditations on a given situation rather than histories of developing and changing situations. In *Gorboduc*, though the violent action was kept strictly out of sight, there was a firm basis of story from which arose the scenes of discussion which were presented to the audience. In Garnier this structure is whittled down to such fine proportions that it almost disappears from view. The unity of place is not always strictly observed, but neither time nor place seems to have any significance in the plays and the action is nearly as elusive as the locale. Nevertheless there is grace in Garnier, the presentation of the chief figures of famous stories is interesting, even if Garnier shows no particular insight, important themes of politics and morals are treated, and refinement of expression and treatment is aimed at in everything. Whether Garnier's plays were ever acted or intended for production or not, it is certain that they could never be popular entertainment. They need a close and loving study of individual graces and the patient application that only a cultivated and sophisticated mind would ever be prepared to give.

'The *ethos* of Garnier's drama is Greek rather than Senecan', writes a modern critic, 'and still more characteristically Christian and French than either Greek or Senecan. In its seriousness of purpose, and its efforts to inculcate patriotism and morality, it has much more in common with the medieval spirit than the ancient'.[4] All this, substitute English for French, is equally true of *Gorboduc*, and the Sidney group did not need Garnier to teach them high seriousness. What Garnier did suggest to them, which *Gorboduc* did not, was the graceful and lyrical treatment of such themes and the general idea of spinning a cocoon of words round a chosen situation in the faith that a thing of beauty would emerge and soar into the intense inane of pure Art. English neo-

---

4. A. M. Witherspoon, *The Influence of Robert Garnier on Elizabethan Drama* (Yale University Press, 1924), p. 64.

classical drama as the Pembroke circle practised it is usually dismissed as a tedious aberration but its intentions, at any rate,
should not be too easily despised. What it aimed at was a highly
sophisticated art form, capable of the utmost refinement, full of
opportunity for the exercise of eloquence, ingenuity and cultivated taste. It was not meant to be dynamic but a shapely and
complete artefact that could be fingered piece by piece and admired
for its skill and polish. Not least of its attractions for a literary
côterie, it is susceptible to theorising and the business of defining
the exact proportions of their ideal could well give, to them at
any rate, the very satisfying impression that what they were
engaged on was the creation of a living and life-enhancing art.
It is not difficult to be mistaken in this way and at least their
serious concern for culture and the critical intelligence in literature
is wholly admirable.

Lady Pembroke's translation of *Marc-Antoine* sticks, in the
main, close to Garnier's text. She translates Garnier's rhyming
alexandrines into blank verse which is by no means without skill
although it sometimes stumbles, but her best work is in the
choruses. Here she feels free to leave literal translation and to
reconstruct Garnier's lyrics in a form and to some extent even a
vocabulary chosen by herself. When she can add a touch out of
her own imagination she does so and the chorus at the end of
Act 2, in particular, shows her composing fluently and with some
force.[5] If she expected her translation to provoke an interest in
Garnier and the possibilities he suggested for the development
of neo-classical tragedy in England, she may not have been
wholly disappointed, for within a year or so of the publication of
her translation another play of Garnier's appeared in an English
version. The play was Garnier's *Cornélie* and the translator was
Thomas Kyd.

How far Kyd genuinely admired Garnier's methods we may
question, and no doubt Lady Pembroke did too. Kyd was in very
distressed circumstances at the time, as he makes no scruple of
acknowledging in the dedication to the Countess of Sussex (she
was not Lady Pembroke's aunt, as has sometimes been stated)
and his *Cornelia* is scarcely likely to have been anything else than

5. Compare *Antonie*, ll. 831–41 (ed. Alice Luce, Weimar, 1897. *Litterarhistorische
Forschungen* III) and the passage from Garnier 'Il viendra quelque journée . . . Percent
les cieux éthérez' (*Oeuvres complètes de Robert Garnier*, ed. Pinvert, Paris, 1923, p. 198).

a bid for patronage, although he does promise to go on to translate a third Garnier play, *Porcie*. The translation of *Cornélie* was
done in a hurry and Kyd deals much more cavalierly with his
original than Lady Pembroke had done. Not only does he treat
the choruses freely, for which he had her warrant, but he takes
considerable liberty also with the rest of the play. He makes many
more and graver mistakes of meaning than Lady Pembroke did
and he does not hesitate to omit some of Garnier's lines and to
add passages of his own. The interpolations and omissions appear
to be entirely unsystematic and arbitrary. Occasionally Kyd
heightens an effect or produces a good original line but sometimes
he is taking a leap away from the text merely in order to accom-
modate a mistranslation. Carelessness and haste and also, it
appears, ignorance, leave their mark on the translation and in the
hands of the author of the *Spanish Tragedy* the soigné French
drama acquires a turbulence quite alien to its nature. Kyd is
aware that somehow Garnier has lost some gracefulness in his
englishing, but he hopes, nevertheless, that the translator's sins
will be forgiven him by his lady patron and he must have hoped
that the fact of having trodden in Lady Pembroke's footsteps
would be enough to find favour with her too.

Whether or not the reception of *Cornelia* was warm enough in
the circles it was aimed at to make a further translation of Garnier
worth Kyd's while cannot be certainly decided, for Kyd died in
1595, but *Cornelia* can hardly have been what Lady Pembroke,
at any rate, wanted. Whatever merits the translation has, and Kyd
strikes sparks from time to time, it entirely misses the refinement
and elegance of the original and it is very evidently not the product of studied care and devotion to the task in hand. The scene
is all set for the entry of Daniel as the new champion of the cause,
one who, properly tutored by the Countess of Pembroke herself,
will carry his spear against 'Grosse Barbarisme' with more con-
viction and a better sense of aim, one who, moreover, is a better
poet than Kyd. His task is not mere translation, but the creation
of an original English play, that 'exact model of all Tragedies'
which Sidney desiderated, and for which the Countess of Pembroke has been carefully preparing the ground.[6]

6. Fulke Greville, Sidney's friend, also had a hand in the attempt, during these
years, to create a non-theatrical drama. Bullough (*Poems and Dramas of Fulke
Greville*, Edinburgh and London, 1938, ii, p. 58) puts the date of the first version of
Mustapha as 1594–6 and of *Alaham* as 1598–1600.

The lines on which he should work were fairly clearly laid down for him. His play was to be a companion-piece to the Countess's *Antonie*: he therefore had Garnier as an immediate model, and, further back, there was a handling of Cleopatra's story by the creator of French classical tragedy, the *Cléopâtre Captive* by Étienne Jodelle of which also he made some use.[7] He had, of course, to write within the neo-classic formula.

It is remarkable, in all the circumstances, that anything of any individuality got written at all, and it is hardly surprising that many readers have been too much depressed by the form ever to find the individuality. Yet *Cleopatra* may still be read with pleasure, for there is life and humanity in it and considerable skill in the handling of the material.[8] The play is conceived as a unity in the fullest, as distinct from a merely conventional sense: its theme is the character of Cleopatra and its whole purpose is to illuminate that character, chosen for attention at a moment of greatest crisis, from a variety of angles. To that end, the material of outward action is pared to a minimum. Jodelle chooses the same moment of crisis for his Cleopatra, but he includes more tangential material than Daniel, all of which tends to dissipate attention and by introducing extraneous emotions to weaken the concentration of interest and sympathy on Cleopatra at which Daniel very deliberately aims. Once the full power of the concentration on Cleopatra is realised, the essential coherence of the play is revealed. The Philostratus-Arius scene, for example, which Daniel works up from a hint in Garnier, gives him scope for the exercise of what Saintsbury called his 'almost unsurpassed faculty of ethical verse-writing',[9] but its true purpose and its justification is to serve as a commentary on Cleopatra's resolve to die and to put the story of individuals into the wider context of society as a whole. Arius has saved Philostratus from death and Philostratus, a fellow philosopher, is a little ashamed that he has clung to life so eagerly in a time of disaster when his country's honour is laid low. Yet, he says, even amidst wretchedness:

7. For a detailed comparison of Daniel's play with his French predecessors, see my article 'Samuel Daniel's *Cleopatra* and Two French Plays' in *M.L.R.* XLVII, 1952, pp. 1–10.

8. Bonamy Dobrée (*Restoration Tragedy*, Clarendon Press, 1929) has some interesting comments on form and diction in *Cleopatra* in the course of his comparison of *All for Love* and *Antony and Cleopatra*.

9. Grosart iii, p. xi.

> . . . yet we reckon life our dearest good.
> And so we live, we care not how we live:
> So deepe we feele impressed in our blood,
> That touch which nature with our breath did give.

The pertinence of this to Cleopatra's situation and the contrast between the abjectness of the philosophers and her courage are obvious. Arius then takes up the discussion, agrees that 'Though we speake more then men, we are but men', and goes on to speake of the state of the whole country, to paint the wider background to the personal tragedy of Cleopatra and to draw more general morals:

> . . . never any age hath better taught,
> What feeble footing pride and greatnesse hath.
> How improvident prosperitie is caught,
> And cleane confounded in the day of wrath.
> See how dismaid Confusion keepes those streetes,
> That nought but mirth and musique late resounded,
> How nothing with our eye but horror meetes,
> Our state, our wealth, our pride, and al confounded.

It is instructive to compare this whole scene with the soliloquy which Garnier gives to his Philostratus. Daniel's philosophers are much more philosophical and it is noticeable that for the signs and wonders which Garnier retails from Plutarch, foretelling the downfall of Antony and Cleopatra, Daniel substitutes auguries of a different nature: pride and riot grown overweening, dissolute impiety seizing the minds of Prince and people, insolent security and wanton thoughts, all ministering to 'fat-fed pleasure'.

This scene has a legitimate place in the play then, not merely because it offers an example of Daniel exercising his gifts in a species of writing in which he excelled, but because, far from dispersing attention, it concentrates it even more firmly on the fate of Cleopatra and reveals implications as yet not touched on.

Another scene, that between Seleucus and Rodon, which may at first glance appear superfluous, is likewise revealed on closer examination to be deliberately contrived as an integral part of the development of the play. Jodelle made Seleucus repent of his betrayal of Cleopatra but the whole episode is treated by Jodelle half-comically and the interchange between Seleucus and the

SAMUEL DANIEL

Chorus, though no doubt meant seriously, hardly escapes a hangover of comedy:

> Lors que la Roine et triste et courageuse
> Devant Cesar aux cheveux m'a tiré,
> Et de son poing mon visage empiré:
> S'elle m'eust fait mort en terre gesir,
> Elle eust preveu à mon present desir . . .[10]

Jodelle has Plutarch's authority that Cleopatra 'flew upon him (Seleucus) and tooke him by the heare of the head, and boxed him wellfavoredly',[11] but Jodelle's treatment of the scene strikes a note out of harmony with the play as a whole. Daniel tones down the violence and preserves more dignity, and in the scene which follows between Seleucus and Rodon, he develops the theme of repentance after treachery more fully than Jodelle. Seleucus, tasting the bitterness of remorse, reveals the respect Cleopatra's servants have for her and his sense of obligation to 'such a bounteous Queene as she'. What is more important, he is, with his grief at his own baseness, a convenient and suitable confidant for Rodon, who introduces yet another aspect of Cleopatra's character, and weaves one of the strongest of its strands into the texture of the play.

In *Marc-Antoine* Garnier had made an interesting attempt to intensify the drama and emotion in his story by the introduction of a scene showing Cleopatra parting from her children. Daniel takes up this idea and makes a great deal more of it. He sticks closer to Plutarch and confines the parting to Caesario (Cleopatra's son by Julius Caesar) and he works up to Rodon's account of the parting, moreover, by a series of preparatory references so that, by the time the crisis is reached, the reader is sensitive to its full effect. In the opening speech of the play, the theme of Cleopatra's love and concern for her children is emphatically introduced:

> You lucklesse issue of an wofull mother,
> The wretched pledges of a wanton bed,
> You Kings designed, must subjects live to other;
> Or else, I feare, scarce live, when I am dead.

10. *Cléopâtre Captive* (ed. Ellis, Philadelphia, 1946), ll. 1136–40.
11. North's Plutarch (London, 1896), VI, p. 85.

52

> It is for you I temporize with *Caesar*,
> And stay this while to mediate your safety:
> For you I faine content, and soothe his pleasure,
> Calamity herein hath made me crafty.

Immediately following these lines comes a hint of an emotional conflict involved in this love of her children:

> For come what will, this stands, I must die free.
> And die my selfe uncaptiv'd and unwonne:
> Blood, Children, Nature, all must pardon me,
> My soule yeelds Honor up the victory,
> And I must be a Queene, forget a mother;
> Though mother would I be, were I not I;
> And Queene would not be now, could I be other.

The same ideas are insisted on in the next scene, this time in Proculeius's account of his interview with Cleopatra. Cleopatra has been pleading for her freedom and pleads especially for her children, mentioning Caesario by name. She goes on:

> But if that with the torrent of my fall,
> All must be rapt with furious violence,
> And no respect, nor no regard at all,
> Can ought with nature or with blood dispence:
> Then be it so, if needes it must be so.

And Proculeius adds that she:

> There staies and shrinkes in horror of her state.

Here Daniel again, and with greater emphasis, points to the conflict between Cleopatra's instincts as a Queen and her instincts as a mother. There is no comparable preparation for the Garnier scene. When the moment for parting comes, the children are wailed over, consigned to Euphronius's care, Euphronius says, 'Allons, enfans' and the children dutifully reply, 'Allons'; we have scarcely had time so much as to recognise Cleopatra in maternal guise before it is all over. In Jodelle the children are even more briefly treated and any possible anxiety over their fate is quickly dismissed since before the end of the Caesar-Cleopatra interview Caesar has promised to spare them.

When in Daniel's play, Rodon tells his story, in the exchange of treacheries with Seleucus, the full significance of the earlier references to the children is revealed in the moving narrative of

Cleopatra's parting from Caesario (the other children and their
fates, having served Daniel's purpose, are allowed to remain
obscure). Cleopatra's vacillations, as she tries to dismiss Caesario,
for his own sake and for Egypt's, and struggles against a presenti-
ment of doom, are traced with a humanity that makes the story
genuinely poignant. At last she makes up her mind:

> But stay: there's something else that I would say:
> Yet nothing now. But O God speed thee well,
> Lest saying more, that more may make thee stay.
> Yet let me speake: It may be tis the last
> That ever I shall speake to thee my sonne.
> Doe Mothers use to part in such post hast?
> What, must I end when I have scarce begunne?
> Ah no (deare heart) tis no such slender twine
> Wherewith the knot is tide twixt thee and me;
> That blood within thy veins came out of mine,
> Parting from thee, I part from part of me:
> And therefore I must speake. Yet what? O sonne.

There is an echo of this scene later on, distorted, as echoes are,
and used deliberately to recall this parting at the moment of
Cleopatra's death as she dallies with the asp, procrastinating a
little before the final deed:

> Looke how a mother at her sonnes departing
> For some farre voyage bent to get him fame,
> Doth entertain him with an ydle parling[12]
> And still doth speake, and still speakes but the same;
> Now bids farewell, and now recalles him backe,
> Tels what was told, and bids againe farewell,
> And yet againe recalles; for still doth lacke
> Something that Love would faine and cannot tell;
> Pleas'd he should goe, yet cannot let him goe.

The rest of Rodon's account is concerned with the betrayal of
Caesario and Caesario's lament on the irony of being born great
only to suffer great miseries – a common theme in Senecan
tragedy which, with its inverse, the virtues of mediocrity, finds a
place also in Jodelle. In Daniel it demonstrates yet another implication of Cleopatra's fate and extends the story into the future
when another generation will take up the old quarrels.

12. Grosart prints, erroneously, 'parting'.

Daniel, then, from the slightest of hints in Plutarch, and with Garnier's tentative treatment of it before him, developed a theme which considerably enriches his play. In the scene between Seleucus and Rodon, he opens up a new vista in the character of Cleopatra and suggests that a passionate and tender devotion to her children is included in her personality. It is evident that Daniel became deeply interested in Cleopatra as he revolved the material for his play and his work takes its shape and impulse from that interest so that, ultimately, all his material, from whatever source, is used to give body and life to a conception which is entirely original.

The scene between Cleopatra and Caesar provides a good single example of Daniel's handling of his material. Daniel introduces Dolabella as a witness of the scene and this is a device which is effective in several ways. It serves to bind the play together, as it is Dolabella who is to send the important letter to Cleopatra warning her of Caesar's intention to send her shortly to Rome (in Jodelle, Dolabella's name is mentioned in connection with the letter but without any reference to him before or after); it serves, by paving the way for the Dolabella-Titius scene, to provide a means of linking the action between Cleopatra's last rites at Antony's tomb and the final narrative of her death; and most important of all, it throws still more light on Cleopatra by illustrating the powerful effect of her beauty and her personality even at this time of disaster. It shows, too, how Cleopatra, made more sensitive to true love and friendship in her sorrow, responds now with gratitude, whereas once she had thought that all men owed her love as a duty and she was bound to none.

What Daniel has done, then, is to evolve a closely integrated action out of his material and, above all, to produce a study of character remarkable for its sympathy and insight.[13] Daniel recognised in 1594 that his Cleopatra was not much like the historical figure and in the dedication of the 1611 edition he

13. It is an interesting idea that Shakespeare may have been led to treat the Antony and Cleopatra story in the way he did because Daniel's Cleopatra suggested how much more could be made of her than the mere 'bad woman', as Dr. Dover Wilson calls her, of Plutarch. As A. M. Z. Norman puts it in his article 'Daniel's *The Tragedie of Cleopatra* and *Antony and Cleopatra*' (*S.Q.* IX (1958), pp. 11–18): 'Samuel Daniel's closet drama . . . provides an explanation of Shakespeare's daring use of two climaxes' (i.e. the death of Antony followed by a long act devoted to Cleopatra) 'and of his conception of Cleopatra as the embodiment of a love transcending worldly obligations'.

defends himself in significant words. He has presented her tragedy, he writes:

> In th'habit I conceived became her care
> Which if to her it be not fitted right
> Yet in the sute of nature sure it is
> And is the language that affliction might
> Perhaps deliver when it spake distresse.[14]

Political issues are firmly subordinated to this sympathy and there is even some inconsistency as far as the moral is concerned, for while the Chorus and the philosophers talk about lust and luxury, the Cleopatra who is portrayed is at least well on the way to being purified. In her first speech she recognises a new depth in her love for Antony and she can see now, too, the quality of his love:

> And yet thou cam'st but in my beauties waine,
> When new appearing wrinckles of declining
> Wrought with the hand of yeares, seem'd to detaine
> My graces light, as now but dimly shining,
> Even in the confines of mine age, when I
> Failing of what I was, and was but thus:
> When such as we do deeme in jealousie
> That men love for themselves, and not for us;
> Then, and but thus, thou didst love most sincerely,
> O *Antony*, that best deserv'dst it better,
> This Autumne of my beauty bought so dearely,
> For which in more than death, I stand thy debter . . .

This passage is in direct contradiction to what Plutarch says of Cleopatra's beauty: '. . . Caesar and Pompey knew her when she was but a young thing, and knew not then what the worlde ment: but nowe she went to Antonius at the age when a woman's beawtie is at the prime, and she also of best judgement'.[15] The alteration enables Daniel to illustrate the change he conceives to have taken place in Cleopatra's character under the pressure of sorrow, her ruthless examination of herself, and her new tenderness towards Antony; but such touches make it difficult to identify her with the sinful figure whom the Chorus denounces.

The human touches, the vividness with which some scenes and situations are realised, are among the by no means negligible rewards offered to a sympathetic reading of this play. Caesario

14. Lederer, p. 4. 15. Plutarch, p. 25.

makes the usual comments about the disadvantages of greatness
and the retribution which overtakes tyrants, but he adds, more
feelingly:

> Yet in the meane time we whom Fates reserve,
> The bloody sacrifices of ambition,
> We feele the smart, what ever they deserve,
> And we indure the present times condition.
> The justice of the heavens revenging thus,
> Doth onely satisfie it selfe, not us.

The messenger, who takes the aspics to Cleopatra, tells how he
put them in a basket of figs, covered with leaves:

> And comming to the guard that kept the doore,
> What hast thou there? said they, and lookt thereon.
> Seeing the figges, they deem'd of nothing more,
> But said, they were the fairest they had seene.
> Tast some, said I, for they are good and pleasant.
> No, no, said they, goe beare them to thy Queene,
> Thinking me some poore man that brought a present.

And he describes Cleopatra in her last finery:

> Glittering in all her pompeous rich aray,
> Great *Cleopatra* sate, as if sh'had wonne
> *Caesar*, and all the world beside, this day.

As she sinks in death Charmion sets straight the crown on her
head

> That all the world may know she dide a Queene.

The verse itself labours at times but, as some of the quotations
above have shown, when a congenial opportunity occurs it
comes alight and takes the imagination. There are many single
lines and some longer passages which make moments, if not
immortal, yet certainly memorable. Daniel's eloquence has
greater opportunities here than ever before and the development
has now taken place which was foreshadowed in *Rosamond*, his
'very pure and copious English' (in Edmund Bolton's phrase)
has been brought fully into the service of his sensitive, reflective,
and intelligent mind.

The Choruses deserve some separate discussion.

The members of the Chorus are 'all Egyptians' and although

they do not participate in the action they are naturally deeply concerned about what is going on. At the end of Act 1, which has consisted solely of Cleopatra's soliloquy, they comment severely on the sins of the great:

> The scene is broken downe
> And all uncov'red lyes,
> The purple actors knowne
> Scarce men, whom men despise.

Cleopatra, they somewhat grimly point out, now sees what lies at the end of 'the dangerous way' she took:

> Which led her to decay.
> And likewise makes us pay
> For her disordred lust,
> The int'rest of our blood:
> Or live a servile pray,
> Under a hand unjust,
> As others shall thinke good.
> This hath her riot wonne:
> And thus she hath her state, herselfe and us undone.

Daniel uses a twelve-line stanza form, rhymed ababbcdbcdee, consisting of eleven lines of three iambic feet and a final alexandrine. Far from being graceful, it is an inflexible form which imparts a peculiar harshness to the Chorus's judgements. At times they contrive a moral allegory that sounds as though Daniel has been reading his Spenser recently:

> Their conscience still within
> Th'eternall larum is
> That ever-barking dog that calles upon their misse.
>
> No meanes at all to hide
> Man from himself can finde:
> No way to start aside
> Out from the hell of minde.
> But in himselfe confin'd,
> He still sees sinne before;
> And winged-footed paine,
> That swiftly comes behind ...

For the second chorus Daniel evolves another curious stanza form, consisting this time of fourteen lines rhyming abbaacddcceeff. The subject is the frustrations and miseries of the discontented mind which, whether it seeks the objects of ambition or of lust, is never satisfied but finds only 'destruction, envy, hate'. Even Cleopatra's resolution to die is seen by the Chorus here as nothing more than a last will o' the wisp:

> This is that rest this vaine world lends,
> To end in death that all things ends.

The lines are longer by a foot than those of the first chorus but the high proportion of monosyllables and a certain bleakness of statement, which is not unimpressive, make them appear clipped. The third chorus has four-foot lines, like the third, a twelve-line stanza, ababbccabadd, and, what distinguishes it very markedly from either of the previous two, a very much richer vocabulary and fuller tone:

> O Fearfull-frowning Nemesis,
> Daughter of Justice, most severe;
> That art the worlds great Arbitresse
> And Queene of causes raigning here.

It gives strong lyric expression to the idea of 'inevitable destiny', the 'swift confusion' which will abase 'late proud mounting vanity' and it questions heavenly justice which includes 'The innocent poore multitude' in the punishment of great men's sins. But, resignedly, the Chorus conclude that in the cycle of human affairs, prosperity will ever grow overweening and will ever be punished:

> As we, so they that treate us thus,
> Must one day perish like to us.[16]

The fourth chorus has a four-foot line and a fourteen-line stanza composed as three quatrains and a final couplet. It is again distinguished from all its predecessors this time by the fact that feminine rhyme endings are used throughout except in the final couplets. It is a languid, nerveless poem in which the chorus find slippery excuses for Egypt's humiliation – it is the decree of fate – it is the fault of their rulers – and only rouse themselves to

16. For some interesting comments on this chorus see C. C. Seronsy, 'The Doctrine of Cyclical Recurrence and Some Related Ideas in the Works of Samuel Daniel', S.P. 54 (1957), pp. 387–407.

hope that the conquerors will in time be corrupted by the weaknesses of the conquered:

> Fill full your hands, and carry home,
> Enough from us to ruine Rome.

The last chorus returns to the three-foot line of the first. The stanza has fourteen lines and is rhymed abcdabcddcbaee. The theme is the extinction of all hope for Egypt now that Cleopatra is dead, and the passion of the moment urges the chorus into symbolic language of some imaginative power:[17]

> And canst O Nylus thou,
> Father of flouds indure,
> That yellow Tyber should
> With sandy streames rule thee?
> . . . .
> . . . .
> Draw backe thy waters floe
> To thy concealèd head:
> Rockes strangle up thy waves,
> Stop Cataractes thy fall.
> And turne thy courses so,
> That sandy Desarts dead,
> (The world of dust that craves
> To swallow thee up all,)
> May drinke so much as shall
> Revive from vasty graves
> A living greene, which spred
> Far florishing, may grow
> On that wide face of Death,
> Where nothing now drawes breath.

It ends with unanswered questions to the gods:

> Are these the bounds y'have given
> Th' untranspassable barres,
> That limit Pride so short?
> Is greatnesse of this sort,
> That greatnesse greatnesse marres,
> And wrackes it selfe, selfe-driven
> On Rockes of her owne might?
> Doth Order order so
> Disorders overthrow?

17. It owes something to the third stanza of the Chorus to Act II of Garnier's *Marc-Antoine* (*Oeuvres*, p. 196).

The choruses, as this account of them has shown, combine commentary on the moral implications of the drama with statements appropriate to the individuals composing the Chorus, the ordinary Egyptian people. They are carefully worked in form and diction and each is devised to make a particular impression and an individual contribution to the play as a whole. Great care has evidently been devoted to them, but the result is only intermittently successful: perhaps, indeed, they try to do too much.

A great deal of effort has undoubtedly gone into the whole play. Daniel is forcing his poetic gifts to expand in the directions that Lady Pembroke and her friends wished, leaving the love-melancholy of *Delia* and *Rosamond* for the fall of kingdoms and the tragedies of the great, and for the cultivation of rarefied dramatic and lyric form. His poetry runs, naturally, more easily into some of the new channels than others. Some of the better passages have already been quoted and it is especially interesting to see the characteristics of the later Daniel emerging in such things as his patient and sympathetic elaboration of the character of Cleopatra, the reduction of the violence of the Seleucus scene in favour of a more adult and dignified treatment, and the serious reflection on human life and character, which leads him, for example, to reject a count of supernatural phenomena and replace it by a history of moral degeneration. As a work complete in itself Daniel's *Cleopatra* deserves much better than to be dismissed merely as an aberration from the path of true drama; in its relation to Daniel's career, it is a very important document, for in the composing of it Daniel developed the character by which he is now best known.

When he began *Cleopatra* he was 'Sweete hony-dropping Daniel'; by the time he finished it, he was Coleridge's 'sober-minded Daniel' and he knew much better than he had where his aptitudes and inclinations in this 'higher straine' lay.

IV

New Patrons: 'Musophilus', 'A Letter from Octavia' and 'A Defence of Ryme'

Cleopatra was entered on the Stationers' Register on the 19th October, 1593, and the first instalment of Daniel's long historical poem, *The Civile Warres betweene the two houses of Lancaster and Yorke*, was entered almost exactly twelve months later, 11th October, 1594. This was a momentous, nearly a disastrous year, for in the course of it some great change took place in Daniel's fortunes which drove him away from Wilton and threatened to overwhelm him completely. In the event, new patrons came to his rescue, Fulke Greville, courtier and poet, the man who cherished to the end of a long and active career the memory of his friendship with Sir Philip Sidney, and Charles Blount, Lord Mountjoy, friend of Essex. Internal evidence in *The Civil Wars* and a letter of Greville's put the existence of a crisis in Daniel's affairs at this time beyond question but what caused it remains doubtful.

The first reference occurs in Book 1, stanza 5 of the early editions of *The Civil Wars* in which Daniel dedicates the poem to Lord Mountjoy in these terms:

> And thou *Charles Mountjoy* borne the worldes delight,
> That has receiv'd into thy quiet shore
> Mee tempest-driven fortune-tossed wight,
> Tir'd with expecting, and could hope no more:
> And cheerest on, my better yeares to write
> A sadder Subject, then I tooke before;
> Receive the worke I consecrate to thee
> Borne of that rest, which thou dost give to mee.[1]

1. *See opposite page.*

The third book in 1595 ends with another reference to Mount-joy's 'remorse of mine estate' and a plea to him to continue his favours.[2]

A letter from Fulke Greville to Robert Cecil, dated April 8th, 1595, adds a little more to the picture. The postcript of this letter runs as follows: 'The parsonage in the Isle of Wight, which I moved Her Majesty for Samuel Danyel, and which she was pleased to be certified of by you from your father, is called Shaw-flete. There is some twelve years to run; he desires so many in reversion as she shall think fit. Sir, you shall do a good deed to help the poor man; many will thank you.'[3] The point of this negotiation is evidently this: the parsonage Greville refers to would be a lay holding comprising the tenancy of the glebe lands and property of the church – including perhaps the vicarage – and also the right to receive tithes.

If he had the reversion, Daniel could either come to some arrangement with the then holder by which he would succeed to the property before the twelve years of the current lease were expired or, and this would be the real value of the reversion to a man desperately in need of money, he could sell it to someone else for ready cash.

Though Greville's appeal was successful, for the Patent Roll records (38 Eliz., pt. iv) that the property was handed on from Daniel to one Nicholas Browne in 1602, there was evidently some delay before Daniel could get any benefit from it and in 1595 Mountjoy's offer of shelter came just in time to save him from destitution. Whatever the cause of the breach with the Pembrokes, it did not cause permanent ill-feeling for in 1603 Daniel addressed his *Defence of Ryme* to William Herbert who had by then succeeded his father as Earl and in 1609 Lady Pembroke was again his patron when he resumed his protracted labours on *The Civil Wars*. Possibly it was some rift with the old Earl which

1. Later, after Mountjoy's death in 1606, Daniel altered the wording, but not the sentiment:

> And thou *Charles Mountjoy* (who didst once afford
> Rest for my fortunes, on thy quiet shore;
> And cheerd'st mee on, these measures to record
> In graver tones, then I had us'd before)' . . .

2. Michel, p. 322.

3. Historical Manuscripts Commission (Hatfield House), part v, p. 166. I am indebted for the explanation of this document to my former colleague, Mr. E. Ives, now of Liverpool University.

SAMUEL DANIEL

caused the trouble. Daniel may have expected some post in the
Earl's gift which never came his way and grown tired of a depen-
dency which perhaps bound him too strictly. There are some
feeling lines about poverty in *Musophilus* (1599) which say rather
more than the context requires, and reveal an almost morbid
revulsion. There may be something, Daniel says (though doubt-
fully), even worse than 'the shame Of vile and unregarded pover-
tie' –

> Which I confess, although I often strive
> To cloth in the best habit of my skill,
> In all the fairest colours I can give;
> Yet for all that me thinks she lookes but ill,
> I cannot brooke that face, which dead-alive
> Shewes a quicke bodie, but a buried will.[4]

Poverty and the galling nature of dependence are strong motifs
also in the *To M.P.* sonnet of *Delia*: possibly Daniel had expected
something from the Pembroke connection which would save
him from these humiliations in the future and, being disappointed,
angered the Earl by his discontent. Certainly he was cast adrift
and his situation was for a time serious.

Whatever the reason for his leaving Wilton, the circumstances could not have been much to his discredit since Greville
was ready to appeal to Cecil for him and Mountjoy took him in.
Through Mountjoy he met Essex and came to love him and this
attachment was to have a profound effect upon Daniel in the
years that followed; but the immediate influences were those of
Greville and Mountjoy and they are reflected at once in his
poetry. *Musophilus*, first published in the *Poetical Essays* of 1599,
is in a sense their poem and claims attention, consequently, at
this point.

The poem takes the form of a debate between Musophilus,
the champion of the Muses, and Philocosmus, who believes that
the cultivation of the arts is a waste of time in 'This wiser profit-
seeking age' (l. 13). Greville's part in the inception of the poem
is acknowledged fully by Daniel, and the comments he makes in
addressing his friend and patron throw a good deal of light on his
attitude to his subject and are relevant also to his personal circumstances at the time of composition. In the editions of 1599,
1601, 1602 and 1623, *Musophilus* is dedicated to Greville in a

4. Sprague, p. 73, ll. 135–40.

64

sonnet which stresses the personal nature of the poem, 'the forme of mine owne heart', Daniel calls it. He is urged to defend his occupation, he explains, by the present contempt of poetry and it is evident that his primary concern is to reassure and justify himself in his literary career. In the earliest edition, the poem concluded with another reference to Greville (ll. 995f.) in which Daniel speaks of his friend's 'learned judgement', which he esteems above all others, and of his 'mild grace' and 'gentle hand', which first encouraged Daniel's 'Infant Muse'. These lines were omitted in later editions but the acknowledgement of indebtedness to Greville was repeated in the thirty-nine lines of dedication addressed to him which in 1611 replaced the original sonnet.[5] These lines give a more extensive account of the *raison d'être* of the poem and make an important, though not altogether luminous, contribution to Daniel's biography. Greville, Daniel says, was the first to encourage his poetic gifts and he:

> Did first draw forth from close obscuritie
> My unpresuming verse into the light
> And grac'd the same, and made me known thereby.
>
> (ll. 9–11)

This may mean that Greville first drew Lady Pembroke's attention to the merits of Daniel's sonnets in the 1591 edition and so secured him her patronage, but in the *Defence of Ryme* (Sprague, p. 129, already quoted) Daniel speaks as though it was the Countess of Pembroke herself who took the initiative. Or the *Musophilus* lines may possibly refer to *Cleopatra* and constitute perhaps an acknowledgement that Greville brought the verse-play to Mountjoy's attention. If so, 'close obscuritie' is an unfriendly description of Wilton and so is the parallel phrase in the 1599 text (ll. 1002–3). It would suggest that Lady Pembroke had offered Daniel her patronage on the strength of *Delia* and *Rosamond*, and that Greville had been led to take an interest in him through *Cleopatra* and to rescue him from what, in spite of the initial encouragement which he never forgot to acknowledge, had grown to be a stifling atmosphere. Whichever of these explanations is right, Greville's honour is involved in the defence which Daniel offers in *Musophilus* since Greville 'holds an interest' in Daniel's pursuit of poetry.

5. Sprague, pp. 203–4.

The 1611 dedication goes on to acknowledge Daniel's gratitude for Greville's praise but in spite of this and the fact that Greville is in his view well qualified to judge, he has still had doubts:

> ... for my part I have beene oft constraind
> To reexamine this my course herein
> And question with my selfe what is containd
> Or what solidity there was therein.
> And then in casting it with that account
> And recknings of the world, I therein found
> It came farre short, and neither did amount
> In valew with those hopes I did propound
> Nor answer'd the expences of my time
> Which made me much distrust my selfe and ryme.
>
> (ll. 20–9)

Self-distrust and diffidence were traits of Daniel's character which N. W. was acquainted with years before and Daniel himself acknowledges them in a passage from the *Defence of Ryme*: '. . . irresolution and a selfe-distrust be the most apparent faults of my nature, and . . . the least checke of reprehension, if it savour of reason, will as easily shake my resolution as any mans living . . .'[6] These words occur in much the same sort of connection as those in the lines to Fulke Greville quoted above and Daniel's doubts, it is clear, go beyond lack of confidence in himself. A man may well feel his own inadequacy and yet have faith in his métier but Daniel is open to suspicions about both, and part at least of the impulse behind *Musophilus* and the *Defence of Ryme* is an attempt to establish the worthiness of the objects to which his efforts are directed.

Daniel's words in the dedication to Fulke Greville, that he *has been* often constrained to re-examine his choice of a career in poetry, suggest a state of mind recurring up to the time of writing, and no doubt the mood of self-distrust was constitutional. But the passage continues in terms which suggest a special reference:

> And I was flying from my heart and from
> The station I was set in, to remaine:
> And had left all, had not fresh forces come
> And brought me backe unto my selfe againe,
> And furnisht my distrusts with this defence

6. Sprague, p. 130.

66

This armor wherewith all the best I could
I have made good, against the difference
Of fortune, and the world, that which I told.

(ll. 30–7)

The tense of the verbs here indicates that he has in mind some crisis of dejection in the past from which he has now been rescued. The whole passage from line 20 onwards ('And for my part, I have beene oft constraind' etc.) and especially the second part of it, is awkward and obscure, giving the impression of a story half told and half concealed, and it cannot be interpreted with certainty. But possibly there is a clue in some lines which occur towards the end of the poem in the earliest editions. Lines 989–94 in 1599, 1601 and 1602 read (Musophilus is speaking to Philocosmus):

Now to what else thy malice shall object,
For schooles, and Arts, and their necessitie:
When from my Lord, whose judgement must direct
And forme, and fashion my abilitie
I shall have got more strength: thou shalt expect
Out of my better leasure, my reply.

This 'Lord' must be identified with the unnamed supporter of the 1611 dedication who brought 'fresh forces' to Daniel's aid (ll. 32f, see above), since Daniel ascribes to both the same function of furnishing his defence against the attacks of those who scorned letters; and he can be no other than Mountjoy to whom the whole volume of *Poetical Essays* of 1599 was dedicated. It is possible, therefore, that the crisis hinted at in the 1611 dedication to *Musophilus* is the same as that which drove him from Wilton in 1594 and if so perhaps the explanation of the Wilton débâcle is that Lady Pembroke was forcing Daniel in directions where he did not want to go and thus precipitating a mood of doubt and depression in which he nearly threw up the whole business of writing.

Thus the specifically personal addenda to *Musophilus* establish the importance of Greville and Mountjoy in Daniel's life and thought at this time. Mountjoy died in 1606 and Daniel omitted from the 1607 and 1611 editions the lines in the body of the poem relating to his 'lord' and the need to seek further advice from him,[7]

7. They were restored in the posthumous edition of 1623 supervised by John Daniel.

but the 1611 dedication supplies the now missing reference to Mountjoy. It perhaps appeared pointless to Daniel to make the reference more explicit when Mountjoy himself was dead, but it was sufficient to complete the background of his poem and to satisfy his own sense of obligation to the memory of his former patron.

Since Mountjoy then, by Daniel's acknowledgement, had so large a part in stimulating him to write *Musophilus*, the sort of influence he was likely to have on Daniel's thinking becomes a subject of some interest. Charles Blount, Lord Mountjoy, 'an ornament equally to the characters of soldier, statesman, scholar and courtier'[8] was born in 1563. He became Lord Mountjoy in 1594 on the death of his elder brother and was created Earl of Devonshire by James I in July 1603. In his *Funerall Poeme upon the Earle of Devonshire*,[9] Daniel describes him as one who had made:

> . . . a general Survey
> Of all the best of men's best knowledges,
> And knew as much as ever learning knew

and who was also an accomplished and successful soldier and governor of Ireland. He conducted his affairs with 'a quiet calme sincerity' and the elements were so mixed in him as to make an harmonious and perfectly controlled whole:

> And never man had heart more truely serv'd
> Under the regiment of his owne care
> And was more at command, and more observ'd
> The colours of that modesty he bare
> Then that of thine, in whom men never found
> That any shew, or speech obscene, could tell
> Of any veine thou hadst that was unsound,
> Or motion of thy powers, that turn'd not well.

He embodies, in fact, for Daniel, an ideal of the cultivated man, a scholar, a man of action, and a moral nature which retains its integrity unshaken by the storms of the world:

> . . . he ever flies
> That Maze of many waies, which might disperse
> Him, into other mens uncertainties,

8. Lodge's *Portraits* (London, 1823–34), iii, p. 77.
9. Grosart i, pp. 171–88.

and he has attained something like that sufficiency and serenity of
conscience which Daniel describes in his epistles to the Countess
of Cumberland and the Countess of Bedford.[10]

How much Daniel might have gained from the friendship and
conversation of such a man can be imagined. Mountjoy gave him
not only money to live on (see *Funeral Poem*, ll. 30–1) and encouragement to pursue his poetry, but also a new faith in the
dignity and virtue of letters.[11] It is of that faith that *Musophilus*
speaks in some of its best moments:

> Soule of the world, knowledge, without thee,
> What hath the earth that truly glorious is?
> Why should our pride make such a stir to be,
> To be forgot? what good is like to this,
> To do worthy the writing, and to write
> Worthy the reading, and the worlds delight?

The 'states soule', he writes, is Learning and 'the weapons of the
mind' are 'states best strengths, and kingdoms chiefest grace'.
'True knowledge can both speak and do' and the possibilities of
the research it may, with encouragement, undertake, are vast and
wonderful:

> Discov'ring dayly more, and more about
> In that immense and boundlesse Ocean
> Of Natures riches, never yet found out,
> Nor fore-clos'd with the wit of any man. (ll. 827–30)

Daniel describes his poem as 'Containing a generall defence of
all learning' and it is indeed a defence of the things of the mind

---

10. Daniel cannot, of course, help but take notice of the scandal over Mountjoy's
marriage with the divorced wife of Lord Rich (*née* Penelope Devereux) which em-
bittered the end of his life; but he pleads that one defect should not be allowed to
obscure so much merit:
> But yet his vertues, and his worthinesse
> Being seene so farre above his weaknesses,
> Must ever shine, whilst th' other under ground,
> With his fraile part, shall never more be found . . .
These lines occur only in 1606 but the same general point is made in all editions of
the poem.

11. In his reference to 'my worthy Lord, the fosterer of mee and my *Muse*' in the
Defence of Ryme (Sprague, p. 126), it is far more likely that Daniel was referring to
Mountjoy than to the old Earl of Pembroke with whom this 'Lord' is usually
identified. The description certainly fits Mountjoy and we do not know that it is
applicable to the Earl of Pembroke.

against materialism and narrow utilitarianism, ranging from an exposure of the shallow foundations of worldly grandeur (ll. 105–32 *et passim*) to a plea for the preservation of a spirit of reverence (ll. 677–754). On this last point, Daniel fears that innovation and reformation will too readily pull down good with bad and leave nothing sacred even in religion. This theme is to recur in Daniel's work, notably in *The Civil Wars*, book VI, stanzas 31–9 and in *The Queenes Arcadia* (see pp. 14–16), and it represents a fear of the arrogant scientific spirit which:

> . . . makes men fore-setled to become
> Curious to know what was believ'd before:
> Whilst faith disputes that used to be dombe,
> And more men strive to talke then to adore.
>
> (ll. 727–30)

This strain of conservatism verging on the obscurantist is the reverse side of the medal which shows the 'bold *Plus ultra*' of the reinvigorated Academies in ll. 821–30 and celebrates the virtue of knowledge, but there is no real contradiction. Knowledge goes hand in hand with humility in Daniel's concept of the ideal, just as great learning and great modesty exist side by side in the character of Mountjoy (*Funeral Poem*, ll. 59–63 *et passim*). Over all, in Daniel's mind, stands the awful figure of

> Sacred *Religion*, mother of forme and feare.[12]

The state of contemporary literature naturally comes in for attention in the poem, and a recurrent theme is the itch for writing which seems to have spread inordinately:

> Do you not see these *Pamphlets, Libels, Rymes,*
> These strange confused tumults of the minde,
> Are growne to be the sicknes of these times,
> The great disease inflicted on mankind?   (ll. 446–9)

'So many' now 'so confusedlie sing' that the 'mysterie' of poetry is brought into contempt (ll. 62–71) and the jostling for position among the crowd of candidates for the honours of literature and

12. Wordsworth quoted the line in the 18th of the River Duddon sonnets and Daniel's attitude to the rationalists of his day struck a responsive chord in Wordsworth's mind when he wrote in *The Prelude* about Godwinism. He echoes there the language of *The Civil Wars*, book VI, sts. 35–6. (See Joan Rees, 'Wordsworth and Samuel Daniel', *N.Q.*, January 1959, pp. 26–7.)

learning engenders jealousies and controversies, and this in its turn:

> Contempt and scorne on all in th'end doth bring
> Like scolding wives reckning each others fault
> Make standers by imagin both are naught.   (ll. 471-3)

The field is too wide open. Entry should be reserved only for the 'choicest wits' whose skill is matched by their 'milde discretion' (ll. 474-85). As it is, good and bad are confounded in 'a deepe distast' arising from a surfeit (ll. 253-8) and it can only be hoped that 'another spring of praise' will come when 'th' infection of distempred daies' has passed (ll. 171-6). Yet Daniel in the end is optimistic: 'this swelling tide And streame of words' now rising so high above its usual banks, is not to be condemned even if it contains some impurities (ll. 927-38). Eloquence is a 'Powre above powres':

> That with the strong reine of commanding words,
> Dost manage, guide and master th'eminence
> Of mens affections, more then all their swords.   (ll. 939-42)

It ill becomes the national pride to neglect its writers and yield the palm to other countries:

> When as our accents equall to the best
> Is able greater wonders to bring forth:
> When all that ever hotter spirits exprest
> Comes bettered by the patience of the North.
>
>   (ll. 953-6)

Our language is at present confined within narrow limits, but who knows what its future may be:

> What worlds in th'yet unformed Occident
> May come refin'd with th' accents that are ours?

and who knows for what great work it may be destined? (ll. 957-68).[13] The whole passage from l. 939 to l. 968 is a superb statement of faith rising to prophecy and its sustained passion makes it a high-water mark of *Musophilus*.

One other passage approaches it, and part of it has already been quoted. The subject is again poetry but the angle this time is a

13. *See footnote on following page.*

much more individual one. Musophilus is anticipating the time
to come when poetry will be once more appreciated:

> When as perhaps the words thou scornest now
> May live, the speaking picture of the mind,
> The extract of the soule that laboured how
> To leave the image of her selfe behind,
> Wherein posteritie that love to know
> The just proportion of our spirits may find.
> For these lines are the vaines, the Arteries,
> And undecaying life-strings of those harts
> That still shall pant, and still shall exercise
> The motion spirit and nature both imparts,
> And shall, with those alive so sympathize
> As nourisht with their powers injoy their parts.
> O blessed letters that combine in one
> All ages past, and make one live with all,
> By you we do confer with who are gone,
> And the dead living unto councell call:
> By you th' unborne shall have communion
> Of what we feele, and what doth us befall.
> Soule of the world, knowledge, without thee,
> What hath the earth that truly glorious is?
> Why should our pride make such a stir to be,

13. Daniel was very conscious of the narrowly restricted use of English. In the
1594 version of the dedication of *Cleopatra* he writes:

> O that the Ocean did not bound our stile
> Within these strict and narrow limites so:
> But that the melodie of our sweete Ile,
> Might now be heard to *Tyber*, *Arne*, and *Po* :
> That they might know how far Thames doth out-go
> The Musicke of declined *Italy* :
> And listning to our Songs another while,
> Might learne of thee, their notes to purifie.
>
> O why may not some after-comming hand
> Unlocke these limites, open our confines,
> And breake asunder this imprisoning band,
> T''inlarge our spirits, and publish our designes;
> Planting our Roses on the *Apenines*?
> And teach to *Rheyne*, to *Loyre*, and *Rhodanus*.
> Our accents, and the wonders of our Land,
> That they might all admire and honour us.

(Grosart iii, p. 26.)

Perhaps Florio gave his regrets a special sting with remarks such as that in the *First
Fruits*: 'What thinke you of this English tongue, tel me, I pray you? It is a language
that wyl do you good in England, but passe Dover, it is worth nothing.' (*Florio's
First Fruits*, ed. A. del Re, Formosa, Japan, 1936, p. 123).

To be forgot? what good is like to this,
To do worthy the writing, and to write
Worthy the reading, and the worlds delight?

(ll. 177–200)

The passion in these lines gathers momentum as it does in the passage on eloquence, and its source, the emphasis on intimate knowledge of the individual as he was and as he felt is characteristic of the mature Daniel. His Cleopatra, Richard II (in *The Civil Wars*), and Henry II (in *Rosamond*), most notably among many, testify his interest in realising the experience of others, especially in the past. The poet, he argues in *Musophilus*, is sensitive enough to be able to pick up these vibrations from the past, and he may also leave to posterity the picture of his own soul, part of a great record of human experience preserved alive, so to speak, in poetry.

Of the two godfathers of the poem it must have been Mountjoy, not Greville, who encouraged, even inspired, the humanity and the elegance of the ideal of learning and of poetry. Greville's view of learning, as Professor Bullough comments,[14] had little in common with Daniel's. He would never have written that knowledge was the soul of the world, and as for the truly glorious, in reference to human affairs the words had no meaning at all for him. Human wisdom, science, power and arts were to him but 'fleshly idols' raised by man 'Upon the false foundation of his Guilt'[15] and Daniel's 'Powre above powres, O heavenly *Eloquence*' which is a more effective ruler of men's affections than any sword, is accorded at best a grudging esteem, provided it indulge in no 'craft of words' and that its subject is the description or praise of God. 'Poesie and Musicke' are 'Arts of Recreation', 'not pretious in their proper kind' but of possible allowance if not given exaggerated importance:

Both, ornaments to life and other Arts,
Whiles they doe serve, and not possesse our hearts.[16]

Nevertheless, some trace of Greville's thinking is discernible in *Musophilus*. It would be surprising on the whole if this were not so, given Daniel's diffidence in defending his own views and his

14. *Poems and Dramas of Fulke Greville*, ed. G. Bullough (Edinburgh and London, 1938), i, p. 61.
15. Greville, *A Treatie of Humane Learning*, st. 55.
16. Ibid., sts. 110–15.

sensitivity to those of other people. The courtier-scholar of the
Renaissance, the Humanist ideal, typified in Daniel's own day by
such men as Sidney and Essex and Mountjoy, lends warmth and
colour to *Musophilus* but the sense of human sinfulness which was
so strong in Greville has its place also in the poem:

> And see how soone this rowling world can take
> Advantage for her dissolution,
> Faine to get loose from this withholding stake
> Of civill science and discretion:
> How glad it would run wilde, that it might make
> One formelesse forme of one confusion?   (ll. 677–82)

These lines introduce Daniel's warning, already discussed,
against the unlicensed application of the spirit of enquiry, and
they represent, if not a retreat from the vision splendid, at least an
anxious glance at the darker shadows in the human picture which
Greville insisted so much upon. Bullough points out that in his
poem written for Florio's *Montaigne* (1603) Daniel speaks of the
suspicion cast on knowledge 'Seeing what uncertainties we build
upon' and the divalence in Daniel's attitude which is hinted at in
Musophilus grew more marked as time went on. Greville's stanza
39 of *Of Humane Learning* would apply very well to the distrust of
'swelling Sciences' expressed in both *The Queenes Arcadia* and *The
Civil Wars*, Book VI:

> And in the best, where Science multiplies,
> Man multiplies with it his care of minde:
> While in the worst, these swelling harmonies
> Like bellowes, fill unquiet hearts with winde,
> To blow the flame of malice, question, strife,
> Both into publike States and private life.

But the influence of Greville's mind on Daniel's at the time of the
composition of *Musophilus* is to be seen less in such things as this,
where Daniel's ideas, though they show perhaps some impress of
Greville's, are assimilated into a philosophy quite different in kind
from his, than in an attitude, to be defined with increasing clarity
as time goes on, towards the nature of poetry and the material of
poetry. Daniel himself thought *Musophilus* a very ambitious poem.
In his 1611 dedication he half apologises for it (ll. 1–4) and the
concluding lines of the 1599 edition make plain how daring the
whole undertaking seemed to him. 'So bold and ventrous' an

attempt he calls it (1. 1008), 'beyond example', an experiment in 'waies That malice from our forces thinkes exempt' (ll. 1009–10):

> And if herein the curious sort shall deeme
> My will was caried far beyond my force,
> And that it is a thing doth ill beseeme
> The function of a *Poem* to discourse:
> Thy learned judgement which I most esteeme
> (Worthy *Fulke Grevil*) must defend this course
>
> (ll. 995–1000)

This certainly suggests affiliations with Greville's attitude to poetry. Greville's verse treatises, originally designed as choruses to his plays (Bullough puts the dates of the first versions of both plays before 1600) were to deal with 'the largest subjects I could then think upon'[17] and Daniel's 'generall defence of all learning' is certainly a large subject too. It is, like Greville's treatises, an adventure into territory which, as Daniel says, was thought to be outside the poet's scope. He has sought to use poetry for the exposition and elucidation of intellectual themes and so, by showing it capable of handling weighty matters, to raise it 'Above the reach of lightnesse and contempt' (1. 1012). Greville, at least after Sidney's death, was not concerned to raise the status of poetry, but he did use it as an instrument of cerebration. Daniel, it is clear, was excited by Greville's views and experiments, and seized on the idea of poetry as thoughtful discourse for the possibilities it offered of increasing and enhancing the domain of poetic eloquence.

Musophilus is, nevertheless, very different in effect from any of Greville's treatises. Its language and its feeling impart a richness to the arguments which Greville's treatises are without: in this fact lies both the strength of *Musophilus* as a personal testament and its comparative weakness as a poem of 'discourse'. Daniel was not the man to take all knowledge to be his province. His mind was not dispassionate and ratiocinative. His thoughts had to be touched by human sympathy before they became effective and imaginative. The consequence is that *Musophilus* as a poem of 'discourse' is less taut and sinewy than Greville's treatises though it reaches peaks of poetic expressiveness which are quite out of Greville's range.

17. Greville *Life of Sir Philip Sidney*, ed. Nowell Smith (Oxford, 1907), p. 150.

Also appearing for the first time in 1599 was the poem entitled
A Letter from Octavia to Marcus Antonius[18] which Daniel dedicated
*To the right Honourable and most vertuous Lady, the Lady Margaret
Countesse of Cumberland.* This marks another stage in Daniel's
career, for about this time he became tutor to the Countess's
daughter, the Lady Anne Clifford (1590–1676), an association
which seems to have left pleasant memories on both sides.[19] There
is some evidence that the poem was written before October 1598
(see below p. 79) and the dedicatory sonnet to *The Letter
from Octavia* implies that Daniel had already at the time of writing
made the acquaintance of the Countess, for he acknowledges his
gratitude to her for valuing his poetry and offering patronage to
him.[20] It appears too that he is already familiar with the circumstances of her unhappy marriage. Her husband was too occupied
in making piratical voyages to the West Indies or the Mediter-
ranean to spend much time with her, but his infidelities were
notorious: the whole story of Octavia, as Daniel treats it, is an
oblique comment on the Countess's personal situation.

The poem is related to *Rosamond* in that its subject is a woman,
and that it is a 'complaint' of one 'highly preferred to affliction'
(The Argument), but Octavia suffers undeservedly whereas
Rosamond brought her tragedy upon herself.

> ... as thy hopes attend happie redresse,
> Thy joyes depending on a womans grace,
> So move thy minde a wofull womans case,

18. Grosart i, pp. 117–38.
19. It is usually said that the scene of Daniel's tutorship was Skipton Castle in
Yorkshire, but this is certainly wrong. Lady Anne Clifford left Skipton Castle early
in 1590 when she was eight weeks old and did not go back there until July 18th, 1649:
six months previously the Castle had been partly demolished by order of Parliament,
having been used as a garrison during the civil wars. (See Historical Manuscripts
Commission Report for 1888, Rep. II, App. vii, p. 87, and G. C. Williamson, *Lady Anne
Clifford* (Kendal, 1922), pp. 418–19. I am most grateful to the Reverend J. Breay of
Royston, Herts., for drawing my attention to these references.) Lady Anne spent
much of her childhood at Lillford House in Northamptonshire and also at a house
on Clerkenwell Green which the Countess of Cumberland acquired in 1596 (Williamson, *op. cit.*, pp. 66 and 494–5) and it must have been at one, or possibly both, of
these places that Daniel supervised her education.
A letter by Daniel to Sir Thomas Egerton, dated 1601, and complaining of the
hard fate which made him a tutor to children when he should have been concerned
with the actions of men, is thought to be a forgery. Grosart prints it in i, pp. 10–11.
20. 'Rosamond' was also, of course, a Clifford. His choice of her story as a subject
may suggest that Daniel had some contact with the family in 1592 or earlier.

Rosamond had urged him in the earlier poem, and Daniel seems to have done his best to establish himself as a sympathetic interpreter of distressed women. His championship of Octavia, indeed, reads at times like an anticipation of much later battles over the 'position of women'.

The occasion of the *Letter*, as the Argument states, is Antony's return to Egypt after his marriage to Octavia and after great efforts made by her to bring about a reconciliation between him and Octavius Caesar, her brother. The substance of the *Letter* is an appeal to Antony to return and free himself from 'the fetters of Egypt'[21] but it becomes more than a personal complaint of a husband's infidelity as Octavia's own unhappiness leads her to think of the injustice suffered by women in general and to make a passionate protest against a double code of morality and the popular opinion of women as 'unconstant, fickle, false, unkinde'. She speaks frankly and forcefully against the system which represses women and allows men liberty to do as they please. 'Thrice happy you', she says, to Antony as representative of his sex:

> Thrice happy you, in whom it is no fault,
> To know, to speake, to doe, and to be wise,   (st. 17)

while:

> We, in this prison of our selves confin'd,
> Must here shut up with our owne passions live,
> Turn'd in upon us, and denied to find
> The vent of outward meanes that might relieve:
> That they alone must take up all our mind,
> And no room left us, but to thinke and grieve.   (st. 18)

It seems, she comments, an odd situation that women, accounted so weak and frail, must nevertheless stand firm against all assaults on their virtue while men, the strong, have licence to stray as they will. The sixteenth-century Octavia speaks more plainly and directly than nineteenth-century women always dared:

> Thinke that there is like feeling in our bloud

---

21. R. C. Bald (*T.L.S.* Nov. 20th, 1924, p. 776) draws attention to the echo of this in *Antony and Cleopatra*, Act 1, sc. ii, ll. 125–6. For another point in the *Letter from Octavia* which seems to have influenced Shakespeare, see Joan Rees 'Shakespeare's Use of Daniel', *M.L.R.* LV (1960), pp. 79–82.

she says and

> If you will have us good, be you then good   (st. 21)

Altogether the *Letter from Octavia* makes a notable attack on male privilege, not, of course, because Daniel was a feminist born out of his due time, but because when he worked on a story he began to enter into the hearts and minds of the characters who roused his interest.

> Yet have I here adventur'd to bestow
> Words upon griefe, as my griefes comprehend;
> And made this great afflicted Lady show,
> Out of my feelings, what she might have pend,

he writes in the dedication to Lady Cumberland, and in the 1611 dedication to the revised *Cleopatra* (1607), he writes to Lady Pembroke in similar vein of his attempts to present the miseries of his Egyptian queen (see p. 56). This capacity for imaginative sympathy with the people he writes about is an attractive quality in Daniel and brings some of his best results. It is, though, essentially sub-dramatic, for it is a process of identification with the characters rather than creation: in other words, the possible range of character and emotion is limited by the kind of person Daniel himself was. He has a good deal of positive capability in his treatment of his subjects, because he was a sensitive, humane and deeply thoughtful man, but he has no negative capability. His *Cleopatra* goes no further than his *Letter from Octavia* towards real drama, and if *Philotas* tries to go further, as I shall argue later, it is at the cost of artistic cohesion, even of intelligibility.

Nevertheless, he can elucidate a character with discrimination and a fineness of touch. With all her forcefulness, his Octavia is no virago and she has amiable weaknesses. She reproaches Antony that even if he could not continue to love her, at least he might have kept up appearances and not shamed her so publicly (st. 25), and she finds the sympathy of the world hard to bear:

> Cannot the busie world let me alone
> To beare alone the burthen of my griefe,
> But they must intermeddle with my mone,
> And seeke t'offend me with unsought reliefe?   (st. 44)

Daniel's *Octavia* seems to have had literary offspring, triplets, in fact, in the form of Samuel Brandon's play *The Tragicomoedye of the vertuous Octavia* and his verse letters, one from Octavia to

Antony, one from Antony to Octavia.[22] Brandon's work was entered on the Stationers' Register on October 5th, 1598, and Daniel's *Letter* did not appear in print till 1599, but it seems very probable nevertheless that Brandon had seen Daniel's work before he composed his own. There are a number of passages in Brandon's play and letters, not deriving from Plutarch, which look very much as though they were suggested by a reading of Daniel, and while it might be that Daniel was the debtor all the evidence goes to show that of the two Daniel had by far the more original mind and the nature of the similarities is such as to suggest that ideas more or less incidentally introduced into Daniel's *Letter* were extracted and worked up at greater length by Brandon.[23] These instances of parallels of idea in the two works point with a fair degree of probability to Brandon's having carefully taken up hints scattered in Daniel's *Letter*, but it is only fair to Daniel to point out the great gulf that in fact divides his work from that of his disciple.

The *Vertuous Octavia* is neo-classical drama of the French school. It is written in quatrains, like Daniel's *Cleopatra*, with, as in Daniel, lyrical choruses at the end of each act. The plot consists of no more than the reception by Octavia of a number of messages from Antony and of her noble reactions to each of them. This, spread out over five acts, is a thin mixture and Daniel must be held partly responsible for the poverty of action. He, in dealing with the Cleopatra story, chose only a very small fraction of it, a point at which most of the action was over, but he does make something

22. Malone Society Reprints, 1909. Both Daniel's and Brandon's letters are indebted to Drayton's *England's Heroicall Epistles* which first introduced the form into English.

23. The passages in question are: Stanza 14, of Daniel's *Letter* which deals with the obligations which high place entails, how eminence of station should be grounded on eminence in virtue: this theme is elevated to a dominant place in Brandon e.g. in the play at ll. 1764f., and in the letter from Octavia, ll. 336–7; stanza 12 in Daniel's *Letter* in which Octavia reminds Antony that her decision to remain faithful to him in spite of his obvious defection is by no means a matter of course, and ll. 873f. of the letter to Octavia in which Brandon's Antony suggests in a thoroughly nasty way and at some length that after all Octavia may console herself in his absence; stanza 41 of Daniel's *Letter* which contains in little the theme of several of the choruses of the *Vertuous Octavia*, the wretched dilemma of man in a world where sin seems sweet and virtue 'undelightfull'; stanzas 20–1 of Daniel's *Letter* with its idea that if men are indeed the superior sex they should behave the better, and the chorus to Act I of Brandon's play where, as is Brandon's wont, it receives more extended treatment; and, finally, it seems to have been some hints in stanzas 22–3 of Daniel's *Letter* which gave Brandon the theme of Act II, sc. ii, of his play.

of the particle he chose to work on. In the interview between Caesar and Cleopatra, for example, there is a real conflict of wills and wits and the Nuntius's account at the end of Cleopatra's death stirs the imagination and engages the interest of the reader because it relates to a central character with whom we have become intimately acquainted. In Brandon's *Vertuous Octavia* there are no such occasions and the whole weight of the play falls on the conflict within the heroine between pride, anger, desire for revenge, and her sense of duty and dignity. The situation is rendered hopeless by the fact that Octavia never deviates into humanity. When she hears of Antony's unfaithfulness, her first reaction is a string of rhetorical questions and classical allusions. When she learns of his death, she is equally ready with a rhetorical flourish. In her soliloquies on her situation, she is proud and hard in her virtue. Her struggles of conscience are purely formal, her reactions merely words. The Octavia of the letter to Antony is entirely the same person. She hectors Antony from a height of unfallen and infallible virtue and takes some relish in painting the doom which will befall him unless he mends his ways. How very meagre both the poetry and the humanity are may be estimated from these closing lines of the letter from Octavia:

> How canst thou ever hope to pay
> The forfait of thy misse:
> When powerfull Justice shall impose,
> The just revenge of this
> Which makes me pittie more thy state,
> Then greeve at mine owne wrong:
> To thinke how he whom I have lov'd,
> Shall plagued be ere long.
> Yet know, though I detest thy fault,
> I beare thee no ill will:
> For if *Antonius* will returne,
> He shall be loved still.

It speaks a great deal for Daniel's charity that we can believe that *his* Octavia is capable of genuinely forgiving Antony.

At one point in the play Octavia makes explicit the dominant motif of Brandon's work:

> O traytor passion, if thou couldst subdue
> Thy soveraigne reason, what ill tragedies
> Wouldst thou soone acte . . .

80

This explains why Brandon labelled his play 'Tragicomoedye', because in it Octavia's reason triumphs over circumstances tempting her to passion, and it also exposes Brandon's essential attitude towards his work: for he sees in the whole Antony and Cleopatra story nothing but an illustration of this text and he preaches on it with a severity unrelieved by warmth of human sympathy and almost completely unlighted by imaginative glow. Play and letters are produced from an attitude to people and things which is much more rigid and much less responsive than Daniel's. Daniel could enter into Octavia's grief but also see a kind of splendour in Cleopatra and he was both a better poet and a wiser man than Brandon. The morals to be drawn from his handling of the story, in *Cleopatra* and in the *Letter from Octavia*, are not dogmatic nor simple, and the reflective treatment which he gives it is, in its own way, an enrichment of his material.

Daniel did well by the Cumberland ladies. In addition to the *Letter from Octavia* he wrote for them two of the finest of his verse epistles, published in 1603.[24] The high-minded stoicism of the epistle to the Countess drew Wordsworth's admiration (he quoted ll. 92–9 in *The Excursion*, Book IV, ll. 324–31) and it has been often praised. Personal integrity and a refusal to commit oneself to the things of the world, under whatever high-sounding names they masquerade, are, Daniel argues, the pillars on which virtue is sustained and he treats his theme with a lofty dignity which is very impressive. This is one of his best things, for the serious reflection on chequered experience which has developed in him of late years and the gift of sober eloquence which is his in his maturity show to great advantage within the restrictions of the form he has here chosen. The epistle to Lady Anne Clifford preaches a no less exalted ethical code but the tone is milder as befits the tender years of the young lady. It takes its place worthily beside the epistle to the mother.[25]

24. Sprague, pp. 111–15 and 119–21. For a discussion of the verse epistles see M. H. Shackford, 'Samuel Daniel's Poetical *Epistles*, especially that to the Countess of Cumberland' (*S.P.* 45, 1948, pp. 180–95). This article is critically sound but not completely accurate biographically.

25. The posthumous (1623) edition of Daniel's works, issued with a dedication to Prince Charles signed by John Daniel, contains a *Letter Written to a Worthy Countess* which is evidently meant for Lady Anne Clifford. She, like her mother, was embroiled in a protracted lawsuit and found little happiness in married life. The letter is, in effect, a prose paraphrase of the verse epistle to the Earl of Southampton (Sprague, pp. 122–3) with the blessings of adversity as its theme. Trial and suffering

Lady Anne became in later life a formidable character. 'She was one of the most illustrious women of her own or of any age. By the blessing of a religious education, and the example of an excellent mother, she imbibed in childhood those principles which, in middle life, preserved her untainted from the profligacy of one husband and the fanaticism of another; and, after her deliverance from both, conducted her to the close of a long life in the uniform exercise of every virtue which became her sex, her rank, and her Christian profession.'[26] So, with masterly conciseness, the historian of Craven sums up her career. She was fond in her old age of erecting monuments to commemorate episodes or people in her life. She did not forget Daniel and she had a monument to him erected in the church at Beckington, where he died, with the following inscription: 'Here lies expecting the second coming of our lord and saviour Jesus Christ, the dead body of Samuel Daniel Esq., that excellent poet and historian, who was tutor to the Lady Anne Clifford in her youth. She that was sole daughter and heir to George Clifford, Earl of Cumberland, who in gratitude to him erected this monument to his memory a long time after, when she was Countess Dowager of Pembroke, Dorset, and Montgomery. He died in October 1619.'[27] There exists at Appleby, one of the Yorkshire castles of the Cliffords, a family picture which includes a portrait of Lady Anne as a young girl with bookshelves behind her and two small portraits above the shelves. The small portraits are of her governess and of Daniel. An explanatory tablet records: 'Samuel Daniel, Tutour to this Young Lady a man of an upright and excellent Spirit as appeared by his Workes was borne in the yeare of our Lord 1563. He died at Redge in the parish of Beckington in Somersetshire about the 9th of October in the year 1619 and lyeth buried in the Chancell of

exercise the soul in virtue and 'Not to b' unhappy is unhappinesse' as Daniel writes in the epistle, or, as the same sentiment appears in the letter: '. . . it seemes God hath set you as a marke of tryall, that you may be numbred amongst the examples of patience and substancy to other ages; and that it may be hereafter your felicity to have had so little to do with felicity.'

Extracts from Daniel's letter are reprinted by Sellers in *M.L.R.* xi (1916), p. 29.

26. T. D. Whitaker, *The Histories and Antiquities of the Deanery of Craven* (Leeds and London, 1878, pp. 383–4).

27. Dr Pevsner writes in the Somerset volume of *The Buildings of England* that if this monument was made shortly after Daniel's death it was 'the first monument in the county designed in a fully understood classical taste. For not only are there volutes and garlands and an open segmental pediment, but the man represented in the bust in the pediment wears a kind of Roman toga and a wreath.'

DANIEL'S MEMORIAL
Photograph by Clifford L. Bennett, Frome

the sayd Church, leaving no issue.' His works in verse and prose
are included among the volumes on the shelves.[28]

Evidently Daniel was well-liked and respected by the Cliffords,
but he kept up his earlier connections too and the familiar names of
Greville and Pembroke reappear in connection with the *Defence of
Ryme*, which was published in 1603. In 1602 Campion had published his *Observations in the Art of English Poesie* attacking rhyme
and setting up a form of classical scansion as the proper mode of
English poetry. Daniel thereupon wrote 'a private letter, as a
defence of mine owne undertakings in that kinde, [i.e. rhyme] to a
learned Gentleman a great friend of mine, then in Court'.[29] In
1603, encouraged to believe that the new King was interested in
such things, Daniel amplified his letter and published it as
A Defence of Ryme. The learned Gentleman to whom the
original letter was written is identified by tradition,[30] probability and internal evidence in the *Defence* itself as Greville, and
the published work is dedicated to Lady Pembroke's elder son
William Herbert, who had by then succeeded his father as Earl
of Pembroke.

Daniel's *Defence* was specifically 'against' Campion, setting out
to prove 'that Ryme is the fittest harmonie of words that com-
portes with our Language'. The rhyme verses quantitative scansion controversy had bedevilled Elizabethan criticism from
Puttenham onwards, the most unrewarding as well as the most
obsessive of its preoccupations. Daniel, in saying what is, in effect,
the last word, gives for the first time depth and meaning to the
whole controversy and expounds, courteously but incisively,
some bold critical attitudes. Rhyme is to be defended, he says, on
the grounds that it both gives pleasure and has proved itself

28. Details of the picture are given by Whitaker, *op. cit.*, pp. 339–54, and by
Williamson, pp. 334–45. The picture is reproduced as the first plate in Williamson's
book.

29. Sprague, p. 127.

30. The *Biographia Britannica* of 1750 has the following note: 'Between whom
(Daniel) and Sir Fulk Grevil, there passed an intercourse of several letters, upon
some improvements or reformation that had been proposed to be made, in the masques, interludes, or other dramatical entertainments at Court; which were in great
request in their time, especially in the reign of King James I they being much encouraged by Queen Anne, and the Ladies who attended upon her. Their sentiments
they also exchanged in writing, upon the topic of our English versification, about
the time that Daniel had his controversy with Dr. Campion thereupon, and Sir Fulk's
judgement is often applauded, with his munificence to several practitioners therein.'
(iii, p. 2400).

effective to achieve the ends of poetry; that it is sanctioned by custom and by nature; and that the alternative of quantitative scansion offered by Campion (latest among many) violates the nature of the language.

It is worth examining Daniel's handling of these points more carefully. '... I see not,' he writes (p. 134), 'howe that can be taken for an ill custome, which nature hath thus ratified, all nations received, time so long confirmed, the effects such as it performes those offices of motion for which it is imployed; delighting the eare, stirring the heart, and satisfying the judgement in such sort as I doubt whether ever single numbers will do in our Climate, if they shew no more worke of wonder then yet we see.' He goes on (p. 135): 'suffer then the world to injoy that which it knowes, and what it likes. Seeing that whatsoever force of words doth moove, delight and sway the affections of men, in what Scythian sorte soever it be disposed or uttered: that is true number, measure, eloquence, and the perfection of speach: which I said, hath as many shapes as there be tongues or nations in the world, nor can with all the tyrannicall Rules of idle Rhetorique be governed otherwise then custome, and present observation will allow.'

'Custome that is before all Law, Nature that is above all Arte' (p. 131) are sounder arbiters than the ancients. The Greeks and Latins were not infallible, neither had they the monopoly of wisdom: '... all our understandings are not to be built by the square of *Greece* and *Italie*. We are the children of nature as well as they, we are not so placed out of the way of judgement, but that the same Sunne of Discretion shineth uppon us, wee have our portion of the same vertues as well as of the same vices' (p. 139). We should not deify the ancient world; by the same token, we should not vilify the middle ages, as the classical enthusiasts, including Campion, did: 'The distribution of giftes are universall, and all seasons hath them in some sort . . . We have but one body of Justice, one body of Wisedome throughout the whole world, which is but apparaled according to the fashion of every nation.' (pp. 143 and 145). Therefore we should honour our past, and beware of being misled by the foreshortening effects of time into unwarranted pride in ourselves and scorn of others.

The details of Campion's proposals for the 'reform' of English poetry Daniel deals with briefly and effectively. He attacks the unnaturalness and the uncertainty of the alleged rules and condemns the whole pamphlet as a piece of self-exhibition on Campion's part, at the same time mischievous in its general argument and trivial in the results it offers. 'Accent' is in English 'the chiefe Lord and grave Governour of Numbers' (p. 152), not 'those imagined quantities of sillables' (p. 151) and 'every Versifier that wel observes his worke, findes in our language, without all these unnecessary precepts, what numbers best fitte the Nature of her Idiome, and the proper places destined to such accents, as she will not let in, to any other roomes then into those for which they were borne' (p. 151).

Daniel's capacity as an apologist is impressive. He sees the wood in clear outline whereas his predecessors had lost themselves in the trees and undergrowth. Only when he has defined and effectively discussed the real issues involved does he come to minutiae and his comments on them gain in clarity and force because of the background of critical statement to which they are related. But there is another aspect of the *Defence*, a current of ideas working through it which must be taken into account.

It may be dangerous and is certainly foolish to defy what custom has endorsed, Daniel has argued, and rhyme is the acustomed mode of English poetry: 'And being now the trym, and fashion of the times, to sute a man otherwise cannot but give a touch of singularity, for when he hath all done, he hath but found other clothes to the same body, and peradventure not so fitting as the former. But could our Adversary hereby set up the musicke of our times to a higher note of judgement and discretion, or could these new lawes of words better our imperfections, it were a happy attempt; but when hereby we shall but as it were change prison, and put off these fetters to receive others, what have we gained . . .' (p. 135). A little later he says 'It is not the observing of *Trochaicques* nor their Iambicques, that will make our writings ought the wiser: All their Poesie, all their Philosophie is nothing, unlesse we bring the discerning light of conceipt with us to apply it to use. It is not bookes, but onely that great booke of the world, and the all-over spreading grace of heaven that makes us truely judiciall' (p. 139). And later still he adds: 'Eloquence and gay wordes are not of the Substance of wit, it is but the garnish of a nice time, the Ornaments that doe but decke the house of State, *et imitatur publicos mores*: Hunger is as well satisfied with meat served in pewter as silver. Discretion is the best measure, the rightest foote in what habit soever it runne. *Erasmus, Rewcline,* and *More,* brought no more wisdome into the world with all their new revived wordes then we finde was before, it bred not a profounder Divine than Saint *Thomas,* a greater lawyer than *Bartolus,* a more accute Logician than *Scotus:* nor are the effects of all this great amasse of eloquence so admirable or of that consequence, but that *impexa illa antiquitas* can yet compare with them' (p. 145).

A complex of motives is operating in these passages. Partly Daniel is trying simply to deflate Campion and all who argued like him, as though classical scansion were the only light-giver to ignorance. Partly he is concerned to explode the arrogant myth of the Dark Ages. Yet, praiseworthy as these objects may be, it is disturbing to find eloquence, so finely celebrated in *Musophilus,* demoted to 'the garnish of a nice time', to be told that the manner of expression scarcely matters (what of the 'powre of wordes' in *Musophilus,* 'the treasure of our tongue', and 'the greatnes of our stile'?) 'The out-side of wordes' and the sound of them are now negligible in comparison with the matter (p. 154-5) which may appear 'in what habite it will' and 'all these pretended proportions of words, howsoever placed, can be but words, and peradventure serve but to embroyle our understanding, whilst seeking to please our eare, we inthrall our judgement . . .' (p. 136). In *Musophilus* 'the weapons of the mind' of which eloquence, the art of words, was one, were 'states best strengths' (ll. 841-2) but the *Defence* tells a different story. 'The Art of men' is the only *Ars Artium,* 'the great gift of heaven, and the chiefe grace and glory on earth . . . Had not unlearned *Rome* laide the better foundation, and built the stronger frame of an admirable state, eloquent *Rome* had confounded it utterly . . .' (p. 144).

It appears that in the interval since *Musophilus* Daniel's attitude has hardened, and for the continual sliding away from literary to moral judgements Greville's influence may be responsible. A *Times Literary Supplement* reviewer wrote some years ago that Greville's manner of thinking can be traced everywhere in the *Defence of Ryme* and that Greville and Daniel, while 'nominally defending rhyme, were introducing a philosophy which made poetry futile'. Really, the review claims, both Daniel and Greville were opposed to poetry, its metaphor, its hyperbole, its rhetoric: 'they had both developed to a degree beyond any of their con-

temporaries save Francis Bacon the prose mind'.[31] This is a judgement that will be considered in a final survey of Daniel's work but
in the meantime the latent ambiguity of the *Defence of Ryme* must
be recorded. It is, in fact, largely concealed by the quality of the
writing. Daniel's prose is strong and unaffected, restrained to the
purpose in hand by a sensitive feeling for decorum and yet at the
same time vigorous and imaginative. He concludes for example,
the particular refutation of Campion with these words: 'And
power and strength that can plant it selfe anywhere, having built
within this compasse, and reard it of so high a respect, wee now
imbrace it as the fittest dwelling for our invention, and have thereon
bestowed all the substance of our understanding to furnish it as it
is: and therefore heere I stand foorth, onelie to make good the
place we have thus taken up, and to defend the sacred monuments
erected therein, which containe the honour of the dead, the fame of
the living, the glory of peace, and the best power of our speach, and
wherin so many honorable spirits have sacrificed to Memorie
their dearest passions, shewing by what divine influence they
have been moved, and under what starres they lived' (p. 155).

The few pages which follow this passage contain some independent comments on problems of poetic technique. There is room
for reform, Daniel believes, in the handling of rhyme. '. . . to mine
owne eare,' he confesses, 'those continuall cadences of couplets
used in long and continued Poemes, are very tyresome, and un-
pleasing, by reason that still, me thinks, they runne on with a
sound of one nature, and a kinde of certaintie which stuffs the
delight rather then intertaines it.' (p. 155). And, he adds, 'my
Adversary hath wrought this much upon me, that I thinke a
Tragedie would indeede best comporte with a blank Verse, and
dispence with Ryme, saving in the *Chorus* or where a sentence shall
require a couplet'. He has experimented, he says, in some of his
epistles, with deferring the expected rhyme in order to avoid
'over-glutting the eare with that alwayes certaine, and ful incounter of Ryme' but he has not entirely satisfied himself in his
experiments. The alternate or cross rhyme which he has so con-
sistently used still holds the best place in his affections. 'Besides,'
he goes on, 'to me this change of number in a Poem of one nature
sits not so wel, as to mixe uncertainly, feminine Rymes with
masculine, which ever since I was warned of that deformitie by

31. *T.L.S.*, 5.6.30, p. 475.

my kinde friend and countriman Maister *Hugh Samford*,[32] I have alwayes so avoyded it, as there are not above two couplettes in that kinde in all my Poem of the Civill warres: and I would willingly if I coulde, have altered it in all the rest, holding feminine Rymes to be fittest for Ditties, and either to be set certaine, or else by themselves.' All this is interesting as evidence of Daniel's care for poetic craftsmanship even while he scorned 'mere literature', but the technical discussion soon changes into something else: 'But the greatest hinderer to our proceedings, and the reformation of our errours, is this Selfe-love, whereunto we Versifiers are ever noted to be especially subject; a disease of all other, the most dangerous, and incurable, being once seated in the spirits, for which there is no cure, but onely by a spirituall remedy' (p. 157). It is not altogether surprising after this, to find innovations in language, 'idle affectation of antiquitie, or noveltie' being described as moral deformity, and the whole essay concludes with this last comment: 'But this is but a Character of that perpetuall revolution which wee see to be in all things that never remaine the same, and we must heerein be content to submit our selves to the law of time, which in few yeeres will make al that, for which we now contend, *Nothing.*'

A similar sudden, unexpected change of focus, revealing a blank or alien future, has occurred before, at the end of *Rosamond* in a passage where also the theme was literary immortality (see p. 40). To remember this is to realise how from the beginning a strain of pessimism has shown in Daniel's temperament and how, in particular, his devotion to literature has always been qualified by distrust or rejection of what seem to him over-enthusiastic claims. The noble statements of *Musophilus* arise out of temporary whole-hearted commitment to the ideals of learning and writing which made so deep an appeal to some things in his nature, but the doubts inevitably come back, sooner or later, and as he grows older they grow stronger.

A Defence of Ryme is Daniel's only formal critical document. It is intellectually and stylistically admirable and it is, besides, a living record of the complex, sensitive, and, in important respects, deeply troubled man who wrote it and whose works, from *Delia* on, bear witness to his efforts to find a way to emotional and intellectual equilibrium.

---

32. Hugh Sanford was William Herbert's tutor, the old Earl of Pembroke's secretary and Robert Parker's friend (see pp. 11–12 and 16–17).

V

Court Patronage 1604–7: Masques, 'Philotas', the revised 'Cleopatra' and 'The Queenes Arcadia'

In the same year that the *Defence of Ryme* appeared, Daniel published also *A Panegyrike Congratulatorie* on the accession of James I to the throne of England.

There used to be a legend that Elizabeth had appointed Daniel poet laureate in 1599 in succession to Spenser but it is unlikely that there was any such official post at that date. There is clear evidence, all the same, that the Queen was graciously disposed towards him during these years. The 1601 volume of *Works* contains a dedicatory poem 'To her sacred Majestie' in which, referring to the first six books of *The Civil Wars* then published, Daniel writes:

> I, who by that most blessed hand sustain'd,
> In quietnes, do eate the bread of rest:
> And by that all-reviving powre obtain'd
> That comfort which my Muse and me hath blest,
> Bring here this worke of Warre . . .[1]

Other references to Elizabeth as patron occur in the last stanza of Book III as printed up to and including 1601 (Michel, p. 322) and in stanza 78 of Book VIII published in 1609. But while Daniel was still tutor to Lady Anne Clifford, the old Queen was failing. Daniel had an eye to the new reign and hastened to greet James on his accession with his *Panegyrike*, delivered, so the 1603 title-page declares, to the King at Burleigh Harrington in Rutlandshire.

The poem is a bid for favour, but it does not descend to mere flattery. Daniel praises James for the virtues he thinks he should

1. Grosart i, p. 9.

have or acquire – a kind of anticipation of merit which is severe in its requirements and has a stern as well as a complimentary facet. He does not hesitate to express the love and admiration of her people for Elizabeth, but he realises that it is not now enough to rely on supreme personalities alone: there must be the security of good laws and good practices if England is to achieve her true and full greatness. The tone of the elder statesman is heard as much as that of the poet and fervour of feeling is directed here not to lovers' meetings, but to the union of England and Scotland and the historic concept of Great Britain. It was tactically appropriate, of course, that Daniel should present himself to James as a scholar poet and an historian poet and a moralist poet, but the character is by no means an assumed one and the grave and thoughtful note of the poem is authentic.

In spite of all this, James evidently made no very satisfactory response to the *Panegyrike* and, the King failing him, Daniel cast about for other ways to win himself Court favour. The way was opened for him by the Countess of Bedford. One of the verse epistles of 1603 was addressed to this lady and it was at the house of her father at Burley-on-the-Hill that the *Panegyrike Congratulatorie* was read to the King during his progress into England (the father's name was Sir John Harington, but he was not the translator of Ariosto). The *Panegyrike* missing the result it was aimed at, Lady Bedford provided Daniel with an opportunity to gain the interest of the Queen though in a guise this time, we may suspect, which was from the beginning less congenial to him than that in which he had sought the King's favour.

The tone of the verse epistle to the Countess of Bedford is similar to that of the epistle to the Countess of Cumberland. The ladies were related and the poems are companion pieces, both dealing with the integrity of the individual, the mind's inviolate retirement achieved in the one case through resolution in the face of suffering and in the other through devotion to studies. Fine as both poems are, they are hardly the sort of thing, one would have thought, to suggest that the writer was a potential creator of Court masques. Lady Bedford, nevertheless, who had charge of the Queen's masque for the first Christmas of the new reign, recommended Daniel to the Queen, and his work, *The Vision of the Twelve Goddesses*, was presented on January 8th, 1604, at Hampton Court. The Queen herself and eleven of her ladies took

part in it, it was lavishly produced, and Queen Elizabeth's ward-
robe was drawn upon freely for the dresses. There was the usual
trouble about invitations to the French and Spanish ambassadors
and probably additional trouble in handling the large caste of
ladies, all of whom were busily jockeying for position in the
favour of the new Queen.[2] It cost a great deal of money, and Sir
Dudley Carleton remembered it especially for two things: the
goddesses descending a winding stair three by three 'which being
all seene on the stayres at once was the best presentacion I have at
any time seene'; and the costume of the Queen: 'Only Pallas had
a trick by herself for her clothes were not so much below the knee,
but that we might see a woman had both feete and legs which I
never knew before.'[3] In 'pompe and splendor', Daniel himself
notes, the occasion 'by the unpartiall opinion of all the beholders
Strangers and others . . . was not inferior to the best that ever was
presented in Christendome'[4] and the revels ended with dancing
and the usual wild confusion of a banquet. Altogether, it must
have been a strange experience for Daniel who had been poring
over the affairs of kings for some nine years in the writing of his
Civil Wars but had not before been on the inside of their 'feastes,
and shewes, and triumphs'.

Historians of the masque are severe on *The Vision of the Twelve
Goddesses*. 'The truth is,' as Jonson's editors sum up the modern
verdict, 'that the *Vision* was by no means qualified to satisfy the
standards applied, in January 1604, to a Court masque. In invention it falls far behind the best Elizabethan examples – a mere
procession of goddesses, introduced (since they are seen in a
'Vision') by Night and Sleep. Even the verse and phrasing are
stiff and hard, throwing into vivid relief the supple strength of
Jonson's 'well-torned lines'.[5] The truth is, equally, that Daniel's

2. See the edition by E. Law (London, 1880), pp. 22–4. See also Mary Sullivan,
Court Masques of James I (New York and London, 1913), for the diplomatic background of the masques of the reign.
3. *State Papers (Dom.) James I*, vi, p. 21. Quoted E. K. Chambers, *The Elizabethan
Stage* (Oxford, 1923), iii, p. 80, and Law, pp. 33–7, 45–6.
4. Grosart iii, p. 195.
5. *Works of Ben Jonson*, ed. Herford and Simpson (Oxford, 1925–52), ii, p. 270.
See also on Daniel's masques R. Brotanek, *Die Englischen Maskenspiele* (Wien und
Leipzig, 1902) *passim*, and E. Welsford *The Court Masque* (C.U.P., 1927), pp. 171–3,
189–91. H. A. Evans has a good brief history of the masque in his collection of
English Masques (London, 1897) among which he prints *The Vision of the Twelve
Goddesses*.

heart was not really in this work and his qualities were not adaptable to this sort of use. The masques and mummeries of the world show better by candlelight and Daniel has no capacity for evoking the glamour of half-light and flickering shadow. He had already written in Book v of *The Civil Wars* of his contempt for:

> ... imaginarie ground
> Of hungry shadowes, which no profite breed;
> Whence, musicke-like, instant delight may growe;
> Yet, when men all do knowe, they nothing knowe.
>
> (Bk. v, st. 5)

But the art of the masque was essentially an art of 'shadows' and Daniel several times described it so. He was uneasy with it from the beginning, as the attempts at justification in the dedication of the *Vision* to the Countess of Bedford show: '... these ornaments and delights of peace are in their season, as fit to entertaine the world, and deserve to be made memorable as well as the graver actions – both of them concurring to the decking and furnishing of glory and Majesty, as the necessary complements requisit for State and Greatnesse' (p. 188). The 'intent and scope' of his masque, he writes, is 'to present the figure of those blessings, with the wish of their encrease and countinuance, which this mightie Kingdome now enjoyes by the benefite of his most gracious Majestie; by whom we have this glory of peace, with the accession of so great state and power'. In other words, Daniel is seeing, or trying to see, this present employment in relation to his task of long standing, *The Civil Wars*, for the time has come now, in theory at any rate, for rejoicing at the blessed outcome of those internecine struggles and for celebration of a union even more inclusive than that of York and Lancaster. His 'shadows', consequently, represent 'the Hieroglephick of Empire and Dominion, as the ground and matter whereon this glory of State is built' (p. 189) and 'those blessings and beauties that preserve and adorne it'.

This is all very well, but Daniel is very conscious at the same time that his masque, after all, numbers but among 'Dreames and shewes'. He is content, therefore, to dress up his central idea with what trappings he and the architect and the musicians and the dancers can provide, but he is impatient with those who would pretend to bring a weight of scholarship to bear on these trifles:

'... whosoever strives to shew most wit about these Pun[c]tillos of Dreames and shewes', he writes acidly, 'are sure sicke of a disease they cannot hide, and would faine have the world to thinke them very deeply learned in all misteries whatsoever. And peradventure they thinke themselves so; which if they do, they are in a farre worse case then they imagine; Non potest non indoctus esse qui se doctum credit' (p. 196).

This preface of Daniel's, with its attempt to justify the masque form by pointing to its connection with affairs of state and his refusal, nevertheless, to take it very seriously as a work on which the maximum effort should be expended, reveals his essential uneasiness with it, and even his contempt for it. As a piece of critical writing it contrasts very strongly with the preface which Jonson wrote for his *Hymenaei*, the wedding masque which he composed for the Twelfth Night of 1606. Jonson stands on the absolute value of the masque, for, he says, it has not only 'body,' but also 'soul'. If it had not been so, then indeed 'The glorie of all these *solemnities* had perish'd like a blaze, and gone out, in the *beholders* eyes' but, as it is, the Princes and great persons who are commonly concerned in masques have taken care for 'the inward parts' of the masque as well as for the 'outward celebration, or shew' and they have required 'heartie *inventions*' which must be 'grounded upon *antiquitie*, and solide *learnings* which, though their *voyce* be taught to sound to present occasions, their *sense*, or doth, or should always lay hold on more remov'd *mysteries*'. Thus for Jonson masques have substance and value on their own account and not merely 'as the necessary complements requisit for State and Greatnesse' and he is very willing to put forth all his powers in composing them. His confidence in the masque form puts him in a far stronger position than Daniel and he does not trouble to disguise his contempt for Daniel's deprecating, left-handed efforts: 'And,' he writes, 'howsoever some may squemishly crie out, that all endevour of *learning*, and *sharpnesse* in these transitorie *devices* especially, where it steps beyond their little, or (let me not wrong 'hem) no braine at all, is superfluous; I am contented, these fastidious *stomachs* should leave my full tables, and enjoy at home, their cleane emptie trenchers, fittest for such ayrie tasts'.[6] Jonson told Drummond of Hawthornden that 'Daniel was at jealousies with him',[7] and also that 'next himself only Fletcher and Chapman

6. *Works of Ben Jonson*, vii, pp. 209–10.   7. Ibid., i, p. 136.

could make a Mask',[8] which is as much as to say that Daniel could not, and it is evident that some personal animosity crept into their disagreement about the nature and value of the masque form. It echoes again in the preface to *Tethys Festival* (1610), Daniel's second masque, with Daniel's blunt statement of the subordination of the poet to the architect: 'But in these things wherein the onely life consists in shew; the arte and invention of the Architect [it was Inigo Jones] gives the greatest grace, and is of most importance: ours, the least part and of least note in the time of the performance thereof'.[9] To give up the citadel to the enemy in this way must have been most galling to Jonson, and one more proof to him of Daniel's pusillanimity.[10]

The preface to *Tethys Festival*, like the dedication of the *Vision*, is revealing of Daniel's mind and characteristic attitudes. He does not publish his account of the masque, he says, out of the 'disease of ostentation', for he has already more publicity than he cares for. Nor does he wish 'to give it other colours then those it wore, or to make an Apologie of what I have done', for, he goes on, 'my long experience of the world, hath taught me this, that never Remonstrances nor Apologies could ever get over the streame of opinion, to doe good on the other side, where contrarie affection and conceipt had to doe: but onely served to entertaine their owne partialnesse, who were fore-perswaded; and so was a labour in vaine' (p. 306). He has in mind in these comments the undesired notoriety he had incurred over his play *Philotas* (see pp. 98–100), and it is typical of Daniel that the masque itself does not occupy him for long even in a formal preface. He could not find in the masque form the depth of meaning which Jonson claimed for it and he could justify it only as a minor accessory of majesty and state. His real preoccupations emerge in his comments, and the poetry which is lacking in the masques themselves is to be found in a passage of splendid prose which touches characteristic themes with that reflective humanity which is his richest and most rewarding mood: 'And shall we who are the poore Inginers for shadowes, and frame onely images of no result, thinke to oppresse

8. Ibid., p. 133.   9. Grosart iii, p. 307.
10. In *Tethys Festival* Daniel includes what he calls an "Ante-Maske or first shew" (Grosart iii, p. 311). The use of the term ante-masque may be intended as a deliberate repudiation of the Jonsonian anti-masque for in the Prologue to *Hymns Triumph* (Grosart iii, p. 331, ll. 15–17) Jonson's theory of the grotesque is explicitly rejected.

the rough censures of those, who notwithstanding all our labour
will like according to their taste, or seeke to avoid them by flying
to an Army of Authors, as idle as our selves? Seeing there is
nothing done or written, but incounters with detraction and
opposition; which is an excellent argument of all our imbecilities
and might allay our presumption, when we shall see our greatest
knowledges not to be fixt, but rowle according to the uncertaine
motion of opinion, and controwleable by any surly shew of reason;
which we find is double edged and strikes every way alike. And
therefore I do not see why any man should rate his owne at that
valew, and set so low prises upon other men's abilities. *L'homme
vaut l'homme*, a man is worth a man, and none hath gotten so high
a station of understanding, but he shall find others that are built
on an equall floore with him, and have as far a prospect as he;
which when al is done, is but in a region subject to al passions and
imperfections' (pp. 306–7). The theme of decent humility occurs
also in *Musophilus* and *A Defence of Ryme* and if it has here some
personal edge and is coloured also by a sombre Grevillean sense
of passions and imperfections, this is nevertheless an impressive
piece of writing.

Only once in the masques do the 'shadows' themselves touch a
lyric spring of comparable depth, but this passage for the subtlety
and range of its comment is worth quoting entire:

> Are they shadowes that we see?
> And can shadowes pleasure give?
> Pleasures onely shadowes bee
> Cast by bodies we conceive,
> And are made the thinges we deeme,
> In those figures which they seeme.
> But these pleasures vanish fast,
> Which by shadowes are exprest:
> Pleasures are not, if they last,
> In their passing, is their best.
> Glory is most bright and gay
> In a flash, and so away.
> Feed apace then greedy eyes
> On the wonder you behold.
> Take it sodaine as it flies
> Though you take it not to hold:
> When your eyes have done their part,
> Thought must length it in the hart. (pp. 320–1)

Some comments on *Tethys Festival* have been added out of chronological order, but back in 1604, in spite of Jonson, *The Vision of the Twelve Goddesses* and perhaps the *Panegyricke* had brought Daniel what he wanted, a post in the royal gift. The Children of the Chapel were reestablished as Children of the Queen's Revels by patent of February 4th, 1604, and Daniel was appointed licenser. The terms of the royal patent create the company for 'the Queene our deerest wief . . . for her pleasur and recreacon when she shall thinke it fit to have any playes or shewes' and Daniel's function is described as follows: 'Provided allwaies that noe such Playes or Shewes shalbee presented before the said Queene our wief by the said Children or by them any where publiquelie acted but by the approbacion and allowaunce of Samuell Danyell, whome her pleasure is to appoynt for that purpose.'[11]

The appointment may well have appeared a promising one, but in the event it brought Daniel a great deal of trouble in more ways than one. The patent grants the licence for training the children and presenting their plays to four men, Edward Kirkham, Alexander Hawkins, Thos. Kendall and Robert Payne, and Daniel, it appears, had been to great trouble and expense to obtain this licence for them. In return, Kirkham and the others became bound, on April 28th, 1604, in a bond of £100 for a yearly payment to Daniel of £10. There was an attempt, on October 25th of the same year, to agree on a different system of payment but it apparently came to nothing. Daniel, however, received the annuity for just one year only, for on April 28th, 1605, the bond and annuity were made over to one John Gerrard and Daniel renounced all claims on Kirkham and his associates. This information is available because of a bill of complaint filed by Kirkham and the widow of one of his partners, Anne Kendall, on May 9th, 1609, and an answer by Daniel setting out the details of his association with the licensees. Kirkham, it seems, had for some time before this date discontinued payment of the annuity to Gerrard and Gerrard had sued, using Daniel's name, for the forfeiture of the bond. Kirkham's Bill of Complaint was an attempt to present the story to his advantage but Daniel's reply has every appearance of being effective.[12]

11. Chambers, ii. p. 49.
12. R. E. Brettle, 'Samuel Daniel and the Children of the Queen's Revels 1604–5', *R.E.S.* 3 (1927), pp. 162–8, prints the relevant documents.

Much of the transaction is obscure, but one thing at least is clear: that Daniel was again in acute financial difficulty. One sentence of Kirkham's Bill brings his situation before us vividly. Referring to the original agreement, he writes: 'After which bond soe made the said Danyell haveinge occasion to use monye woulde still importune and Request the said Kyrckham and Kendall to pay to him his mony before the day did come that the same was due and somtymes to pay the same to others to whom the said Danyell did stande indebted . . .'

But financial troubles and litigation were not the only accompaniments of the brief period with the Queen's Revels. The choice of plays presented during Daniel's term as licenser was singularly unfortunate. The first trouble (of unknown nature) arose over the presentation of Marston's play *The Dutch Courtesan*, then over Daniel's own play *Philotas* and lastly over *Eastward Ho!* The Company did not appear at Court during the winter of 1605–6 and was thereafter known as the Children of the Revels, having forfeited Anne's patronage through its indiscretions.[13] Whether Daniel severed his connection with the company in the April of 1605 because of disagreement over policy, or whether as licenser he had by that time made too many mistakes or if there is some other explanation of this rather curious story, there are at present no means of knowing. It is certain, however, that the production of *Philotas* brought about the climax of what must have been a very anxious period for him.

Philotas was probably performed before the King by the Children of the Queen's Revels early in January 1605.[14] The play seems to bear some marks of Campion's influence, for Daniel had confessed in the *Defence of Ryme* that his 'Adversary' had persuaded him that 'a Tragedie would indeede best comporte with a blank Verse, and dispence with Ryme, saving in the *Chorus* or where a sentence shall require a couplet'. Daniel uses his favourite alternate rhyme and also rhymed couplets in *Philotas* but a new departure is the number of long unrhymed passages he introduces into the play. The mixture of rhymed and unrhymed passages is evidently a further extension of the experiments to which he refers in the *Defence* and by which he endeavours to avoid the monotony which he recognises may result from the 'always certaine, and ful incounter of Ryme'.

13. Chambers, ii. p. 51.   14. See Michel's *Philotas*, p. 36, fn. 1.

But there were more dangerous issues than a modification of verse form involved in Daniel's treatment of *Philotas*, and they resulted in Daniel being called before the Privy Council charged with having, under the cover of an ancient story, commented seditiously on the trial and execution of Essex in 1601.[15] Two letters of Daniel's survive from this period.[16] One is addressed to Robert Cecil under the title of Lord Cranborne. Cecil became Earl of Salisbury in May, 1605, so that Daniel's letter must have been written before that date. It is a plea to Cecil to 'let no misapplying wronge my innocent writing' and a protestation that he had no intention in writing his play but the literary ambition to 'reduce the stage from idlenes to those grave presentments of antiquitie used by the wisest nations' and to give a just account of 'those tymes' and of human behaviour. 'But yf', he adds, 'it shall seeme sknendulous [scandalous] to any by misconceiving it, and yr ho: be so pleased I will finde the meanes to let it fall of it self, by wtdrawing the booke & mee to my pore home, prtending some other occasion, so yt the suppressing it by autoritie might not make the world to ymagin other matters in it then there is.'

The second letter is addressed to Mountjoy who was by this time Earl of Devonshire, and like the letter to Cecil it affirms Daniel's innocence of any intention to comment on the handling of the Essex affair. Its special interest is the personal tone which Daniel adopts in writing to this old and respected patron and friend. He had, it appears, pleaded before the Privy Council in his own defence that Mountjoy had seen the manuscript of *Philotas* and would speak for him, but Mountjoy, who had been too closely associated with Essex to enjoy the possibility of a new reckoning of old scores, had taken offence at this use of his name. Daniel's letter is an attempt to excuse himself and to set himself right with one whose friendship has meant so much to him, not only in a monetary sense. 'Understanding yor ho: is displeased wt mee, it hath more shaken my harte then I did thinke any fortune could have donne', he begins and the letter ends on the same note: '... good my L. mistake not my harte that hath bene & is a

15. See *Calendar of State Papers (Dom.) James I, 1603-10*, p. 182.
16. Printed by H. Sellers *Oxford Bibliographical Society Proceedings and Papers II* (1927-30), pp. 51-2; also by Grosart i, pp. xxii-iii and iv, pp. liii-iv, and Michel's *Philotas*, pp. 37-9.

sincere honorer of yow and seekes yow now for no other end but to cleare it self, and to be held as I ame (though I never more come nere yow) yor honors pore follower & faithfull Servant Samuel Danyel'.

Both letters are moving and rather painful documents. They reflect the humiliation of a man who knows that he cannot afford to be proud but who respects himself too much to grovel. He rejects the charges brought against him: if there is any coincidence between Philotas's situation and that of Essex, he writes to Cranborne, it is because 'No tyme but brought forth the like concurrencies, the like interstriving for place and dignitie, the like supplantations, rysings & overthrowes, so yt there is nothing new under the Sunne, nothing in theas tymes yt is not in bookes, nor in bookes that is not in theas tymes.' But while he defends himself with spirit, he is deeply depressed by the situation, wishing only to 'bury my self, and my writings out of the way of envie' since 'the tyme will yeald me no grace nor comfort & yt my studies, my faculties are unnessarie complements of the season'. In the letter to Mountjoy he writes more freely: 'the world must, & shall know myne innocencie whilst I have a pen to shew it. and for yt I know I shall live inter historiam temporis as well as greater men, I must not be such an abject unto my self as to neglect my repution [sic], and having bene knowne throughout all England for my virtue I will not leave a stayne of villanie uppon my name whatsoever error els might skape me unfortunately thorow myne indiscreation, & misunderstanding the tyme'.

The printed version of *Philotas* was dedicated to the young Prince Henry and in 1605 the hope that when he should grow to maturity 'this now neglected Harmonie' of verse would be graced by his sympathetic patronage is accompanied by a good deal of personal gloom:

> ... I the remnant of another time
> Am never like to see that happinesse,   (ll. 65-6)

Daniel writes somewhat sourly and comments on the efforts of all the poets in the new reign, himself, of course, included:

> ... all our labours are without successe,
> For either favour or our vertue failes.   (ll. 97-8)

As for himself in particular:

> ... since I have out-liv'd the date
> Of former grace, acceptance and delight,
> I would my lines late-borne beyond the fate
> Of her spent line, had never come to light.
> So had I not beene tax'd for wishing well,
> Nor now mistaken by the censuring Stage,
> Nor, in my fame and reputation fell,
> Which I esteeme more then what all the age
> Or th' earth can give. But yeeres hath done this wrong,
> To make me write too much, and live too long.
>
> (ll. 100–9)

These lines of personal despondency were omitted from the 1607 and 1611 editions, but in 1605 Daniel's anguish of mind was obviously considerable. He had always been particularly sensitive to adverse criticism and his natural reaction is heightened here by a deep bitterness that he, of all men, who had taken pride in his 'virtue' should be accused of any manner of 'villanie'.

Philotas reappeared in 1607 and 1611 along with other poems of Daniel's so that his declarations of innocence must have been accepted. A modern editor, however, Laurence Michel, in his edition of *Philotas*, has made a new assessment of the evidence for believing that Daniel had Essex's trial and execution in mind in writing his play and concludes, in spite of Daniel's own protestations, that the Privy Council were right to suspect that he was making propaganda for Essex and against his accusers. Certainly the play is a curious one. Philotas himself can be taken at first as simply an ambitious man with some noble and generous impulses. Alexander is shown at first as wise and willing to love. Then there comes a change, and Philotas appears as victimised innocence and Alexander and his counsellors as a tyrant and his corrupt ministers. And at the end Philotas confesses that all along he has harboured a secret plot against Alexander and that he has been a traitor from the beginning. This is confusing on any reading. To keep Philotas's treachery secret even from the audience, supposing the revelation of the treachery to be the main thing in the play, may well be bad dramatic practice but even when the play is read with the final revelation in mind, the inconsistencies are not removed. The explanation which Michel offers is that Daniel began the play, perhaps with Essex in view, with the

intention of portraying through an historical figure the temptations and dangers of high place; and that the trial and execution
of Essex made him return to the subject with a different emphasis,
making it now an indictment of tyranny and the intrigues of
courtiers. Daniel's own story (as told in the *Apology*) is that as
early as 1596–7 he had been thinking of writing a play on the
subject of Philotas. Later in 1600, 'neere half a yeare before the
late Tragedy of ours' (i.e. the Essex affair) he wrote three acts of
his play. In 1604, being short of money (as has already been seen,
p. 97), he finished the play for stage production, believing the
subject, he says, to be especially acceptable being set 'so farre
from the time, and so remote a stranger from the climate of our
present courses,' so that he 'could not imagine that Envy or
ignorance could possibly have made it, to take any particular
acquaintance with us, but as it hath a generall alliance to the
frailty of greatnesse, and the usuall workings of ambition, the
perpetuall subjects of bookes and Tragedies'. Certainly it was
daring of Daniel, if indeed Essex had been his theme, to close the
Apology with a reference to Essex couched in such terms as he
uses: '. . . for mine owne part having beene perticularly beholding
to his bounty, I would to God his errors and disobedience to his
Sovereigne, might be so deepe buried underneath the earth, and
in so low a tombe from his other parts, that hee might never be
remembred among the examples of disloyalty in this Kingdome,
or paraleld with Forreine Conspirators'. These words echo a
passage in Philotas's defence of himself:

> Let not my one dayes errour make you tell,
> That all my life-time I did never well,
> And that because this falles out to be ill,
> That what I did did tend unto this ill   (ll. 1569–72)

and the natural presumption is that Daniel would only dare such
a comment on Essex in the circumstances and such an echo if he
had been utterly sure of his innocence of any attempt at subversive
propaganda in his play.

A reading of *Philotas* which does not depend on the Essex
business to account for its perplexities is possible and has the
advantage of drawing attention to the play as a piece of literature
rather than as a political document.

In *Philotas* Daniel is taking the development of the story as

the stuff of his play in contrast to his method in *Cleopatra* where
he was hardly at all concerned with the events of the Antony and
Cleopatra story but only with the reflections they gave rise to
after they had occurred. The approach to the material is different
in the two plays and the handling is different but Daniel's serious
and contemplative mind is the governing factor in both, and in
Philotas as much as in *Cleopatra* he is concerned far more with the
moral implications of the story than with the sensational value of
the events themselves. He intends that a background of philo-
sophic commentary shall be built up as the story works itself out
but he does not, as in *Cleopatra*, concentrate on the background
and diminish the story. What he had in mind was a work of some
complexity, and the Chorus, consisting of three Grecians and a
Persian, has an important part to play in his scheme. The Chorus
of Egyptians in *Cleopatra* had been involved with the fate of the
principals in obvious ways and had commented accordingly, but
the significance of the Chorus in *Philotas* is much more subtle.
They represent, as the Argument explains, 'the multitude and
body of a People, who vulgarly (according to their affections,
carried rather with compassion on Great-mens misfortunes, then
with the consideration of the cause) frame their imaginations
by that square, and censure what is done'. Philotas's affliction
draws their compassion because they look on 'mens fortunes, not
the cause', and they are incapable of the wide view that takes in
all the issues. When they talk amongst themselves they divide into
men of narrow views and war-weary soldiers who have their own
troubles and sorrows in the light of which they see Alexander's
career and Philotas's downfall:

> What get we now by winning, but wide minds
> And weary bodies, with th'expence of blood?
>
> (ll. 1839-40)

they ask, and in their dejection they can see no period to the
disturbance of the state and their own toil. Yet they are, in their
very narrowness and simplicity, sometimes 'capable of truth'. In
Cleopatra Daniel was sensitive to the effects of the decline of great
kingdoms and monarchs on the small man, and in his use of the
Chorus in *Philotas* he seems to be trying to thicken the weave of
his plot by developing the idea of the interdependence of all
estates in a realm and by pointing out the conclusions the common

man may draw from the flurries among the mighty. On the whole the conclusions that the Chorus draws from the affairs it sees enacted in *Philotas* are disillusioned and somewhat cynical.

In the character of Alexander, as Daniel paints it, there is again complexity. 'Alexanders drawing a Pedigree from Heaven, with assuming the *Persian* magnificence, was the cause that withdrew many the hearts of the Nobilitie and people from him,' Daniel writes in the *Apology* but in the early part of the play this very question of the title reveals Alexander in a favourable light. Alexander is remembering Philotas's objections to his assumption of the title of son of Jupiter, and he comments:

> Alas good man, as though what breath could give
> Could make mine owne thoughts other than they are!
> I that am Arbiter betwixt my heart
> And their opinion, know how it stands within,
> And finde that my infirmities take part
> Of that same frailty other men live in. (ll. 463–8)

He goes on to justify his consent that men should think him other than he knows he is by the consideration that majesty 'Needs all the props of admiration That may be got, to beare it up on hie' and his own position, especially,

> Needs all the complements to rest upon
> That rev'rence and opinion can bring forth. (ll. 479–80)

During these early scenes Alexander has every appearance of being a genuinely affectionate man and one who has not been deluded by his own majesty so as to forget his own frailties and his human sympathies; but later his desire to preserve himself and his throne leads him to persecute like a tyrant and to prosecute Philotas's trial with inhumanity and a ruthless disregard for even the forms of justice.

The counsellors, too, are equivocal studies, Craterus in particular, who has a larger part than Ephestion. Their behaviour at first may plausibly spring from a laudable desire to serve Alexander, but the Chorus all along suspects motives of personal jealousy and self-aggrandisement, and as they proceed in the play their behahaviour does indeed seem to be dominated by sheer malice and a desire, now that they have him in their power, to destroy Philotas, regardless of his innocence or guilt. In the *Apology* and the Argument Daniel describes the parts played by the counsellors as follows: 'Which [Philotas's treason] being by *Ephestion* and *Craterus*, two the most grave and worthy Councellors of *Alexander* providently discerned, was prosecuted in that manner, as became their neerenesse and deerenesse with their Lord and Maister, and fitting the safety of the State in the case of so great an aspirer', but this by no means squares exactly with the impressions which the play itself produces. It was perhaps natural, after the difficulty his play had caused him, that Daniel should attempt to simplify his treatment of Craterus and Ephestion and emphasise only the honest motives for their actions but it is the mixture of good and bad as it appears in the play itself which contributes to the distinctive quality of the whole.

As for Philotas, he is from the beginning a proud man and it is part of his pride that he sees himself as the only honest man among all those who surround Alexander, not afraid to criticise the king to his face, and refusing to flatter or to truckle to anyone. So far does he convince himself of this part, that he plays the trial scene nobly: and yet all the time he is nursing the secret of the plot hatched with his father '. . . though the affection of the multitude . . . discerned not his ends', writes Daniel, 'nor peradventure himselfe, that knew not how large they might be, nor how much his heart would hold, nor of what capacity would be his ambition, if occasion were offered: Yet some . . . saw well, to how hie a straine he had set his hopes by his affected carriage.'

In these people, in Alexander, in the counsellors, and in Philotas, Daniel is describing the effects of fear and ambition in high places, fear and corruption which work upon even the best and noblest qualities in men's natures and pervert them, and which encourage men to practise fraud and deception even on themselves. Thus Alexander's better nature is submerged, the Counsellors, with a genuine reason for vigilance and anxiety, become unscrupulous and cruel as unexpected power and the opportunity for the gratification of personal jealousies are thrust upon them; and Philotas is corrupted at the heart by his position and the ambition which makes him aspire to be even higher and all his attractiveness and generosity become false and hypocritical.

On this reading 'the frailty of greatnesse, and the usuall workings of ambition' are in a very full sense the themes of the play and the characterisation, with its use of motives only half recognised by the characters themselves, is seen to be conceived with considerable subtlety. Here the Chorus have their principal usefulness in pointing out a second 'soul-side' of the chief characters. Thus as 'the common man', they are sympathetic towards Philotas because of his graces, his bravery, his bluntness, his generosity. So too they are suspicious of Craterus and Ephestion, naturally so, for they are 'the vulgar', distrustful of privileged counsellors who talk secretly with the king and exercise great power behind closed doors. And when Alexander is putting forth a despotic power to crush his enemies they, because they are themselves harried and deprived of comfort by his restlessness, see instinctively that he likewise is doomed to be unhappy and frustrated.

Daniel's handling of character elsewhere is subtle enough to make it by no means impossible that he might have planned such a treatment of what he calls 'the perpetuall subjects of bookes and Tragedies' and he was certainly capable of thinking deeply into his themes and seeing them from more than one angle. Daniel was, besides, so scrupulous a writer, taking such care to polish his work and to examine questions of literary craftsmanship, that it is difficult to imagine him allowing his play to be dragged apart by ungovernable feeling, as the Essex interpretation requires. The attitude toward his material which has been suggested above is at least in harmony with Daniel's characteristic attitudes in other works and this reading provides a coherent and unified design for the play, a thing which Daniel, assuredly, unless he was suffering from some very serious aberration, would never have been content to neglect.

'. . . as good As not to write, as not be understood', wrote Daniel, dedicating *Philotas* to the Prince, and his bitterness is understandable, for if indeed he had intended in *Philotas* a dramatic representation of ideas as complex and deeply studied as has been suggested, it must have been very galling to have it taken as no more than a common piece of political propaganda. Yet after all, the intentions and development of the play are not luminously clear and *Philotas* is not as a whole successful. Much of it is admirable and all of it is interesting but, perhaps because Daniel was trying to put too much into it, the mechanics of the plot as well as the general outlines of the characters tend to become confused.

The whole question of Daniel's approach to drama at this date is an interesting one. There are some striking differences between the technique of *Philotas* and that of the 1594 *Cleopatra*. In the later play, the stage is positively crowded at times with far more than the three characters allowed by neo-classical prescription and Dymnus dies on the stage. There are very few monologues, none lengthy. Passages of reported action are introduced very sparingly (the first reporting an event supposed to have occurred contemporaneously with the action of the play does not come till Act IV, scene i), and at one point Daniel makes use of a flash-forward, a device more dramatically effective than the recitals of things past so prominent in *Cleopatra*. There is altogether much more dramatic tension in *Philotas* than in the earlier play. Daniel emphasises the idea of struggle and potential danger from the beginning and works the situations up to a climax in the trial scene. He provides, for emphasis, a sub-plot of internal conflict in the small but effective scene between Antigona and Craterus.

This is, of course, not closet drama. It was meant for the stage, and there is a strong presumption that it was acted. Daniel's own comments on this departure are worth collecting. 'my necessitie', he writes to Cranborne, 'I confess hath driven me to doo a thing unworthy of mee, and much against my harte, in making the stage the Speaker of my lynes ...' '... driven by necessity,' he repeats in the *Apology*, 'to make use of my pen, and the Stage to bee the mouth of my lines, which before were never heard to speake but in silence ...' In other words, he was impelled into the theatre by the need to get some money, not because he yearned to see his creations come to life on the stage. But given that he was to write an acting drama, what were his aims to be? '... I sought to reduce the stage from idlenes to those grave presentments of antiquitie used by the wisest nations', the letter to Cranborne continues and the *Apology* amplifies this a little: 'I thought the representing so true a History, in the ancient forme of a Tragedy, could not but have had an unreproveable passage with the time, and the better sort of men, seeing with what idle fictions, and grosse follies, the Stage at this day abused mens recreations.' The form of closet-drama is to be modified to some degree, it appears, in order to make it presentable on the stage but the modifications are not to be by any means so radical as to risk confusion either in tone or form with the popular drama. And the result, as has been noted, was not a success. Daniel was attracted to the story in the first place, so he says (*Apology*), partly because of 'the aptnesse, I saw it had to fall easily into act . . .' but in fact his mind soon discovers and dwells on aspects of the story which do not fall easily into drama at all.[17]

These considerations are of particular interest because two years later, in 1607, Daniel republished his *Cleopatra* 'newly altred' and altered so much and in such ways as to raise a number of interesting questions. The revised *Cleopatra* has received a good deal of attention in recent years because of its relationship with Shakespeare's *Antony and Cleopatra*.[18] The precise nature of this relationship has not yet been firmly established but the main question, as concerns Daniel, is whether, after his arm's length approach to the theatre in *Philotas*, he did not come more under the spell of the stage and attempt to revitalise *Cleopatra* under the influence of the supreme popular dramatist, Shakespeare; or to put it a different way, whether, remaining short of money, he did not try to recast his *Cleopatra* in the hope of profiting, financially, by another man's example. In any case, the revised *Cleopatra* would seem to be a retreat from the Pembroke purism of the 1594 *Cleopatra*.

The first thing to be said about this is that *Philotas* already shows significant departures from the form and manner of the 1594 *Cleopatra* so that there is no absolute need to postulate a blinding flash of Shakespeare in order to account for the revision of *Cleopatra*. *Philotas*, moreover, is a more thoroughly dramatic piece of work than even the revised *Cleopatra*. The effect of the revisions in *Cleopatra* can, in fact, easily be overemphasised. Some long speeches of the original are split up as dialogue, though many remain, nevertheless, very long. New scenes are introduced, but Dircetus's narrative of Antony's death, the biggest and one of the best additions to the play, is in form entirely in the neo-

17. Since this chapter was written G. A. Wilkes in "Daniel's *Philotas* and the Essex Case" (*M.L.Q.* Sept. 1962, pp. 233–42) has questioned Michel's reading of the play in terms of the Essex troubles. His last paragraph contains some interesting comments on the difficulty of adapting Daniel's characteristically meditative habit of mind to the demands of dramatic form.

18. See especially Ernest Schanzer, 'Daniel's Revision of his *Cleopatra*', *R.E.S.* 7–8, (1956–7), pp. 375–81; and A. M. Z. Norman, 'The Tragedie of Cleopatra and the Date of *Antony and Cleopatra*', *M.L.R.* LIV (1959), pp. 1–9.

As these articles show, there has been much quoting of alleged parallel passages but since the search for verbal echoes is at best a slippery exercise and since in this particular case nothing conclusive has been brought forward, it has not seemed necessary to reproduce the arguments and suggestions here.

classical tradition, and two long passages of reported action remain from the original (the Proculeius-Gallus episode and Titius's account of the reading of Dolabella's letter). The play as revised hardly ranks as theatrical drama either in point of action presented or speed and liveliness of dialogue.

Since much has been made from time to time of Daniel's alleged dependence on Shakespeare in his revisions, some comments may be made on specific points that have been considered cogent.

Diomedes appears in the revised *Cleopatra* but not in the original. Yet he hardly discharges the same function in Daniel as he does in Shakespeare, or, for that matter, as he does in Plutarch or in Garnier's *Marc-Antoine*. In each of the last three versions, he is employed as the messenger whom Cleopatra sends to tell Antony that she is still alive. Very little more is made of him. In Daniel's play it is to Diomedes that Cleopatra turns when she realises that death is the only alternative to going to Rome as Caesar's captive and she asks Diomedes to procure the asps for her. He does as she bids him and returns to her later in the monument, disguised as a countryman and bringing the asps concealed in a basket of figs. Plutarch leaves the exact manner of Cleopatra's death in doubt, only suggesting that the countryman and his figs had something to do with it, but Daniel had wanted, from the beginning, to tie the story up neatly. In the original version of his play the messenger who relates Cleopatra's death at the end reveals that he himself was instructed by Cleopatra to provide the asps. In the revised version the death scene is played out on the stage, so there is no messenger. Daniel has to find someone else to take over the part in the final catastrophe which the messenger had previously played and it is in no way remarkable that he should think of Diomedes. He has Plutarch's word that Diomedes was 'a secretarie' and employed by Cleopatra in personal missions for her and he may very well have appeared a suitable person for Daniel's purposes. There seems little need to call in the memory of Shakespeare's Diomedes when everything about the two men is different except the name.

Gallus is added to a scene in the revised version of *Cleopatra*. There is no apparent reason for his presence since he says nothing, unless Daniel thought that the presence of both the participants in the action to be described (the surprising of Cleopatra in the monument by Gallus and Proculeius) might add liveliness to the scene. The most that editors of *Antony and Cleopatra* assign to Gallus is two lines. It hardly seems necessary to suppose that Daniel was so impressed with the effectiveness of this small part that he felt urged to introduce Gallus into his play on that account, although he had nothing for him to say.

The rôles of Eras and Charmion are extended in the revised as compared with the original version of the play. Hints for this enlargement of their parts could quite well have been found in Jodelle's *Cléopâtre Captive* and Garnier's *Marc-Antoine* which were important sources in the earlier *Cleopatra*.

The part played by Dircetus in the revised version is a more interesting subject for in his circumstantial account of the death of Antony he introduces a whole new slice of material and material, moreover, which Shakespeare works up into some of the most striking and memorable scenes of his play. It has been suggested, and with some plausibility, that the reworking of his play more or less obliges Daniel to introduce this material.[19] In the earlier version it was quite unnecessary to tell this part of the story for it had been dealt with in the Countess of Pembroke's *Antonie* and the audience for the two plays was to be the same. But the 1607 play is an independent one, intended presumably for presentation on the stage, and the story as originally told is perhaps not self-sufficient but needs filling in with an account of the death of Antony. This seems a very reasonable explanation as far as it goes, but it does not meet the whole of the situation. The part of the Dircetus speech which deals with the hauling up of Antony into the monument and his reception by Cleopatra (Act 1, sc. ii, ll. 238-66) is remarkably vivid and what is more, some of its detail is surprising in itself and cannot be accounted for by any known source. Daniel might have been expected to go to *Antonie* for the details of this scene but, in fact, his whole account of the operation of drawing Antony into the monument is quite different from Lady Pembroke's. He is remarkably precise in his account of the working of a 'pulley' and of Antony's body, swinging in mid-air, the blood from his wound 'showring out', meanwhile, 'on th'under lookers', and whereas Plutarch says that Antony was

19. Johannes Schütze, 'Daniel's *Cleopatra* und Shakespeare', *Englische Studien*, 71, (1936-7), pp. 58-72.

drawn up by means of 'chains and ropes', Daniel says that he is drawn up 'in rowles of taffaty'.[20]

Perhaps this speech gives a clue to what Daniel's objects were in the revision of his play as a whole. It is clear that he intends to give his play greater vitality and movement than it had before and he sets about it by replacing reported speech and action by the scenes themselves and by increasing the number of characters and extending minor rôles. He has already, with *Philotas*, emancipated himself from strict adherence to the Countess of Pembroke's principles and practice and the revised *Cleopatra* is another step in what seems to be an attempt to arrive at a new form in English drama, one which will have greater vigour than Garnier's, more complexity and subtlety than *Gorboduc*, and yet be capable of appealing to 'the better sort of men', those whose taste is too refined and fastidious to be delighted by the 'idle fictions and grosse follies' of the contemporary drama. One of the essentials of this new mode, as Daniel apparently saw it, was vividness of detail. To replace the more flamboyant attractions of 'romantic' dramatists, he would offer description in depth, a profound realisation of his characters and their situations. There is evidence of this in *Philotas*; there is more in the revised *Cleopatra* and Dircetus's speech is a case in point for the whole business of hoisting Antony up is done with an extraordinary degree of visual imagination. The 'rowles of taffaty' are also perhaps to be accounted for by the same intensity of realisation for Cleopatra withdrew much of her treasure into the monument with her,[21] amongst which costly materials might be expected to be included, and her willingness to swathe the bloody Antony in this may be a measure of the

20. See my letter in *R.E.S.* 9, Aug. 1958, pp. 294–5. I have previously suggested that this scene embodies an eye-witness account of a performance of *Antony and Cleopatra* (*Shakespeare Survey* VI (1953), pp. 91–3). I now think that this explanation is less likely than the one offered above.

21. This is stated in Act 1, sc. ii, ll. 305–8 of the revised text where Caesar expresses anxiety lest Cleopatra should destroy

... the treasure which she hath amast
Within that vault of all the precious stuffe
That Egypt yields ...

There is no such reference in the earlier version although Plutarch has: 'Cleopatra had long before made many sumptuous tombs and monumentes.... Thither she caused to be brought all the treasure and pretious things she had of the auncient kings her predecessors...' (*North's Plutarch*, vi, p. 77) and (after the death of Antony, Caesar) 'sent Proculeius and commaunded him to doe what he could possible to get Cleopatra alive, fearing least otherwise all the treasure would be lost' (p. 81).

new devotion to him which Daniel particularly emphasises in his picture of her character in adversity. Whether or not Daniel was influenced by Shakespeare is, consequently, of less importance in the study of Daniel than might appear since the object of the revision in any case was not to emulate Shakespeare nor to compete with him on his own ground, but to show how the bounds of neo-classic drama could be enlarged beyond the narrow limits of the earlier Pembroke examples and yet remain uncontaminated by sensationalism and technical 'licence'.

In fact, the revised *Cleopatra* is not so satisfactory a piece of work as the original version. The essential unity which gives strength to the 1594 play is shattered by a multiplication of claims to attention and a variety of focal points. Some fine passages are omitted in the interest of shortening speeches and others are broken up in a way that destroys their total, cumulative effect. Rodon's account, for example, of his treachery and of Cleopatra's parting from Caesario derives some extra poignancy in the original version from the fact that both Rodon himself and Seleucus, in whom he confides, are suffering agonising remorse for their betrayals of Cleopatra. The Nuntius's account of Cleopatra's death and of the whole final scene in the monument contains much that has to be sacrificed in the revised version with no compensating gain. In short, Daniel's words speak better and more fully when they are written to be heard 'in silence', but his effort to externalise, to fill in a scene, produces some good things, including one of the most charming of his effects. It is the arrival of Diomedes, disguised as a countryman, at the beginning of the last act. The little scene between him and the guard has a simple beauty very effective in its context:

Gua.	And whither now sir, stay, what have you there?
Diom.	Good sirs, I have a simple present here,
	Which I would faine deliver to our queene.
Gua.	What ist? lets see?
Diom.	And please you sirs it is
	Onely a few choice figs which I have growne
	In mine owne garden, and are soonest ripe
	Of any here about, and every yeare
	I use to bring a few unto our queene.
	And pray my masters take a taste of them
	For I assure you they are very good.
Gua.	No, no, my friend, goe on, and beare them in.

(v. ii. 1669–76)

On a small canvas such as this Daniel sometimes achieves among his most delicate and telling strokes.

Philotas and the revised *Cleopatra* need to be considered together since they represent the fruits of Daniel's mature and independent thinking about the nature of 'right tragedy', but in the years between the publication of *Philotas* and that of the revised *Cleopatra* he began to work on an entirely new *genre* of dramatic entertainment. The 'captious Censurers' on whom he comments in his account of *The Vision of the Twelve Goddesses* had soured the business of masque-writing from the beginning, and it was in any case a commission which Daniel scarcely welcomed, but he was not exhausted as a purveyor of court entertainment. He could not compete, and disdained to try, with the novelties and developments which Jonson was introducing into the masque, but he had another resource in the contest for court favour, to provide novel entertainment by bringing the manner and matter of Italian pastoral drama to the English stage.

'Which of your poets?' demands Lady Politick Would-Be of a harassed Volpone:

> . . . Petrarch, or Tasso, or Dante?
> Guarini? Ariosto? Aretine?
> Cieco di Hadria? I have read them all,

but especially *Pastor Fido*:

> . . . All our English writers,
> I mean such as are happy in the Italian,
> Will deign to steal out of this author, mainly:
> Almost as much as from Montaignié:
> He has so modern and facile a vein,
> Fitting the time, and catching the court-ear!

This, written in 1605–6, is certainly a jibe at Daniel, an attempt to disparage the Italianate pastoral drama which he had contrived, perhaps as a deliberate counter-stroke to the Jonsonian masque.

The Queenes Arcadia,[22] originally called *Arcadia Reformed*, was written for the visit of James and the Queen and Prince Henry to Oxford from August 27th to 31st, 1605. Latin plays were given on the first three days and Daniel's, the only English production, was performed on the 30th and was especially a play for the

22. Grosart iii, pp. 213–300.

Queen and the ladies. The King did not attend, though it is to
hoped that someone reported to him the tirade against tobacco
which Daniel inserted for the royal gratification. What charm it
may have had has been of less interest to literary historians than
its unique quality as 'the first avowed attempt to reproduce the
conventional Italian pastoral drama on the English stage'.[23] It is
heavily indebted to Tasso and Guarini and also to Luigi Groto,
the 'Cieco di Hadria' whom Lady Politick has on her reading-list
and from whose play *Il Pentimento Amoroso* (1575) a large part of
Daniel's Act 1, scene ii is translated.

But *The Queenes Arcadia* is Daniel's own work, nevertheless,
moulded and given character, for better or worse, by his habits
of thought and poetic style. So much is this so, in fact, that the
Italian motifs sometimes take on a very odd look in their English
guise.

The play deals with the complications introduced into the lives
of a number of Arcadian nymphs and shepherds by one Colax, 'a
corrupted traveller', and Techne, 'a subtle wench of Corinth',
both of whom seek to undermine the purity and simplicity of
Arcadian life. Techne teaches the women to paint their faces and
to adorn themselves, stirs up trouble among true lovers, and
would be Colax's bawd. Colax himself is the complete rake, quite
without moral standards:

> Tush, wrong is as men thinke it . . .,   (1. iii. 246)

a seducer who boasts an impudent metaphysic of lust and beauty:

> Some thing there is peculiar, and alone
> To every beauty, that doth give an edge
> To our desires, and more we will conceive
> In that we have not then in that we have.
>
> .   .   .
>
> So that we see how beauty doth consist
> Of divers peeces, and yet all attract,
> And therefore unto all my love aspires;
> As beauty varies, so doth my desires.   (1. iii. 221–42)

Their efforts are supplemented by Alcon and Lincus, a quack-
doctor and a quack-lawyer respectively, who hope to make a

23. V. M. Jeffery, 'Italian and English Pastoral Drama of the Renaissance III
Sources of Daniel's *Queen's Arcadia* and Randolph's *Amyntas*', M.L.R. 19, (1924),
pp. 435–44.

plump living out of the Arcadians by medicining them into sickness (and by the introduction of tobacco) and by urging them
into litigation. These four aliens all discuss their plans within the
hearing of Meliboeus and Ergastus, 'two ancient Arcadians', who
are able, when the complications have run their due course, to
expose the prime movers, and put right the damage done.

The Queenes Arcadia has, then, a serious theme, the contrast
between the demoralising effects of sophistication and the whole-
some goodness of simpler, less pretentious ways. In itself the
theme is commonplace, but Daniel's treatment of it makes plain
that he was not merely paying lip-service to a conventional attitude, but expounding a seriously held idea with far-reaching
implications. In Act III, scene v, Meliboeus and Ergastus exclaim
indignantly over the 'artificiall knowledge' with which the in-
truders seek to disrupt Arcadian tranquillity, and Ergatus adds:

> And evermore we see how vice doth grow
> With knowledge, and brings forth a more increase,
> When skilfull men begin, how good men cease.
> And therefore how much better do we live,
> With quiet ignorance, then we should do
> With turbulent and ever working skill,
> Which makes us not to live, but labour still. (ll. 1426–32)

The tenor of this is very similar to the passage in Book VI of The
Civil Wars in which Nemesis is instructing Pandora in ways of
breaking up the peace and prosperity of the West, the first
essential being to break up religious faith:

> Goe therefore thou, with all thy stirring traine
> Of swelling Sciences, the gifts of griefe:
> Go loose the links of that soule-binding chaine;
> Inlarge this uninquisitive Beliefe:
> Call-up mens spirits, that simplenes retaine:
> Enter their harts and knowledge make the thiefe
> To open all the doores, to let in light;
> That all may all things see, but what is right.   (st. 35)

Knowledge, it is implied, unless allied to faith and to humility, is
a curse and not a blessing, and the same link between the 'artificiall knowledge' by which Colax and Techne and Alcon and
Lincus seek to corrupt Arcadia and the disturbance of religious
faith is made in the play with the appearance of Pistophoenax.

Pistophoenax does not appear in the cast list and he does not enter the play until near the end when Meliboeus and Ergastus have summoned the Arcadians to hear the perfidy of the conspirers against their peace. Ergastus suddenly realises that there is another with them whom he has not seen before and Meliboeus explains that he found him

> Maintaining hote dispute with *Titerus*
> About the rites and misteries of *Pan*   (v. iii. 2282–3)

'For sooth', says Techne, 'he is a very holy man', whereupon Ergastus, suspecting that he is not what he seems, has his mask plucked from him revealing

> . . . a most deformèd ougly face,
> Wherewith if openly he should appeare,
> He would deterre all men from comming neere.
>   (ll. 2293–5)

Pistophoenax himself speaks only once, and not until the very end of the play, just before Meliboeus's final speech. Lincus has bidden him not to be discouraged by the rebuff he has received in Arcadia, and Pistophoenax answers in a significant speech:

> Tush *Lincus*, this cannot discourage me,
> For we that traffique with credulity
> And with opinion, still shall cherisht be;
> But here your errour was to enter first
> And be before me, for you should have let
> Me make the way, that I might have dislinkt[24]
> That chaine of Zeale that holds in amity,
> And call'd up doubt in their establisht rites;
> Which would have made you such an easie way,
> As that you might have brought in what you would,
> Upon their shaken and discattered mindes;
> For our profession any thing refutes,
> And all's unsetled whereas faith disputes.   (v. iv. 2542–54)

Once again reference to the Nemesis-Pandora passage in *The Civil Wars* makes the background of thought plain. Nemesis describes the devoutness of the West and outlines the plan of corruption:

24. 'dislinkt' is the reading of the first edition of 1606. Later editions misprint. 1623 has 'mislikt'. Grosart prints correctly.

SAMUEL DANIEL

For, see what workes, what infinite expence,
What monuments of zeale they edifie;
As if they would, so that no stop were found,
Fill all with Temples, make all holy ground.

But wee must coole this all-believing zeale,
That hath enjoy'd so faire a turne so long;
And other revolutions must reveale,
Other desires, other designes among:
Dislike of this, first by degrees shall steale
Upon the soules of men, perswaded wrong
(*The Civil Wars*, Bk. VI, sts. 33-4)

Greg[25] notes of Pistophoenax that 'the discovery that he is
wearing a mask to hide the natural ugliness of his features passes
altogether the bounds of dramatic satire, and carries us back to
the allegorical manner of the middle ages'. His own description
of him as 'the disseminator of false doctrine ... perhaps the
favourite object of contemporary invective' hardly seems quite
to meet the case, for it is evident that Pistophoenax's existence in
the play does not derive solely from a wish on Daniel's part for a
piece of contemporary satire to gratify the audience but that his
appearance becomes necessary, so to speak, as the play progresses,
because of deep-rooted ideas in Daniel's own mind.[26] In other
words, Daniel may have begun *The Queenes Arcadia* with no more
in mind than a reshuffling of themes and incidents from Italian
pastoral drama but the introduction of the cynics and the pur-
veyors of bastard knowledge led him gradually and characteristically to deepen the tone until the play ends, with Meliboeus's last
speech, on a note of moral severity worlds away from the romantic
episodes culled from the Italians.

Midway between the deep seriousness of this part of the play's
structure and the romantic episodes is the contemporary satire
proper. The passage on the evils of tobacco (Act III, sc. i, ll. 12-

25. W. W. Greg, *Pastoral Poetry and Pastoral Drama* (London, 1906), p. 256.
26. The name Pistophoenax suggests two Greek words, pistos = trusty, faithful,
and phĕnax = cheat, imposter. This makes an example of oxymoron, which Daniel
liked. The peculiar form of the latter part of the compound may indicate that he had
in mind the quibble introduced in the *Acharnians* of Aristophanes, l. 89, when play
is made with phĕnax and phoinix (phoenix). I am indebted for this note to my
colleague, Mr. E. W. Whittle.
The ideas of constancy in deceit and also of ever-springing vitality would both be
ppropriate to Daniel's conception of the evils of doubt and contention in religion.

116

64) has already been mentioned and there is a pleasant scene immediately following in which Alcon, the quack, interviews Daphne, a patient:

Alc. It seemes faire nimph you dream much in the night.
Dap. Doctor, I doe indeed.
Alc. I know you doe;
    Y'are troubled much with thought.
Dap. I am indeed.
Alc. I know you are.
    You have great heavinesse about your heart.
Dap. Now truly so I have.
Alc. I know you have.
    You wake oft in the night.
Dap. In troath I doe.
Alc. All this I know you doe;
    And this unless by physicke you prevent,
    Thinke whereto it may bring you in the end.

(III, ii. 1195-1208)

The satire is not often as sprightly as this. The complaints of the corruption of manners and the accounts given by Alcon and Lincus of the tricks of their trades follow rather heavily in well-worn paths. When he has a more serious object in view, Daniel is much more telling, as in the perverted intelligence of Colax's philosophy of lust and the insinuating lasciviousness of Techne's advice to Cloris (2. ii). He can also make a shrewd point as in describing the discomfiture of the over-confident would-be seducer when his prey escapes him:

    . . . in troth me thought
    I never heard a man more vainely talke,
    (For so much as I heard) for up the hill
    I went with such a pace, and never stayd
    To give regard to anything he sayd:
    As at the last I scarse had left him breath
    Sufficient to forsweare himselfe withall.

(IV. iii. 1677-83)

Colax is neatly mocked for

    . . . having cast away
    Much foolish paines in tricking up himselfe
    For this exploit . . .

(ll. 1690-2)

As for the romantic episodes themselves, they have their moments of sweetness and grace. The nymphs talk on the whole like sensible young women, which has its charm, but accentuates the ludicrousness of some of the situations they find themselves in. Techne runs to report to Cloris that Amyntas, mad with despair, is about to make away with himself and perhaps has done it already, to which Cloris with devastating common-sense replies:

> If it be done, my help will come too late;
> And I may stay, and save that labour here.
>
> (IV. iiii. 1814–15)

Her relenting is not much more romantic:

> Well *Techne*, come, I would not have him yet
> To perish, poore *Amyntas*, in this fit,   (ll. 1864–5)

to which Amarillis, blunt and matter-of-fact, replies:

> Well *Cloris* yet he may, for ought I see
> Before you come, unlesse you make more hast.
>
> (ll. 1866–7)

The spirit of romance can hardly expect to flourish on such fare as this and so great is the confusion of Latin fervour in matter and Anglo-Saxon phlegm in manner that when Palaemon, after some four pages of bewailing the supposed unfaithfulness of his lady excuses Mirtillus from further attention to his 'tedious tale', promising to confine himself in future to

> . . . beasts, and trees, whose sense I shall not tyre
> With length of mone; for length is my desire,
>
> (II. iii, 894–5)

it is impossible to tell whether Daniel has his tongue in his cheek or is simply making a stolid statement of a sentiment appropriate to the occasion. On the whole, and such lapses apart, the pitch required by the material is too high for Daniel and he can only bring it down an octave or so where sweetness and sentiment have to do duty for ardour and lyricism. His reversion to his more serious speculations about life is the most interesting thing in the play from one point of view, but it hardly helps to unify what is already a hotch-potch of satire, high-flown romantic situation and solid common-sense.

Daniel does not indeed claim very much for his play. The dedicatory poem to the Queen insists on the modest aspirations of the production and makes some rather curious observations on the impropriety of men who, being 'below the Sphere of action, and the exercise Of power' presume nevertheless to comment on the conduct of state affairs. They will inevitably be wrong in their conclusions, says Daniel, and may sow sedition in the minds of the people. 'The eye of practise', meantime, looking down on it all, will see the dangers and also the malice of the attempt:

> And how though th' Woolfe, would counterfeit the Goate,
> Yet every chinke bewrayes him for a Woolfe. (ll. 41–2)

The unaptness of humble men fully to understand the affairs of the great is commented on elsewhere by Daniel, for example in the dedication of the *Letter from Octavia* to the Countess of Cumberland, but the comment in the dedication to *The Queenes Arcadia* runs to much greater length and generates a surprising amount of feeling. The passage might perhaps be taken as a confession of error with reference to the *Philotas* trouble but the last two lines make this explanation improbable. Daniel is hardly likely to have described himself as a wolf, or even a goat, and he never ceased to proclaim his innocence of seditious intentions in *Philotas* and his sense of injury at being accused. It is much more likely that he is referring to somebody else and that the somebody was Jonson, his great rival at this time. In 1605 Jonson was going through a difficult period in his career. When *The Queenes Arcadia* appeared on the Stationers' Register in November, Jonson was just emerging from prison where indiscreet allusions to the Scots and to the King in *Eastward Ho!* had put him and it was not long since he had been examined before the Privy Council for his *Sejanus*. *Sejanus* was produced in 1603 and was entered on the Stationers' Register in November 1604 but it was not published till nearly a year later i.e. September or October 1605, just after the performance of *The Queenes Arcadia* at Oxford and just before its entry on the Stationers' Register – about the time, in other words, when Daniel was preparing the dedication to the Queen. The publications of *Sejanus* and *Eastward Ho!* nearly coincided and if the trouble over *Sejanus* had by that time been smoothed over, fresh doubts may have been stirred about it when *Eastward Ho!* caused a louder commotion.

Daniel's remarks in the dedication of his *Queenes Arcadia* become distinctly pointed if, in fact, he had Jonson in mind. This claimant of court favour, who set himself up as so much Daniel's superior, had been involved in public insults to the King and his favourites and had presumed to comment satirically on affairs of state under cover of a scholarly treatment of ancient history: whereas the righteous Daniel has known his place and preserved respect and humility. There is even an echo of Jonson's own words in all this from Tiberius's speech (*Sejanus*, 1. ll. 537–40):

> Princes have still their grounds rear'd with themselves,
> Above the poore low flats of common men,
> And who will search the reasons of their acts,
> Must stand on equall bases . . .

These lines are marked off in inverted commas in the quarto (1605) edition and it would be a stroke of some malice on Daniel's part thus disingenuously to turn Jonson's 'sentence' against himself.

The oddness of these passages in the dedication to *The Queenes Arcadia* is not, of course, diminished if they represent a bout in a running battle with Jonson. For at the same time as Jonson was busily addressing letters from prison to influential persons protesting his innocence of any desire to affront the King, Daniel was writing similar letters pleading the innocence of his intentions in *Philotas*. Both appealed to Robert Cecil, Jonson's letter being later than Daniel's as his use of the title 'Earl of Salisbury' indicates. Both recognise some sort of connection with Lord Northampton. Jonson reported to Drummond that 'Northampton was his mortall enimie for brauling on a St. Georges day one of his attenders, he was called before ye Councell for his Sejanus and accused both of popperie and treason by him'.[27] Daniel, in his letter to Cecil, offers to withdraw both himself and his book from circulation: 'Onely,' he goes on, 'I would beseach my L: of Northampton and your ho: . . . to bestow some small viaticum to carry me from the world, where I may bury my selfe, and my writings out of the way of envie . . .' What Daniel's relations with Northampton were is not clear. Among the verse epistles of 1603 there is one to Northampton under his former title of Lord Henry Howard which may suggest that Daniel had previously sought his patronage and perhaps had some encouragement from him,

27. *Works of Ben Jonson*, i, p. 141.

but the verse epistle is itself something of a mystery for Howard is praised, not for the wit and learning which he undoubtedly had, but for honesty and straight dealing which were most notoriously *not* his characteristics. The epistle to Howard can be read, in fact, as a kind of commentary on the themes of the suspect play for, like *Philotas*, it describes the evils of corrupt ambition and of devious and dishonourable courses. Lines 65-70 of the Epistle echo very closely the opening lines of the first chorus to *Philotas*, a warning that 'the vulgar', though ignorant, 'wholy never can deluded be'. What Northampton made of this, and what Daniel meant him to make of it, are interesting but unanswerable questions.

Northampton was a notorious intriguer and the connection of his name with both prosecutions may not be accidental; but it is in any case true that the Court and the government were in a very sensitive frame of mind at this date. Calvert wrote to Winwood on March 28th, 1605: 'The plays do not forbear to present upon their stage the whole Course of this present time, not sparing either King, State or Religion, in so great Absurdity, and with such Liberty, that any would be afraid to hear them.'[28] One consequence was that both Jonson and Daniel were charged at about the same time with having made seditious comments under cover of historical drama. It does not appear that they loved each other any better for it and Daniel had evidently sufficiently recovered in the Royal favour to risk a blow at Jonson in the dedication of *The Queenes Arcadia* without fear of a tu quoque.

28. *Memorials of affairs of state in the reigns of Queen Elizabeth and King James I* collected from the original papers of Sir R. Winwood, ed. E. Sawyer (London, 1725), ii. p. 54.

VI

1605–9: 'The Civil Wars'

Mountjoy, Daniel's friend and patron, died in 1606, but Daniel had for some time before that been looking for supplementary patronage. He probably met and first sought the patronage of the Earl of Hertford as early as 1603 and he seems to have entered into his service at about the time of the production of *The Queenes Arcadia* in 1605.[1] The Hertfords and the Pembrokes were the two great houses of Wiltshire and on the death of the old Earl of Pembroke in 1601, the Earl of Hertford had become Lord Lieutenant of Somerset and Wiltshire. Whether or not some local connection drew Daniel to him, Hertford seems to have provided Daniel with the means for withdrawing to the more secluded life of the country for which he had expressed an inclination in his letter to Cranborne. At some date between 1605 and 1608 he retired to a farm of the Earl's[2] whence he wrote a very bucolic letter on May 20th, 1608, confessing that he had eaten '3 dozayn & 9 pigions' and adding: 'thus I am fayne to discend in my pticulars, that in my generall account do somme & cast up the busyneses of princes and convers dayly in my quiet wt the best of the earth . . .' The reference is to his poem *The Civil Wars* and the buoyant tone of the letter, which is addressed to one James Kirton, an officer in the Earl of Hertford's household, reflects Daniel's happiness at having found at last a haven where he may work at this task which has been occupying him on and off for the last fourteen years.

A second letter survives, written eleven days later to the same

---

1. See the article by C. C. Seronsy, 'Daniel's *Panegyrike* and the Earl of Hertford,' in *P.Q.* xxxii (July, 1953), pp. 342–4; and Joan Rees, 'Samuel Daniel and the Earl of Hertford', *N.Q.* (Sept. 1958), p. 408.
2. This may be the 'Farm in Wiltshire nigh the Devises' to which Fuller refers, though he seems to have confused this period of farming with a later one (see p. 150).

man. Since writing the first Daniel had come up to London at the request of the Earl and he writes to tell Kirton that he is staying with his friend and publisher, Simon Waterson, and that he is unwilling to venture far from the house: '. . . to be often seene in ye Cittie, at this tyme, of some I would not see, might much prjudice mee'.[3] This sounds slightly sinister but there is probably a simple explanation. In 1607 Daniel was describing himself as 'one of the Groomes of the Queenes Majesties privie Chamber' and Fuller says she allowed him 'a fair salary' (Wood specifies £60 a year): probably he had special leave of the Queen to absent himself from Court in order to work at his poem in the country and this would account for his reluctance to be seen gadding about the city.

The business which has brought Daniel up to town evidently involves negotiations of some sort with the Earl of Hertford, and although the details are not clear they seem to concern, in part at any rate, the poem of *The Civil Wars*. 'I would,' Daniel writes, 'we might once all agayne meet together conveniently, to cosider [*sic*] thorowly of this good worke, wc were great pittie beeing so worthy & honourable for all parties, should now fall to the ground for want of a little furtherance to hold it up & set it forward agayne. my L. is truly noble and wise & sapiens scit quid velit, & qd semel voluit velle nō desinit. I shall thinke this as meritorious a deed for mee yf it succeed, as pore Peeter the Hermit did to combine in amitie all the Christian princes together, and I would most gladly imploy all my best powres in it.'

The Civil Wars had been hanging fire for a long time, for Daniel first began work on it in 1594 and a manuscript draft of the first two books still exists.[4] Two issues of the first four books of the poem were published in 1595 and in 1599 the poem was republished with the addition of a fifth book. In 1601, a sixth book was added which brought the history to the crowning of Edward IV, and Daniel at this point seemed weary of his task. His Muse, he wrote:

3. Both these letters are printed by H. Sellers, 'A Bibliography of the Works of Samuel Daniel', *Oxford Bibliographical Society, Proceedings and Papers*, 11 (1927–30), pp. 29–54.
4. It has been examined by C. C. Seronsy. See his article, 'Daniel's Manuscript *Civil Wars* with some previously unpublished stanzas' in *J.E.G.P.* LII (April 1953), pp. 153–60.

> . . . but in the midd'st of her long way
> Stands trembling at the horrors that succeed,
> Weary with blood and slaughter, faine would stay
> Her further course, unwilling to proceed,
> And, faine would see that glorious holy day
> Of Union, which this discord hath agreed,
> And knowes not yet what to resolve upon,
> Whether to leave-off here, or else go-on.

(vi, st. 115. 1601 text)

He was reluctant to surrender the poem, however, and in the dedication of *Philotas* to Prince Henry, the incompleteness of what he evidently considers his magnum opus is one thing that he specially regrets when bitterness at the trouble over his play drives him to contemplate giving up writing altogether. It seems fairly clear from the Kirton letters that in 1608 he was again in the full flush of enthusiasm and looking forward to bringing his poem to a conclusion. In the end, though, the Earl of Hertford must have let him down and when in 1609 the final, though still uncompleted, version of Daniel's poem appeared, it was dedicated to the Mary Herbert, now Countess Dowager of Pembroke, who had sponsored his earliest ventures in poetry. 'She', wrote Daniel:

> . . . whose beames do reincense
> This sacred fire, seemes as reserv'd in store
> To raise this Worke, and here to have my last;
> Who had the first of all my labours past. (viii, st. 1)

The 1609 version splits the original Book iii into two books, adds new material ('making-up a part, which (for haste) was left unfurnisht in the former Impressions' as he says in the dedication), and contributes an entirely new book 'continuing the course of the Historie' as far as the marriage of Edward IV to Lady Grey. The total thus became eight books.[5] At the end of Book viii, Daniel is obviously preparing to treat a fresh phase of the history and in the dedication to Lady Pembroke he speaks of his intention to carry the poem down 'unto the glorious Union of Hen. 7.' But in fact,

5. The text of *The Civil Wars*, ed. by L. Michel, is being used for reference in this chapter so that the numbering of the books unless otherwise stated is according to the latest division made by Daniel in 1609. For some notes on the history of the text see James G. McManaway, 'Some Bibliographical Notes on Samuel Daniel's *Civil Wars*', *Studies in Bibliography*, iv (1951), pp. 31–9.

after Book VIII, the poem was never resumed, and when Daniel wrote history again, he wrote it in prose.

The Civil Wars was probably already in Daniel's mind when, between 1592 and 1594 he was writing his *Cleopatra* and when, dedicating his play to Lady Pembroke, he enrolled himself as one of her knights to chase away 'Grosse Barbarisme', and longed that all the world might know the achievements of his native land in poetry and admire 'what great Elizaes raigne hath bred'. Love for his 'deare England' and pride in Elizabeth, 'Deare to her owne, wonder to other Lands' (VI, st. 46), towards whom the whole story moves, are certainly among the original motives of *The Civil Wars*, and the earnestness of purpose of 1594, if not the young enthusiasm, is reflected in 1609 as Daniel writes '. . . this Argument was long since undertaken . . . with a purpose, to shewe the deformities of Civile Dissension, and the miserable events of Rebellions, Conspiracies, and bloudy Revengements, which followed (as in a circle) upon that breach of the due course of Succession, by the Usurpation of Hen. 4, and thereby to make the blessings of Peace, and the happinesse of an established Government (in a direct line) the better to appeare: I trust I shall doo a gratefull worke to my Countrie, to continue the same, unto the glorious Union of Hen. 7: from whence is descended our present Happinesse'.[6]

The increased soberness and weightiness of tone are natural enough. Daniel is not only fifteen years older but the years which have intervened have been far from tranquil. *The Civil Wars*, in one way or another, tells us a great deal about Daniel's development during this central part of his life.

In 1594 Daniel had been at Wilton, writing *Cleopatra*, and in 1595 he was newly received under the patronage of Charles Mountjoy. Through Mountjoy he came to know Essex, for the two men were close friends in spite of an early quarrel which led to a duel. Daniel's imagination seems to have been captured at once by Essex's brilliance and in a sonnet dated 1595 in commendation of William Jones's *Nennio* he speaks in the highest terms of Essex's true nobility. He concludes:

> . . . if men can not true worth discerne
> By this discourse, looke they on him and learne.[7]

Daniel was never a man to indulge in fulsome and easy compliment and what he says here has to be taken as springing from personal acquaintance and sincere admiration. The early editions of *The Civil Wars* add strikingly to this testimony. Book II originally ended with eight stanzas which make it perfectly clear that between 1595 and 1601 Daniel was a whole-hearted admirer of Essex, and the gradual whittling away of these stanzas in successive versions makes a sad commentary on the tragic course of Essex's career.

By the end of Book II the history has reached the point where Richard II has just resigned his crown to Bolingbroke, and Daniel breaks into a lamentation of the woes that will follow this breach of succession. Had Lancaster only been as rightful as he was an able ruler, then England would not have wasted her strength in internecine wars but she would have grown in strength and prosperity and could have undertaken campaigns to beat back 'th' Earths-terror *Ottoman*'. At this point in 1595 and 1599 the poem suddenly launches into a direct address to Essex as Daniel considers how in these fields of Eastern wars, there would have been scope for Essex's courage and prowess, and he would have brought back 'Eternall *Tropheis*' to his Queen, laying the spoil and the glory at her feet. There too, 'Pure-spirited *Mountjoy*, th'ornament of men', would have had 'a large and mightie fielde' for his 'holy guiftes and learned counsels' and between them they would have provided material for a poem quite different from the one that Daniel must write now. Whereas now he must speak in 'bloudie accents' of the horrors of the past, he might have had a theme to celebrate and to rejoice in, and he imagines how Essex and Mountjoy by their exploits in these imagined wars would have:

> ... builded for your great designes
> O you two worthies bewties of our state,
> Immortall tombes of unconsuming lines
> To keepe your holie deedes inviolate:
> You in whose actions yet the image shines
> Of ancient honor neere worne out of date,
> You that have vertue into fashion brought
> In these neglected times respected nought.

(Michel, p. 312)

Mountjoy was very deeply concerned in Essex's later fortunes when the harried favourite was projecting all sorts of schemes for overthrowing his enemies at Court and re-establishing himself. In

1599, when Essex was in Ireland, Mountjoy sent a secret messenger to Scotland to assure James that Essex would support his accession to the English throne: this was presumably intended as a move to win James's support for Essex himself against his enemies. When Essex was confined, after the Irish disgrace, it was to Mountjoy and Southampton that he entrusted the supervision of his affairs. In February 1600 Mountjoy was appointed Lord Deputy of Ireland in succession to his friend and Essex begged him to bring an army from Ireland and in concert with James to come to his assistance; but once in Ireland Mountjoy thought better of this scheme and refused to co-operate. When news of the final attempted coup reached him and of Essex's capture with fellow-conspirators (including Southampton) on a charge of high treason, he was in considerable fear that he also would be drawn in but, in fact, his services in Ireland were too valuable to lose, and the Queen and the government overlooked his association with Essex's earlier plans and even suppressed passages in confessions which implicated him. It is probable that Daniel was sufficiently in Mountjoy's confidence to know a good deal of what was going on and it is certain that he was very sympathetic to Essex and his friends, whatever he thought of their policies. One of his verse epistles of 1603 is addressed to Southampton congratulating him on his release from prison and his conduct in adversity.

In 1601, for obvious reasons, the stanzas relating to Essex were omitted from Daniel's poem and in 1609 all eight stanzas addressed to the 'two worthies' were cut out and a brief reference in the original to the Archbishop of Canterbury's approbation of the deposition of Richard was expanded to two and a half stanzas followed by a generalised regret at the pity of it all. By 1609 both Essex and Mountjoy were dead and both more or less disgraced. Essex had been executed as a traitor and Mountjoy's reputation was tarnished at the end of his life by his marriage to Lady Rich after her divorce from her husband. Daniel has already paid his tribute to Mountjoy in his *Funeral Poem* and pleaded his merits in extenuation of his lapse and he makes one last direct reference to them both at the beginning of Book VIII: 'On yet, sad Verse', he writes:

> . . . though those bright starres, from whence
> Thou hadst thy light, are set for evermore;
> And that these times do not like grace dispense
> To our indevours, as those did before . . .   (VIII, st. 1)

In 1595 the accelerating course of Essex's disasters had scarcely begun and Daniel's verses are sharply ironical in the light of what was to happen. They show, nevertheless, a remarkably shrewd assessment of some of the factors that were to shape the things to come. One of the advantages of the happier times that Daniel imagines is that they could provide legitimate outlets for Essex's energy and ambition and the lack of such outlets goes far to explain Essex's career. It is a paradox of the age that while from one aspect it offered opportunity and adventure with a lavish hand, from another point of view the scope of action of some of its noblest spirits was strictly confined and controlled. Mountjoy was one of those who chafed at the strict and narrow limits and in his early days at Court he was continually contriving his escape abroad until he was kept at home by the Queen's express edict. Sidney, a few years earlier, had found himself everlastingly frustrated in his great projects and desire for a field of action big enough to call out all his powers and the Queen remembered Sidney in one of her reprimands to Mountjoy: 'Serve me so (quoth she) once more, and I will lay you fast enough for running; you will never leave till you are knocked on the head, [i.e. killed in action] as that inconsiderate fellow Sidney was.'[8] To many an energetic, ambitious young man, the spacious times of great Elizabeth must, in fact, have appeared maddeningly confined and cramping. Hence the explosiveness of so much energy in so small room.

All that Essex might achieve in these imagined exploits, Daniel goes on, of course he would lay at Elizabeth's feet for her glory. It is possible that he was practising here what he later defined as policy and certainly applied when he thought it needful:

> . . . often times to greatnesse we are glad
> To attribute those parts we wish they had[9]

and that having observed Essex's proud and stubborn nature, he feared the effect of it in his relations with the Queen and took occasion to slip in a reminder of the necessity of subordination. As Naunton remarks: '. . . my lord of Essex, even of those that

8. Sir Robert Naunton *Fragmenta Regalia* (Arber's English Reprints, London, 1870), p. 33.

9. *Funeral Poem upon the Earl of Devonshire*, Grosart i, p. 173. The lines occur only in 1606.

truly loved and honoured him, was noted for too bold an ingros-
ser, both of fame and favour.'[10]

Daniel is equally clear-sighted in his reference to Mountjoy
when he speaks of him as one capable of exercising the powers of
government, of bringing 'Whole landes and Provinces' into order
and 'calme obedience'. His claim was later justified by the con-
spicuous success of Mountjoy's term of office in Ireland.

Daniel withdrew from *The Civil Wars* his over-sanguine remarks
about Essex but he remained nevertheless remarkably loyal to him
although such loyalty caused him personal discomfort, even possibly danger, in the *Philotas* affair. His remarks about Essex in the
Apology to *Philotas* have already been quoted and only once is
there any record of his having faltered in his loyalty to Essex's
good parts. In the 1606 edition of the *Funeral Poem* for Mountjoy,
in lines which he afterwards suppressed, he is goaded by sneers to
defend himself against a charge which cuts at his pride in his
own rectitude – that he has been indiscriminate in his praises. No
names are named but Essex must be one of those who are meant:

> ... the choyce
> Of those I made did yeald the greatest show
> Of honour and of worth, and had the voyce
> Of present times their virtues to allow.
> And if they have not made them good, it is
> No fault of mine, nor ought it to be layd
> To disrepute these my observances.[11]

Afterwards Daniel omitted this passage and made no apology for
having thought well of Essex only reaffirming, on the contrary,
his belief in his good qualities and his gratitude for his help in the
past.

It is possible that some final comments on Essex and his career
are woven into the last section of the last book of *The Civil Wars*.
Daniel is dealing ostensibly with Warwick the king-maker and his
reactions to the English marriage of Edward IV, but the passage
seems to offer as well a summing-up of his reflections over the
years on the brilliant figure of his own times who had moved his
admiration and even his love. The Warwick passage is dispro-

10. *Fragmenta Regalia*, p. 52.
11. *Funeral Poem upon the Earl of Devonshire*, Grosart i, p. 173.

portionately long in relation to its significance in the history and it is also in manner and matter somewhat out of key with the rest of the poem. It resolves into what is in effect a moral dialogue between the advocates of Withdrawal and Action, represented respectively by Warwick's religious confessor and Warwick himself. The priest takes advantage of the disappointment of Warwick's hopes in the breakdown of the French marriage negotiations to try to reduce the 'fever of ambition' in him. He has, he says, made and established a King, which is what he wanted to do: let him now rest thankful that he is unscathed by the dangers which have beset him. Let him now be himself, the king of his own life, and hanker no more for a wider field of action, having known 'The dangers that on mighty Actors fall'. There is a double significance in the word 'actors' here. It means, of course, those who do, but it means also those who counterfeit, those who are not themselves. Warwick has recently given an example of this kind of acting when on his return from France to the English Court:

> He drawes a Traverse 'twixt his greevances;
> Lookes like the time: his eye made not report
> Of what he felt within: nor was he lesse
> Then usually he was, in every part;
> Wore a cleere face, upon a clowdy hart.   (VIII, st. 89)

Now, says the priest, he may choose to free himself from this sort of necessity by renouncing ambition and living retired. By withdrawing within his own limits, he may be free to be himself. The passage is very close in tenor and even in phrasing to the epistle to the Countess of Bedford, especially lines 50–82, and the priest's whole doctrine that the business of the world is vanity and the only true kingdom is that which a man makes for himself, is common to both the epistle to the Countess of Bedford and that to the Countess of Cumberland.

The ideas are staples of Daniel's thought and their occurrence here is in itself not remarkable; but what is surprising is the care and intensity with which Daniel has framed Warwick's reply. Warwick has twice been mentioned earlier in the poem, first in Book VI, stanza 13 as

> The fatall kindle-fire of those hot daies:
> Whose worth I may, whose work I cannot praise,

and again in Book VIII, stanza 5, where he is described with a similar pun as the

> ... fatall fier-brand
> Of Warre, *Warwicke*; that blazing starre of fight,
> The Comet of destruction, that portends
> Confusion, and distresse, what way he tends.

He would appear to have been definitively summed up in these passages but from about stanza 82 onwards of Book VIII, he unexpectedly becomes the focus of sympathetic attention as he realises that by the English marriage he has lost the interest at Court which he relied on and that past services will count for nothing. He retires to his estates to recoup his energies, and it is then that his confessor's attempt to wean him from his love of power draws from him a striking and moving apology for his life and an account of the springs of action. Warwick acknowledges the soundness of the priest's advice but he cannot follow it. His nature, the place that he was born to, and the extent of his commitment so far, make withdrawal impossible. Recognising the dangers and the disadvantages of his course, he yet cannot change it. It is inevitable that he go on, partly because of external pressures, mainly because of an inner necessity to follow the law of his own being. It is Daniel's attempt to understand the motives and behaviour of a temperament drawn as compellingly to the life of action as he himself was by this time to a life of retirement, and he produces some fine strokes:

> ... action best, I see, becomes the Best.
> The Starres, that have most glorie, have no rest. (st. 104)

> What is our life, without our dignitie?
> Which oft, we see, comes lesse by living long.

> ... Old-age doth give, by too long space,
> Our soules as many wrinkles as our face. (st. 108)

The attempt is a striking piece of imaginative projection but it is curious to observe echoes of an earlier poem and to see how Warwick's defence of the compulsion which makes him what he is finds expression in words very similar to those with which Musophilus replies to Philocosmus's deflating account of the power of letters:

> I know men must, as caried in their spheare,
> According to their proper motions move,

Musophilus acknowledges (ll. 527–8) and, in spite of all that may be said against it:

> This is the thing that I was borne to doo,
> This is my Scene, this part must I fulfill.   (ll. 577–8)

'I have my part', says Warwick, defending his very different proclivities:

> And I must live, in one house, with my hart   (st. 103)

and

> I knowe, that I am fixt unto a Sphere
> That is ordayn'd to move. It is the place
> My fate appoints me; and the region where
> I must, what-ever happens, there, imbrace.   (st. 104)

It would be to over-simplify Daniel's processes of thought to say that he was drawn to such a measure of personal involvement here because when he wrote Warwick he meant Essex. It is a similar over-simplification which reads *Philotas* in terms of the Essex case. One of Daniel's most constant doctrines was that 'there is nothing new under the Sunne, nothing in theas tymes that is not in bookes, nor in bookes that is not in theas tymes'[12] and that

> ... we find that nothing can accrew
> To man, and his condition that is new.[13]

The same sentiments are to be found also in *Musophilus* and *A Defence of Ryme* and in the dedication of the 1609 *Civil Wars*, and they are the basis of Daniel's treatment of his historical characters. The past was very vivid to him as the record of people who had thought and felt even as they did in his own day and in interpreting the past it was inevitable that he should draw on the experience of the present. He would have been less intelligent and sensitive than he was if he had not seen some parallels between the story of *Philotas* and the fate of Essex, but he would also have been less scrupulous a writer than he was if he had allowed this perception to dominate his work to the exclusion of other con-

12. Letter to Cranborne.
13. Dedication to Prince Henry (Michel's *Philotas*, p. 97, ll. 39–40).

siderations. If history repeated itself, as it did, that was not Daniel's fault, as he said somewhat plaintively over and over again: his business as a writer on historical themes was to enrich his subjects with all the possibilities of comment which the experience of ages allowed. What is true of *Philotas* is also true of the Warwick stanzas in *The Civil Wars*. The situations of the fifteenth century and of the sixteenth are allowed to comment on each other and the whole adds up to a view from the heart of the participant, as far as Daniel can make it, in one of 'the perpetuall arguments of bookes and tragedies'. Essex, like Warwick in these stanzas, felt the attractions of a retired life and could willingly have left his 'sphere' if that were possible. 'I have heard him say,' Wotton records, '(and not upon any flashes or fumes of Melancholy, or traverses of discontent, but in a serene and quiet mood) that he could well have bent his mind to a retired course.'[14] The 'acting' necessary in great affairs and especially at Court, on which some emphasis is laid in the Warwick stanzas, was particularly uncongenial to Essex '... so far was he from being capable of dissembling a Resentment,' Camden writes, 'that (as *Cuffe* used to complain to me) he carried his Passions in his Forehead, and the Friend or the Enemy was easily read in his Face'.[15] Consciously or otherwise, Daniel links the two men, Warwick and Essex, by the image of the stars. Essex is one of the 'bright starres' whose fall Daniel mourns in Book VIII, st. 1, and Warwick compares himself to the stars who having most glory have no rest. The priest's final counsel, in which he was interrupted, was such as would have been very appropriate to Essex:

> ... that we are ty'd
> As well to beare the inconveniencie
> And straynes of Kings and States; as to abide
> Untimely raynes, tempests, sterilitie,
> And other ills of Nature that befall:
> Which we, of force, must be content withall (VIII, st. 111)

It has seemed worth tracing the background of the Essex references in *The Civil Wars* at this stage, because this interweaving of

14. Sir Henry Wotton, *Reliquiae Wottonianae* (London, 1672), p. 162.
15. W. Camden, *History of England*, ed. Kennet (London, 1719), ii, p. 637. Both Wood and Fuller note that Camden was among Daniel's closest friends. Camden attended Essex's trial and there is every likelihood that he and Daniel discussed Essex together.

past and present, the research into history going on simultane-
ously with the experience of the pressures of the present, gives
another dimension to *The Civil Wars*. 'Daniell wrott civill warres,
and yet hath not one battle in all his Book';[16] 'too much historian
in verse';[17] the well-known comments of Jonson and Drayton
have encouraged later readers to regard the poem as the product
of an academic seclusion, an assumption which is true neither in
fact nor in spirit, and it is fitting that the poem in its last form
should close with a reminiscence of the man whose career exerted
a powerful hold on Daniel's imagination during the writing of the
greater part of *The Civil Wars*.

The idea that Daniel expanded the Warwick episode to make
room for a final attempt to present a sympathetic and understanding picture of Essex is strengthened by the generally loose
construction of Book VIII in which Daniel seems deliberately to
be picking up personal threads. The Countess of Pembroke, the
patron of his first verse, has now come again to his assistance
while he completes *The Civil Wars*, which he thinks of as his last
work, and the old patronage brings in echoes of the old style as
Daniel sees his end in his beginning. The political preoccupations
of the rest of the poem give way, half way through Book VIII, to a
minute and lingering treatment of the growth of Edward's
passion for Lady Grey, in which style and treatment are reminiscent, at some removes, of *Rosamond* of seventeen years earlier.
The 'Sweet silent Rhetorique of perswading eyes' of the earlier
poem comes to mind when Lady Grey

> ... lifts up her eyes
> (The movingst Mediatours shee could bring)   (st. 54)

and the whole episode, almost a self-contained poem, is really a
Rosamond in reverse, the moral conflict being fought this time in
the King's breast and the lady remaining impregnable in her
virtue and winning (like Richardson's Pamela) marriage as her
prize. The story helps Daniel to a graceful compliment to Lady
Pembroke (st. 76) and to a tribute to Queen Elizabeth (st. 78)
and might well have pleased his aesthetic sense by enabling him
to introduce the last stage of his last work with a brief résumé of
his career so far. Book VIII contains a recollection of one of his
earliest poems, with tributes to his earliest and now his latest

16. *Works of Ben Jonson*, i, p. 138.   17. *To Henry Reynolds*.

patron, and to the Queen whose reign he looked back upon with increasing nostalgia as the winds blew colder round him: and out of this context the Warwick stanzas flow naturally enough with their undertones of the Essex affair.

The aspect of *The Civil Wars* which in recent years has received the most attention is its relationship with Shakespeare's history plays, and the lines of argument and the conclusions to date were neatly summarised by Laurence Michel and Cecil C. Seronsy in 1955.[18] As far as *Richard II* is concerned, they believe that the evidence supports Dr. Dover Wilson's claim that 'Shakespeare had his head full of the poem while he was engaged upon the play'[19] and they add the hope that '*The Civil Wars* will be recognized as the most illuminating background reading yet found for a full appreciation of *Richard II*, and a companion piece not unworthy to stand beside it'. It is also accepted that Daniel's influence on *Henry IV* was substantial although Michel and Seronsy argue that Daniel's revisions in 1609 indicate that he had modified some of his views, notably his 'earlier and harsher view' of Henry IV and his early sympathy for Richard II, after reading Shakespeare. They do not find any substantial evidence of Daniel's use of *3 Henry VI* in the 1609 edition.

No one seems to have remarked on the way Daniel's Henry V exhorts some poet to undertake a national epic to celebrate his deeds although Dr Tillyard suggests that Shakespeare thought of his trilogy as an epic in competition with *The Civil Wars* and the *Arcadia* and *The Faerie Queene*.[20] Daniel's lines could hardly be more categoric. He is about to pass over with a brief reference the reign of Henry V for to him, with his eyes on the theme of the disturbed succession, Henry's military triumphs are an irrelevance when it seems to him that Henry himself comes to reproach him:

> Ungrateful times, that impiously neglect
> That worth, that never times againe shall shew
>
> (Book v, st. 3)

18. 'Shakespeare's History Plays and Daniel: an assessment', *S.P.* 52, 1955, pp. 549–77. See also for the possible influence of *The Civil Wars* on *Julius Caesar*, Joan Rees, 'Shakespeare's Use of Daniel', *M.L.R.* LV (Jan. 1960), pp. 79–82.

19. New Cambridge *Richard II*, p. lxiv.

20. E. M. W. Tillyard *Shakespeare's History Plays* (London, 1944), p. 242. The relevant stanzas in *The Civil Wars* were first published in 1595.

he begins:

> Why do you seeke for fained *Palladines*
> (Out of the smoke of idle vanitie)
> Who may give glory to the true designes,
> Of *Bourchier, Talbot, Nevile, Willoughby*?
> Why should not you strive to fill up your lines,
> With wonders of your owne, with veritie?   (st. 4)

This picks up the first quatrain of *Delia*, Sonnet 46:

> Let others sing of Knights and Palladines;
> In aged accents, and untimely words:
> Paint shadowes in imaginary lines,
> Which well the reach of their high wits records

and tells us something of Daniel's attitude to the proper material of poetry and also, by implication, makes a criticism of misdirected labour in *The Faerie Queene*. Stanza 5 is even more illuminating on both counts as Henry dilates on the possibilities of his triumphs as a theme for poetry:

> What everlasting matter here is found,
> Whence new immortall *Illiads* might proceed!
> That those, whose happie graces do abound
> In blessed accents, here may have to feed
> Good thoughts, on no imaginarie ground
> Of hungry shadowes, which no profite breed;
> Whence, musicke-like, instant delight may growe;
> Yet, when men all do knowe, they nothing knowe.

If only, he says, his own times had produced a poet worthy of the subject, but since they did not, he bids Daniel:

> Tell great ELIZA (since her dayes are grac't,
> With those bright ornaments, to us deni'd)
> That she repaire what darknesse hath defac't,
> And get our ruyn'd deedes, reedifi'd   (st. 9)

and Daniel himself, hearing this impassioned plea of Henry's, sighs, he says,

> . . . and wisht that some would take t'ingrave,
> With curious hand, so proud a worke to reare
> (To grace the present, and to blesse times past)
> That might, for ever, to our glorie last.   (st. 11)

The whole of this passage is worth consideration in relation to *Henry V*, both as a possible stimulus to Shakespeare and as a statement of the contemporary idea of epic material and epic function.

The studies which have been outlined have been undertaken mainly in the interests of Shakespearean scholarship, although in the process of careful reading to assess Shakespeare's indebtedness, the considerable merit of Daniel's poem has often come to light; but Daniel's treatment of his material in *The Civil Wars* is an interesting subject and worth considering for its own sake, free of any Shakespearean entanglements.

Daniel's intention when he began to write is clear enough, to establish himself as an epic poet[21] and a loyal subject of Elizabeth by enshrining the Tudor myth in an extensive historical poem. His subject matter will be the bloody factions of a mighty land and, although such warfare is naturally to be deplored, yet nevertheless out of evil good has come:

> The blisse of thee Eliza; happie gaine
> For all our losse . . .

and in 1595 he continues:

> O sacred Goddesse, I no muse but thee
> Invoke in this great worke I now entend,
> Do thou inspire my thoughts, infuse in mee
> A power to bring the same to happie end:
> Raise up a worke for latter times to see
> That may thy glorie and my paines commend:
> Strengthen thy subject strange thinges to rehearse
> And give peace to my life, life to my verse.   (I, st. 4)

In Book v, stanza 10, through the mouth of Henry V, he reminds the Queen of what he is doing and what is to be expected of her:

> . . . She fosters some (no doubt) that wake
> For her eternitie, with pleasing paine

and in Book VI, added in 1599, he anticipates the eventual inter-

---

21. For a discussion of the claims of *The Civil Wars* to be considered an epic, see L. F. Ball 'The Background of the minor English Renaissance Epics',*E.L.H.* (1934), pp. 63-89. See also the discussion of Daniel's work in E. M. W. Tillyard's *The English Epic and its Background* (London, 1954), pp. 322-37.

marriage of York and Lancaster and forecasts the praise which
will be due to Elizabeth:

> Out of which blessed union, shall arise
> A sacred branch (with grace and glory blest)
>
> .   .   .
>
> For, shee (faire shee) the Minion of the skies,
> Shall purchase (of the high'st) to hers such rest
> ⁀tanding betweene the wrath of heaven and them)
> As no distresse shall touch her Diadem.
>
> And, from the Rockes of Safetie, shall descrie
> The wondrous wracks, that Wrath layes ruined;
> All round about her, blood and miserie,
> Powres betray'd, Princes slaine, Kings massacred,
> States all-confus'd, brought to calamitie,
> And all the face of Kingdomes altered:
> Yet, she the same inviolable stands,
> Deare to her owne, wonder to other Lands.   (sts. 45–6)

The references to Elizabeth in her dual rôle as inspirer of the
poem and supreme peace-maker after the civil wars culminate in
the dedicatory poem of 1601, *To her Sacred Majesty*.

There is no reason to doubt the genuineness of Daniel's
admiration of Elizabeth, and the whole subject as he originally
saw it was a proper one for poetry. He meant to give a coherent
reading of an historical period and he had a moral and political
lesson ready to apply; but before he wrote the last book in 1609,
Elizabeth was dead and Daniel is already projecting another kind
of treatment of history, in prose, and has to remind himself in the
dedication that he is under an obligation to finish his poem; but
in fact he never did complete it.

The length of the task alone is not likely to have deterred him.
The *Philotas* business drained him of energy and enthusiasm for
poetry, the withdrawal of the Earl of Hertford's patronage probably discouraged him further, and James was far from inspiring
him with the same enthusiasm as Elizabeth had done. These things
go a long way towards accounting for the abandonment of his
work but the edginess which increases as the poem progresses
derives from an even more fundamental distress.

The initial situation with which the poem opens lends itself
to relatively simple treatment. It is not difficult to see the fate of

Richard as murder most foul and a gross violation of kingship, with Bolingbroke cast as a great sinner, and this, by and large, is how Daniel treats it. But with the accession of Henry V, difficulties begin to crop up. Book v opens with the vision of Henry V, already quoted from, in which Henry complains that no poet has celebrated his reign, a reign capable of inspiring later generations with 'the love of good' and weaning them from evil 'By good example of faire vertuous acts'. Daniel adds his wish for someone to undertake this worthy task, and then he goes on:

> So should our well-taught times have learned alike,
> How fair shin'd Virtue, and how foul Vice stood;
> When now my selfe am driven to mislike
> Those deedes of worth, I dare not vow for good:
> I cannot mone who lose, nor prayse who seeke
> By mightie Actions here t'advance their Blood.
> I must say, Who wrought most, least honor had:
> How ever good the Cause, the deedes were bad.   (st. 12)

This is an awkward situation for a poet to find himself in, in which he 'dare' not acknowledge one aspect of his material, though it strikes him as more attractive and rewarding than that to which he is committed. He tries to resolve the difficulty by offering the neglected material to another poet, but it cannot be so easily disposed of and the ambivalence which it imposes on Daniel's attitude soon becomes noticeable. Stanzas 14–23 extol Henry's virtues, personal and regal, but at stanza 24 the crucial question of the usurpation rears its ugly head. The Earl of Cambridge has risen to dethrone the King in favour of the Earl of March whom Richard II nominated as his heir, but intelligence of this reaching the King when he is at Southampton embarking for France, he has Cambridge executed. A proper moral judgement is not easily arrived at: the French expedition is a glorious design, an example of Henry's 'careful Virtue' seeking to advance the state, but nevertheless March has strong claims to be Richard's lawful heir. Daniel has refuge temporarily in an evasion:

> That though the Cause seem'd right, and title strong;
> The time of dooing it, yet makes it wrong   (st. 30)

but this sort of equivocation cannot serve for long.

All sorts of questions begin to pour in, and the whole conception of an inevitable Nemesis following the murder of Richard is under fire. Henry is a miracle of a king but it is bitter to reflect how little effect his virtues will have on the course of things to come:

> What? from the best of Virtues glorie, springs
> That, which the world with miserie doth fill?
> Is th' end of happinesse, but wretchednesse?
> Hath Sinne his plague, and Virtue no successe? (st. 38)

The questions raise the most disturbing speculations:

> Either that is not good, the world holdes good:
> Or else is so confus'd with ill; that we
> (Abused with th'appearing likelihood)
> Run to offend, whilst we thinke good to bee:
> Or else the heavens made man (in furious blood)
> To torture man; Allotting no course free
> From mischiefe long: Sending faire dayes that breed
> But stormes; to make, more foul, times that succeed.
>
> (st. 39)

The situation is no longer simple and the orderly pattern of sin and retribution is beginning already to break up.

Another ambiguous situation arises soon after. Henry dies. Nearly sixty years have passed since Bolingbroke seized the throne, and his heirs are now accepted as the 'right possessors'; but fresh disturbance is to come, through Richard, Duke of York, son of that Earl of Cambridge whom Henry V disposed of. His assertion of his right represents an upheaval, a reversal of the order of things which is now established, and Daniel is indignant with him for undertaking it. But at once the other side of the case presents itself: there is some excuse in the circumstances of the time for York to rebel and besides, however well behaved the usurping line may be, it is illegal, and

> ... the now ripe wrath (deferd till now)
> Of that sure and unfayling *Justicer,*
> That never suffers wrong so long to growe,
> And to incorporate with right so farre,
> As it might come to seeme the same in showe (st. 49)

is ready to strike at the offending house. It is all, Daniel now argues, an illustration of the workings of Divine Justice, which strikes at the powerful offender as at the weak. His line of thought

has veered considerably from the regret of a few stanzas earlier
that York had not been content to keep his head bowed but un-
bloody, but the two divergent sets of ideas are brought together in
stanza 51 in more questions:

> But could not yet, for blood-shed, satisfie
> The now well-ruling of th'ill-gotten Crowne?
> Must even the good receive the penaltie
> Of former sinnes, that never were their owne?
> And must a just Kings blood, with miserie
> Pay for a bad, unjustly overthrowne?
> Well; then we see, Right in his course must goe:
> And men, t' escape from blood, must keepe it so.
>
> (st. 51)

This seems conclusive, but the argument is not over. In Book VII,
stanzas 74-8 (written in 1601), the sequence of events from Bolingbroke's return from exile is reviewed and historical precedents
cited for irregular successions. York's claim may be strong but the
crowning of three Lancastrian kings has given some validity to
their succession: this is the argument of Henry VI's ministers but
Daniel's marginal note presents the irreconcileable opposite: *Non
confirmatur tractu temporis quod de iure ab initio non subsistit*. No
compromise is possible, only more disasters.

After such unsatisfactory attempts to wrestle with the moral
issues and so much investigation as the history has led him into
of the selfishness and unscrupulous machinations of both parties
and of the genuine goodness and heroism that have also been
expended for one or the other and all, it seems, futile, it is not
surprising that by the time Book VIII came to be written a mood
of disillusion had set in. The note is struck at the beginning with
the comment on yet another bloody battle:

> ... nor here were any sought
> T'emancipate the State, for publique good;
> But onely, headlong, for their faction wrought.
> Here, every man runs on to spend his bloud,
> To get but what he had already got.
> For, whether *Pompey*, or a *Caesar* wonne,
> Their state was ever sure to be all one.   (st. 7)

A bitterness of spirit has descended on Daniel as he contemplates
it all. Edward's Agincourt-like offer that any man who wishes
may withdraw receives a sour comment:

> ... not one would goe,
> To beare away a hand from bloud; not one
> Defraud the Field of th'evill might be done. (st. 12)

The verse gains bite from the bitter irony of the mood:

> It was upon the twi-light of that day
> (That peacefull day) when the Religious beare
> The Olive-branches as they go to pray,
> (And we, in lieu, the blooming Palme use here)
> When both the Armies, ready in array
> For th'early sacrifice of blood, appeare
> Prepar'd for mischiefe, ere they had full light
> To see to doo it, and to doo it right. (st. 14)

The whole concept of the sacredness of majesty, which was active at the beginning of the poem, has also been lost and Henry VI, at Berwicke, realises:

> ... what a poore distressed thing,
> A King without a people was ...
>
> .   .   .
>
> He sees, what chayre so-ever Monarch sate
> Upon, on Earth, the People was the State. (st. 31)

There is a back reference here to Book VII, stanza 64, when York returns to England from Ireland and sits himself down in the chair of State, a deliberate act, symbolising his intention to claim the crown. The allusion to the chair in the context of Book VIII links both York and Lancastrian claimants in Daniel's disillusion with the mystique of majesty. By stanza 35 of Book VIII the volte-face from the spirit in which he began his poem is almost complete and Daniel marks it with a direct reference to the earlier part of the history:

> Now *Bullingbrook*, these miseries, heere showen,
> Doo much unlode thy sinne; make thy ill, good.
> For, if thou didst by wrong, attaine the Crowne,
> 'Twas without cryes; it cost but little bloud:
> But *Yorke*, by his attempt hath over-throwne
> All the best glorie wherein *England* stood;
> And did his state by her undooing winne:
> And was, though white without, yet red within.

Moral questions have been finally yielded up in despair, and when in stanza 37–8 Daniel remarks that the more things change the more they stay the same, there is another reminiscence of the earlier books and again a striking contrast in the tone. Richard's comments early in Book 11 on the fickleness of the crowd who run to greet Bolingbroke carry some moral weight in that the issue of legitimacy and illegitimacy is still a live one, but here the now dominant cynicism prevails and the rival kings are both described as birds of prey. Soon after this point Book VIII sheers off on to the more congenial themes of the courtship of Lady Grey and Warwick's apology.

When Daniel wrote Book VIII he also went back over the earlier books and made some revisions and filled in some gaps. A large part of the work he did then consisted of that sort of tidying up which can well be done when enthusiasm and creative vitality are at a low ebb. The largest single addition of new material, Book IV, stanzas 55–82, is one of the flattest and dreariest portions of the whole work, a slab of history rendered into verse form without ever catching the poet's interest or imagination except at two points: stanza 77 which describes Henry IV and stanza 82 which describes Henry's son, later Henry V.

It is clear that in looking back over the history Daniel is less disposed than he had been to underplay the virtues of Boling-broke and he has decided, too, to give Henry V more room to shine by introducing him early in terms of emphatic praise. He had already, in 1601, reduced some of the fervour of his first championship of Richard (see the different versions of III, 24, III, 66, ll. 7–8, and the omission of some of Richard's stanzas of self-pity III, 67f.) and the whole movement of Daniel's thought about *The Civil Wars* over the years has been towards a blurring of the distinctions between a 'right' side and a 'wrong' which at the outset had seemed clear-cut. When in VIII, 35 (already quoted) he comments that the crimes of the Yorkists go far in retrospect to extenuate Bolingbroke's original offence, for at least he had shed less blood, the observation is the culminating point of a development that has been taking place throughout the poem. His original reading of the history, he has found through his experience of writing the poem, was not viable. Whether he was indifferent to the difficulty of reconciling his more favourable references to Henry IV and Prince Hal with what still remains of the older material in the early books, or whether he was trying to give the poem some semblance of unity by throwing back hints

143

of his later attitudes into the earlier parts, it would be hard to say; probably the latter. In any event, it seems unnecessary to suppose that these revisions and additions are simply the result, as has been suggested, of deliberate reference to Shakespeare's treatments of the reigns of Henry IV and Richard II. Both the jejuneness of the historical filling-up and the modifications of the attitude to the two kings are in line with the mood of weariness with the poem and disillusion with the original view of the subject-matter which has become dominant in 1609.

Uneasiness with the subject matter makes itself felt as soon as Daniel gets well over the threshold of his poem but it is understandable, even so, that he was unwilling to give it up, for history and the writing of history interested him and he had set his heart on this project as his *chef d'œuvre*, the fulfilling of the ambitions he had faced the world with in 1594. It appealed to him, besides, so long as Elizabeth lived, as a great patriotic work whose motives he could continue whole-heartedly to subscribe to, whatever its drawbacks in other directions. Even as late as 1608, when the chance offers to go on with it, he is overjoyed, for seven years have elapsed since he last added to his poem and his attempts in the meantime to break into the theatre and to establish himself as a writer of court entertainment have been at best only mildly successful and have involved him in a good deal of unpleasantness and unwelcome publicity. But by 1609 his personal circumstances have changed again, and the writing of the poem, when it comes to the point, offers him no more satisfaction than it did in 1601. No longer restrained by his loyalty to and admiration of Elizabeth, his dissatisfaction is given more explicit expression than ever before and now that she is no longer alive to preside over his poem, he adopts – perhaps a significant change – Virtue, not a Royal patron, as his only muse.[22]

He may have remembered Bacon's dictum: 'books ought to have no patrons but truth and reason'.

This analysis of the feelings with which Daniel came to regard his task provides the explanation of why he abandoned it. He found as he went on that the scheme he had drawn up for himself at the beginning was an impossible one, the lines of just retribu-

22. In the pre-1609 versions of Bk. 1, st. 4, the Muse invoked was Elizabeth. In 1609, the first line reads: 'Come sacred *Virtue:* I no Muse, but thee, Invoke . . .' and l. 7 was also suitably altered.

tion for an initial crime could not be traced in that clear course which he had expected and at the same time the plan to which he had bound himself did not allow him to comment freely or fully on the moral and political situations which emerged but drove him on further into the tangle of events and towards a predetermined, but no longer convincing, conclusion. The work becomes sterile and unrewarding to him both as poet and historian and his disgust with it was no doubt deepened by his personal experience of power politics and intrigue in the Essex affair. He made an effort in 1609 to carry on the original scheme, but as the quotations above have shown, he had no heart for it. He had already decided to provide for his interest in history by a work in prose which would be as scholarly as he could make it and free of any fore-announced intention to find a pattern in it. As for his interest in poetry, he has all but surrendered it. He makes no bones about confessing to the Countess of Pembroke that he has become indifferent to the 'weapon of utterance . . . so it may make good my minde, I care not', and apart from *Hymen's Triumph*, an unexpected swan-song in 1615, this is his last major poem.

And, of course, he was right to abandon poetry for prose as far as his history was concerned. Drayton had some justification for his comment that Daniel was 'too much historian in verse', but it was only half the truth, for, when he began *The Civil Wars*, he was also too much a poet for the history.[23] 'I versifie the troth not Poetize', he boasted in the opening stanzas, and though it is easy to see how he came to make it, it is a foolish remark; for of course he poetized, or tried to. He tried to make an artistically complete pattern of the history, to give it a shape and form that he could polish and highlight as his aesthetic sense directed him. This is his justification for writing the poem at all. But he had too much respect for the facts as his studies unfolded them to him to be able to do this. The facts did not fall into his pattern and if any sense was to be made of them at all it had to be at a far deeper level than that offered by the Tudor propaganda to which the original scheme of his poem properly belongs. The poem he was commit-

23. Drayton's comment on *The Civil Wars* has been quoted so often that it is worth pointing out that Drayton himself was impressed and influenced by Daniel's poem. When he recast his *Mortimeriados* in 1603 as *The Barons Warres* he abandoned rime royal for Daniel's ottava rima and the editors of the Shakespeare Head *Drayton* see this as part of a general endeavour to write a poem more like Daniel's: 'That is,' they add, 'a poem more historical, more critical, less romantic, less decorated.' (v, p. 63).

ted to could not be adapted to that sort of enquiry: hence the perpetual tug between the historian bound to deal with the facts of the history and the poet trying to give some artistic shape to a creative work. Inevitably it is sometimes versified history and fragmentarily, when subject and imagination work together, it is a poem. When the theme allows sympathetic commentary on character, it is a poem, as in the Warwick stanzas in Book VIII; or when it provides an emotional situation based on relationships, as in the Richard II – Isabel scenes in Book II or the courtship of Lady Grey; or when there is opportunity for taut, sinewy argument in verse, as in Blount's speech in Book III, stanzas 37–47; or when the action pauses for a reflective comment, as in Book III, stanzas 64–9, which is part lyrical and part dramatic: Daniel treats all these kinds of material very well and the verse lights up when such passages occur. The mood of bitterness in the latest parts of the history proper also induces some keen-edged writing which demands attention.

To put the point in other words, Daniel as a poet needed material which he could shape, whether the shaping spirit was disgust, or admiration, or tenderness, or pleasure in the exercise of the intellectual faculty. *The Civil Wars* cannot be good as a complete poem, but the numerous smaller poems it contains are sometimes very good, and the whole work, versified history and all, provides a fascinating study of a poet's relations with intractable material and of the reactions of a thoughtful, intelligent man to the awakening within himself of the spirit of historical enquiry. This spirit is essentially demythologising and consequently anti-poetic. Among the myths on which Daniel set out to found his poem was the idea that the civil wars could be read as an illustration of the workings of Nemesis (for a treatment of the Nemesis theme in 1594, see the Chorus to Act III of *Cleopatra*), that they could be treated as a sort of bloody prelude to 'the glorious Union of Henry 7', not to be repined at because they were the necessary gestatory period for the peace and the glory and the bliss of the Tudor monarchy; and that a King was something apart from his political function. Of all these ideas Daniel's study of history disabused him and the loss of them broke his poem apart.

VII

Last Years: 'Tethys Festival'
'The History of England' and
'Hymens Triumph'

The last instalment of *The Civil Wars* was published in 1609 and
in the following year Daniel, after his long pondering on the
consequences of a disordered succession, was called upon,
appropriately enough, to participate in a state occasion of dynastic
importance, the creation of Prince Henry, James I's elder son,
as Prince of Wales. Daniel's contribution was his second masque,
Tethys Festival, which was produced on June 5th, 1610, at White-
hall. The fact that it was required for an occasion of some historic
significance probably helped to reconcile him to another experiment in a form he did not much care for, but in general at this time
he much preferred to be left to his own devices. He had a house
in Old Street, St Luke's, and here, according to Fuller, 'as the
Tortoise burieth himself all the Winter in the ground, so Mr.
Daniel would lye hid at his Garden-house in Oldstreet, nigh
London, for some Months together, (the more retiredly to enjoy
the Company of the *Muses*) and then would appear in publick, to
converse with his Friends, whereof Dr. *Cowel* and Mr. *Camden*
were principal'.[1]

Daniel had been signing himself 'one of the Groomes of her
Majesties most Honourable privie Chamber' since 1607[2] and

1. William Camden (1551–1623), the antiquary. John Cowel (1554–1611) was an
eminent authority on civil law who was appointed professor at Cambridge in 1594.
In 1603 and 1604 he was Vice-Chancellor of the University and in 1608 Bancroft,
Archbishop of Canterbury, made him his Vicar-general. His book, *The Interpreter*,
was suppressed and publicly burned in March 1610 because of its unsatisfactory
political doctrines.
2. This signature first occurs on the title-page of *Certaine Small Workes* (1607).

he must have stood very well in the Queen's favour to be asked to prepare the masque for this important celebration. *Tethys Festival*, like *The Vision of the Twelve Goddesses*, was a Queen's masque, Anne herself and the little Duke of York took part, and no expense was spared in producing it.[3] Daniel's principal endeavour, nevertheless, seems to have been to give Inigo Jones as much scope as possible and he freely acknowledges in his Preface to the Reader[4] that the poet's art made a very subsidiary contribution to the total effect. His only concern with his own work was that it should serve its purpose and that it should do so with dignity and decorum and he is proud of the fact that only 'great Personages of State and Honour' took part and there were none 'of inferiour sort'. He draws attention also to his willingness to sacrifice an effect for the sake of the comfort of the company: 'The introducing of Pages with torches, might have added more splendor, but yet they would have pestred the roome; which the season would not well permit.'[5] Later critics[6] have poured scorn on *Tethys Festival*, dismissing it as a feeble effort at a date when the masque form was in its full flower and it is clear from the tone of Daniel's Preface and the concluding comments in his published account of the masque that he had already encountered hostile comments enough to rouse his resentment. He attempts to draw their sting by a 'postcript' added for the benefit of his detractors:

> Praetulerim scriptor delirus inersque videri
> Dum mea delectant mala me, vel denique fallant,
> Quam sapere et ringi

and his attitude throughout is unmistakable: indifference towards the masque form itself and some contempt for those who would take it seriously. The one good lyric *Tethys Festival* contains has already been quoted (p. 95) and, apart from that, only marginal interests can engage the modern reader: the presence of Lady Anne Clifford, for example, by now Countess of Dorset, as one of the thirteen river nymphs who, under the tutelage of Tethys (the Queen herself), pay their homage to the King and Prince, and, alongside her, the Countess of Montgom-

---

3. For details about the preparation and staging of the masque, see Chambers, iii, pp. 281–3.

4. Grosart iii, p. 307.   5. Ibid, p. 323.

6. e.g. Brotanek, *Die englischen Maskenspiele*, p. 131.

ery, wife of Lady Pembroke's younger son whose second wife
Lady Anne afterwards became.

At intervals throughout his career Daniel published collections
of his poems, with revisions and alterations in successive editions.[7]
The last of these appeared in 1611 and among the alterations and
additions are some interesting changes in the dedication of
Cleopatra to the Countess of Pembroke. In 1605 and 1607 the
verse dedication had been omitted altogether, 1607 being the date
of the first appearance of the drastically revised text, but by the
time Daniel republished the play in 1611, the Countess of Pembroke had resumed her patronage of him and he took the trouble
to renew the dedication and make the play over to her in its
recast form:

> And glad I am I have renewd to you
> The vowes I owe your worth . . .

he writes, and he remembers the inspiration Lady Pembroke was
to him in his younger days and the influence of 'the then dilicious
Wilton' (not so delicious later?) upon him as a young man. He
rewords the stanzas which in the earlier dedication deal with
England's place in relation to other European, especially Italian,
literature and makes a more emphatic statement of achievement:

> Let them produce the best of all they may
> Since Rome left bearing, who bare more then men
> And we shall paralell them every way
> In all the glorious actions of the men.
>
> .   .   .
>
> They cannot shew a *Sidney*, let them shew
> All their choice peeces, and bring all in one
> And altogether shall not make that shew
> Of wonder and delight, as he hath done:
> He hath th'Olimpian prize (of all that run
> Or ever shall with mortall powers) possest
> In that faire course of glory and yet now
> *Sydney* is not our all, although our best.

7. *The Poeticall Essayes of Sam. Danyel. Newly corrected and augmented*, 1599. *The
Works of Samuel Daniel Newly augmented*, 1601. Ditto, 1602. *Certaine Small Poems*, 1605.
Certaine Small Workes . . . now againe . . . corrected and augmented, 1607. Ditto, 1611.
There was a posthumous edition of the *Whole Workes* in 1623 under the auspices of
the poet's brother.

He finishes with the now inevitable comment on the decline of poetry under James:

> And if the same come now extinguished
> By the distemperature of time, and cease
> Suffice we were not yet behind the rest,
> But had our part of glorie with the best.[8]

To 1611 also, with Daniel in a mood for reminiscence, belongs the verse dedication of *Musophilus* to Fulke Greville which has already been discussed (see pp. 65–7) and also a prefatory poem written for the enlarged edition of Florio's Italian dictionary, *Queen Anna's New World of Words*. With admirable and ingenious diplomacy Daniel uses the occasion to urge on James and Anne the desirability of the intelligent patronage of letters (he may have particularly in mind his own needs in writing his prose *History*), and he ends 'Thus from my Plow'.

Possibly Daniel was still at the Earl of Hertford's farm but the change of patron between 1608 and 1609 makes this seem unlikely. Fuller says that 'In his old Age he turn'd *Husbandman*, and Rented a Farm in Wiltshire nigh the Devises' but Wood locates the farm he retired to in Beckington, where he is buried. The explanation perhaps is that Fuller, who is in general very vague about Daniel's later years, confused the Earl of Hertford's farm, where Daniel was living in 1608 and which may very well have been in Wiltshire, with the farm that he later retired to. If this is so it would appear from the Florio poem that by 1611 Daniel had taken the farm at Beckington and kept it until his death in 1619.

He was not, of course, completely in retirement, for he was still in the Queen's service and in 1612 he was one of the seven grooms of the Queen's privy chamber who took part in the funeral procession of the Prince of Wales whose creation they had all been celebrating two years before.[9] Daniel had dedicated *Philotas* to this 'most hopeful Prince' entrusting to him 'not as you are, But as you may be', his hopes for the future of poetry:

> . . . that you one day
> May grace this now neglected Harmonie:
> Which set unto your glorious actions, may
> Record the same to all posteritie.   (ll. 61–4)

8. Lederer, pp. 6–7.

9. *The President of ye Funerall of the high and mightie Prince Henrie late Prince of Wales*, P.R.O., L.C., 2. 4 (Quoted Yates, *John Florio*, p. 249).

No doubt he was depressed by the young Prince's death and, with his keen historical sense, he may well have had a special awareness of the tragedy of the occasion as he took his place in the funeral procession.

Certainly the study of history occupied Daniel increasingly in the last ten years of his life and in the year in which Prince Henry died, he printed the first part of his prose *History*, ending with the death of King Stephen. The dedication to Sir Robert Carr, Viscount Rochester, describes Daniel's motives and intentions in writing the history. He has, he says, 'spent much time of my best understanding, in this part of humane Learning, Historie, both in forraine countries where especially I tooke those notions, as made most for the conduct of businesse in this kind, and also at home, where it hath bene in my fortune (besides conference with men of good experience) to have seene many of the best discourses, negotiations, instructions and relations of the generall affaires of the World'.[10] With this preparation he has decided to attempt to remedy the shameful lack of an adequate English history, having specially in mind the needs of statesmen: 'seeing it concernes them most to know the generall affaires of England, who have least leasure to read them'.[11]

Daniel was not alone in recognising the inadequacy of existing work: Bacon in 1605 had been pressing on James the desirability of a good history of England and Scotland, most modern histories he comments, being 'beneath mediocrity', and it is interesting to compare his outline of what he takes to be a suitable period for such a study, 'from the uniting of the Roses to the uniting of the kingdoms' with Daniel's account of his third section which is to contain 'the succession of five Soveraigne Princes of the Line of Tewdor'. It is, writes Bacon, 'a portion of time wherein, to my understanding, there hath been the rarest varieties that in like number of successions of any hereditary monarchy hath been known', and, he concludes, 'now last, this most happy and glorious event, that this island of Brittany, divided from all the world, should be united in itself . . . it seemeth that by the provi-

10. Grosart iv, p. 75.

11. Ibid., p. 76. It is probable that *A Breviary of the History of England*, often ascribed to Raleigh, which deals with the early period up to and including the reign of William the Conqueror, is a first short sketch by Daniel of his longer work. See R. B. Gottfried, 'The Authorship of *A Breviary of the History of England*', *S.P.* 53, (1956), pp. 172–90. Gottfried suggests that it was written between 1605 and 1612.

dence of God this monarchy, before it was to settle in your majesty and your generations (in which I hope it is now established for ever), it had these prelusive changes and varieties.'[12] Daniel agrees that it is 'a time stored with all varietie of accidents fit for example, and instruction' but he stops short of drawing Bacon's conclusion about its triumphant culmination in the reign of James. He has not Bacon's motives for flattering James and besides, he has learnt from his experience of *The Civil Wars* that this sort of reading of history will not work. This time he will let 'example' and 'instruction' arise from the facts themselves: 'This is the scope of my designe', he says firmly: he intends no interpretations of the 'providence of God'.

The 1612 impression was a private one of a few copies to be circulated among friends. Daniel's intention obviously is to engage the attention of people likely to be interested in the work and to put materials at his disposal. He 'invokes' 'all worthy men that are furnisht with matter of this nature' to assist him and by doing so to perform a patriotic duty. He relies especially, he adds, 'upon the ayde of the right worthy and well-deserving Knight, Sir Robert Cotton, who, out of his choyce and excellent store, can best furnish this worke'.[13] A public edition was printed in 1613 and in this year Daniel for the first time signed himself 'one of the Gentlemen extraordinarie of her Majestys most royall privie Chamber.'[14]

In 1618 the history was continued till the end of Edward III's reign and published as *The Collection of the Historie of England*. It was printed *cum privilegio* and a dedication to the Queen replaced the earlier one to Carr. In the dedication Daniel acknowledged that the work was 'for the most part done under your Roofe, during my attendance upon your Sacred Person', so that it appears that Daniel was spending a good deal of his time at Court during these years. In *Certaine Advertisements to the Reader* printed with the *History*, Daniel speaks of ill-health and inadequate means but, although this was printed for the first time in 1618, it appears to have been intended to accompany the private issue and possibly the situation improved between 1612 and 1618 when Anne was

12. *Of the Advancement of Learning*, ed. Case (World's Classics), pp. 83–4.
13. Grosart v, Appendix A, pp. 293–4.
14. Signature to 1613 version of verses on Florio's translation of Montaigne (Grosart i, pp. 285–8).

making it possible for him to work while he was living at Court.

'Pardon us *Antiquity*,' writes Daniel, 'if we mis-censure your actions, which are ever (as those of men) according to the vogue, and sway of times, and have onely their upholding by the opinion of the present: We deale with you but as posterity will with us (which ever thinkes it selfe the wiser) that will judge likewise of our errors according to the cast of their imaginations'. The sense of the continuity of human affairs, the personal humility, and the touch of acerbity at the presumptions of men, make this a fully characteristic statement of the later Daniel. Sprague describes the *History* as 'an incomparable picture of his thought and opinions,'[15] and it is true that the fruits of Daniel's maturity may be found here and the distillation of his experience of 'the generall affaires of the World'.

'Great festivals,' comments the author of Court entertainments and Queen Anne's attendant, 'often-times break up with great discontentments',[16] and as one who has seen much and pondered deeply on the relations between princes and their people, he writes '. . . the preservation of Kings and Kingdomes is to have the ballance of satisfaction, both of the one and other, equall . . . worthily that Prince deserves to bee deceived in his executions, who understands not, as well the Counsailors, as the Councell'.[17] As for the great actions of the past, undertaken by kings and nobles for ostensibly great causes, Daniel has worn out his enthusiasm, and his comments on them, unemotionally and precisely phrased as they are, are nevertheless highly charged with his sense of the shallowness of great professions and the complexity of motive which may pass under one misleading title. Of the dealing of the kings of England and France with Sicily and Cyprus on their way to the Crusades, he writes: 'These mischiefs suffred these two famous Isles of Christendome, in the passage of those mighty Princes against Pagans, who peradventure would have as well used them for their goods, and treasure, as they did; *But Armies and power know no inferior friends*, it was their Fate so to lye in the way of great attempters, who, though in the cause of Piety, would not sticke to doe any injustice.'[18]

This tone occurs again and again, not bitter, but without illusion, combining compassion with a clear perception of man's

15. Sprague, p. xxviii. 16. Grosart iv, p. 289.
17. Grosart v, p. 62. 18. Ibid., p. 7.

vainglory and a sense of justice with a capacity for dropping a touch of acid on what might appear to be an encomium, as in his summing-up of Edward I: 'A Prince of a generous spirit, wherein the fire held out even to the very last; born and bred for action and Militarie affaires, which hee managed with great judgement: ever wary, and provident for his owne businesse: watchfull and eager to enlarge his power: and was more for the greatnesse of *England*, then the quiet thereof. And this we may justly say of him, that never King before, or since, shed so much Christian blood within this *Isle of Brittaine*, as this Christian Warrior did in his time, and was the cause of more in that following.'[19]

Daniel does not forget the present in his treatment of the past. His comments on Edward I's wars against the Scots illustrate the weaving together of ideas which goes to make the characteristic texture of this work. The historical situation is fairly treated and Daniel has very much in mind also the 'happy Union' under James and the need to cement it by ungrudging acknowledgement of the honour due to the weaker and smaller nation which 'seemes never to have been subdued, though often over-come'. But he sees also in the story one more example of the vanity and tragedy of so many of 'the generall affaires of the World': 'Neyther doth it now concerne us to stand uppon any poynts of Honour, whether of the Nations did the bravest exploytes in those times, seeing who had the better was beaten, neyther did the over-commer Conquer, when hee had done what hee could: That little which was gayned, cost so much more then it was worth, as it had beene better not to have beene had at all.' And at another level still, he judges the attempt to bring about the union by force as both futile and iniquitous, for: 'Violence may joyne Territories, but never affections together' and 'God hath fore-decreed to make it his owne worke by a clearer way.'[20]

Daniel's achievement as an historian and his methods of writing history have received some attention in recent years[21] and, though he was not a great historian, he is acknowledged to have been a far from contemptible one. In the course of the sixteenth century many of the source documents of medieval history had been pub-

19. Ibid., p. 176.   20. Ibid., p. 155.
21. See May McKisack, 'Samuel Daniel as Historian', *R.E.S.* 23 (July, 1947), pp. 226–43 and R. B. Gottfried, 'Samuel Daniel's Method of Writing History', *Studies in the Renaissance*, III (1956), pp. 157–74.

lished and Daniel was able to draw on a substantial number of medieval Latin chronicles and also on Berners's Froissart. For the early Norman history and the history of the Norman kings of England he used an anonymous *Croniques de Normandie* published first at Rouen in 1487 and frequently republished at Paris and Rouen until 1610. Daniel was fully aware also of the value of first-hand documents and promised to publish in an appendix 'all Treaties, Letters, Articles, Charters, Ordinances, Intertaynments, provisions of Armies, businesses of Commerce, with other passages of State appertayning to our History'. The promised appendix never materialised but there is no doubt of Daniel's anxiety to give his work ample authority: 'so that', as he says, 'the Reader shall be sure to be payd with no counterfeit Coyne, but such as shal have the stampe of Antiquity, the approbation of Testimony, and the allowance of Authority, so farre as I shall proceed herein'.[22]

He read, in fact, much more widely for this work than he had done for *The Civil Wars*, in the composition of which he seems to have relied mainly on sixteenth-century historians supplemented occasionally by Froissart and Walsingham, but although he apparently had access to some of Cotton's manuscripts, he did not aim at original research. He claims no more for his handling of the material than 'sowing it together, and the observation of those necessary circumstances, and inferences which the History naturally ministers'.[23] But as Miss McKisack puts it: 'Though much less deeply read than many of his learned contemporaries he was what few of them could claim to be – a natural historian, endowed with a rare sense of the past and with an intuitive understanding (almost unique in that age) of the limitations of historical knowledge'.[24] He rejects myths and legends and where he cannot find a creditable authority (as for the early history of England) he refuses to fill in with invented matter. But what is even more remarkable than his dismissal of the legends used by historians from Geoffrey of Monmouth to Holinshed and Stow, is his repudiation of the common English Renaissance view of the medieval period as dark ages of ignorance and superstition. 'He is,' as Miss McKisack points out, 'one of the few Elizabethans to write of the Middle Ages with a sense of loss', and this attitude, rare as it

22. Grosart iv, p. 82.   23. Ibid., p. 83.
24. McKisack, art. cit.

is among his contemporaries, is no new one for Daniel:[25] it has already found noble (and aggressive) expression in the *Defence of Ryme*, as, for example, in the passages quoted above on pages 84 and 85-6.

His refusal to look down on the past and his lack of interest in legendary heroes are natural products of a scholarly and sceptical intelligence but they derive also from another at least equally strong characteristic which produces some of the richest comments in both Daniel's poetry and his prose – that is his imaginative concept of the past as a panorama of human history made up of individual men and women, thinking, feeling and reponding to experience as he himself did. He must have been a sensitive man in his own personal life to have had this delicate, scrupulous and almost tender concern for the past. For him it is an absorbing study, capable of arousing compassion, admiration, and sorrow, full of examples of life for men of all times to ponder and learn from, but never a theme to paint in crude blacks and whites. The clarity with which these conclusions emerge from the prose history throws into sharp relief the strain he was under in composing *The Civil Wars* where his historical sense and the humanity which is his finest imaginative gift in his later work were pulling against the poetical pattern which he had begun by imposing on the material.

The comparison between his two attempts at the writing of history is pointed by the comments made by R. B. Gottfried on the art of the prose history. 'Daniel', he writes, 'frequently uses more than one of his sources in a single episode, and he not only sews them together, as he says, but he condenses, amalgamates and interprets his material into a narrative which is characteristically his own.' He was, he adds, 'both an historian and a poet; his *History of England*, unlike the vast compilations of Holinshed and Stow, was an attempt to reinforce the claims of truth with those of literary art.' Though the initial concern of both Gottfried and Miss McKisack is with the work as a contribution to the writing of history, both conclude by giving their chief praise to it as an accomplished literary expression of a rich and mature mind and character. The last comment quoted from Gottfried is particularly interesting since it touches the sensitive spot at the heart of all but the earliest of Daniel's creative activity: the relation

25. There is a pleasant article on 'Samuel Daniel's Sense of the Past' by William Blissett in *E.S.* xxxviii, 1957, pp. 49-63.

between 'the claims of truth' and those of 'literary art'. In *The Civil Wars*, the form had made claims for literary art which the material, as Daniel saw it, had not often been able to satisfy; but prose is 'the common tongue of the world', an accommodating servant, not an imperious master, and because it was more amenable Daniel chose it for his second attempt at a history. The task he set himself this time seemed to him both modest and arduous for he was: 'Desirous to deliver things done, in as even and quiet an Order, as such an heape will permit, without quarrelling with the Beleefe of Antiquity, depraving the Actions of other Nations to advance our owne, or keeping backe the Reasons of State they had, for what they did in those times: holding it fittest and best agreeing with Integrity (the chiefest duty of a Writer) to leave things to their owne Fame, and the Censure thereof to the Reader, as being his part rather then mine, who am only to recite things done, not to rule them.'[26] The arrangement worked well: the poet subdued to the historian, there were none of the uneasy tensions that had occurred in *The Civil Wars* and Daniel is clearly much happier with this work than he was with the later books of his poem. The critical verdict is ironical, but not surprising: *The Civil Wars* is censured, somewhat scornfully, as being too much history in verse, and the *History* is praised, above all, as being literature, for 'Daniel was both an historian and a poet'.

His interests and aptitudes being so successfully provided for in the prose *History* it is curious to find Daniel appearing once more as a poet and provider of court entertainment in 1615. He was not, of course, his own master and Anne was evidently reluctant to lose altogether his services in catering for the shows she loved. *Hymens Triumph*, Daniel's second pastoral drama, has generally been much more highly praised than *The Queenes Arcadia*, though Chamberlain told Sir Dudley Carleton that in performance it was 'solemn and dull' but he adds, 'perhaps better to be read than represented',[27] whereas he had reported to Winwood in 1605 that the other Oxford entertainments were dull but *'Queenes Arcadia* made amends for all; being indeed very excelent, and some parts exactly acted.'[28]

26. *Certaine Advertisements to the Reader*, Grosart iv, p. 83.
27. Quoted J. Nichols, *The Progresses of James I* (London, 1828). See vol. ii, pp. 747–55 for an account of the marriage festivities.
28. Winwood, ii, p. 140.

The occasion of the production of *Hymens Triumph* was the marriage in February 1614 of Robert Ker, Lord Roxborough,[29] to Jean Drummond, a kinswoman of William Drummond of Hawthornden. The celebrations were postponed once to avoid clashing with the wedding of the Robert Carr, now become Earl of Somerset,[30] to whom the 1612 edition of the *History* had been dedicated, but they were held eventually at Somerset House in the Strand which had recently been altered under Anne's direction. The King came to grace the house-warming and to enjoy the 'fires and chearefull hospitality' which Daniel refers to in dedicating the published work to the Queen.

Edinburgh University Library has a manuscript of Daniel's play given by Drummond himself in 1627. This is probably a presentation copy to the bride and it provides an earlier version of the text than that of the printed edition of 1615. It does not contain the dedicatory verses to the Queen or the dramatic introduction but some corrections and insertions are in Daniel's own hand.[31] In particular, in place of the published dedication to the Queen, it has a poem to the bride, written out and signed by Daniel himself. It is simple, informal, and dignified, speaking of long personal acquaintance – Jean Drummond had been a member of Anne's household – and perhaps this was one reason why Daniel was willing to return to poetry to honour her marriage. Altogether it is in the characteristic style of Daniel's addresses to noble patrons, in which hyperbole and adulation are rigorously excluded in favour of discriminating praise out of personal knowledge. The published dedication to the Queen is written in his state style, much more formal and highly wrought, but even here Daniel does not relinquish his own dignity and his tone is that of one who knows he will be listened to with respect.

The play itself, as published in 1615, is introduced by a Prologue consisting of the figure of Hymen 'opposed by *Avarice, Envy,* and *Jealousie,* the disturbers of quiet marriage'. Hymen bids them all begone for they are unworthy of the company –

29. Grosart (iv. pp. lvi–vii) identifies him wrongly as Sir Robert Ker son of William Kerr of Ancrum. He was in fact the son of William Ker of Cessfurd. Jean Drummond was his second wife.

30. This is the marriage connected with the notorious Overbury murder.

31. For an account of the manuscript, see W. W. Greg, '*Hymens Triumph* and the Drummond MS.', *M.L.Q.*, VI (1903), pp. 59–64.

FACSIMILE OF AN ADDITION IN DANIEL'S HAND
to the Drummond manuscript of *Hymens Triumph*

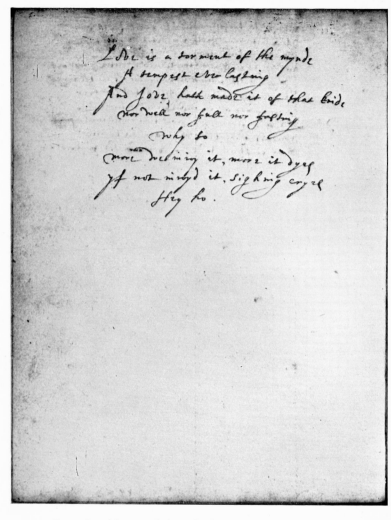

This place is sacred to integrity,
And cleane desires . . .

but Envy has the last word:

HYMEN, thou canst not chase us so away,
For, looke how long as thou mak'st marriages,
So long will we produce incumbrances.
And we will in the same disguise, as thou,
Mixe us amongst the shepheards, that we may
Effect our worke the better, being unknowne;
For, ills shew other faces then their owne.

This sober allegorical introduction seems a curious one for a graceful pastoral but the serious formality of the preface is thoroughly characteristic of Daniel's cast of mind.

Apart from this, the prologue is interesting for its repudiation of some of the coarser materials of pastoral:

Here, shall I bring you two the most entire
And constant lovers that were ever seene,
From out the greatest suffrings of anoy
That fortune could inflict, to their full joy:
Wherein no wild, no rude, no antique sport,
But tender passions, motions soft, and grave,
The still spectators must expect to have.

Montanus with his roughness and his one act of violence does in fact provide some contrast to the delicacy of the main plot (Wordsworth thought the play 'sadly injured' by the Montanus episodes)[32] but the contrast is a very subdued one, and scarcely disturbs the 'motions soft, and grave' of the whole piece.

Daniel's statement of his intentions seems innocent enough but in these years he was continually crossing Jonson's path and when Jonson also wrote a pastoral and introduced it with a prologue he took occasion to reject 'an heresy of late let fall', the heresy being, according to him:

That mirth by no means fits a pastoral;
Such say so, who can make none, he presumes:
Else there's no scene more properly assumes
The sock . . .

32. See C. C. Seronsy, 'Wordsworth's Annotations in Daniel's *Poetical Works*', *M.L.N.* (1953), pp. 403–6.

There is conflicting evidence about the date of the composition
of Jonson's *The Sad Shepherd* but these lines could very appropriately point to Daniel and his *Hymens Triumph*. Certainly
Jonson had Daniel's work in mind when he went on to argue that
there may be different modes of pastoral and each equally good in
its kind:

> But that no style for pastoral should go
> Current, but what is stamp'd with Ah! and O!
> Who judgeth so, may singularly err;
> As if all poesie had one character
> In which what were not written were not right . . .

The Ah's and O's of *Hymens Triumph* are so many as to be a
noticeable and perhaps irritating mannerism and Jonson's satirical
shrewdness gives him a palpable hit. He had already jeered at the
Italian provenance of *The Queenes Arcadia* and now it seems that
the undeniable beauties of *Hymens Triumph* stung him to work on
a rival composition in which deliberate Englishness should be the
key-note, the scene Sherwood Forest, not Arcadia, the characters
Robin Hood and Maid Marian and their company, with 'Maudlin,
the Envious, the Witch of Paplewick', 'Douce, the Proud' and
'Lorel, the Rude' to represent the dark underside of pastoral
pleasures.

> You shall have love and hate, and jealousy,
> As well as mirth, and rage, and melancholy:
> Or whatsoever else may either move,
> Or stir affections, and your likings prove,

Jonson promises, contrasting his own breadth of mind and imagination with Daniel's too exclusive niceness; but whatever his
achievement in *The Sad Shepherd* it cannot detract from Daniel's
own success in *Hymens Triumph*.

'*Hymens Triumph*', wrote Coleridge, 'exhibits a continued series
of first-rate beauties in thought, passion, and imagery; and in
language and metre is so faultless, that the style of that poem may,
without extravagance, be declared to be imperishable English'.[33]
The play has none of the satirical scenes which pleased the audience
of the *The Queenes Arcadia* in 1605, but no one has doubted that it
is much better to read than the earlier pastoral. The romantic

33. Coleridge, *Literary Remains*, ed. H. N. Coleridge (London, 1836–9), ii, p. 360.

episodes are assimilated into a coherent plot fashioned by Daniel himself and the atmosphere is much more harmoniously maintained, though at the sacrifice of the variety of *The Queenes Arcadia*.

When the story opens, Thirsis is found still lamenting his love, Silvia, who, two years before, has disappeared and is believed to have been killed by wild beasts on the shore. She is not dead, however, but captured by pirates and having escaped, she returns to Arcadia disguised as a boy. Her father had originally wished her to marry one Alexis and she now waits till Alexis's wedding to another nymph is safely accomplished before revealing who she is to Thirsis. In the meantime, she takes service with Cloris who is herself in love with Thirsis and who employs her in messages to him, and Phillis, another nymph, falls in love with her as a supposed boy. Montanus, who has been for a long time unsuccessfully wooing Phillis, is jealous and tries to kill the apparent rival; but all ends well and Thirsis and Silvia are united.

There are some pleasant scenes, not without humour, between Cloris and her 'boy', and Silvia's account of her adventures in the past two years (IV, iii) is a beautiful piece of narrative, full of feeling and yet restrained, written in pure, lucid language. Lamb quoted from it in his *Specimens of the English Dramatic Authors* and it is a fair example of the poetic tone of the play. But what gives *Hymens Triumph* its special distinction is the character of Thirsis, the bereaved lover. He uses conventional talk of 'the heates, the colds' of love and makes extravagant lamentation over the torn veil and the lock of hair which are all that is left him of Silvia, he pulls his hat over his eyes and crosses his arms and paces up and down in the woods, and in all these respects he does no more than indicate a type and a situation. But he goes beyond that. His love and his grief are real things. He is more than the show of a melancholy lover for he has a depth of experience too. Palaemon, his friend, reproaches him with weakness for not having put his sorrow behind him and he replies that on the contrary there is greater strength in his constancy of grief which calls for stern self-discipline:

> And thinke *Palaemon* I have combates too,
> To be the man I am, being built of flesh,
> And having round about me traytors too
> That seeke to undermine my powres, and steale
> Into my weaknesses, but that I keepe

Continuall watch and ward upon my selfe,
Least I should be surpriz'd at unawares
And taken from my vowes with other snares

(Act. III, sc. iv, ll. 1201–8)

Palaemon taunts him that it is humiliating for a man of his intelligence to 'pine in love And languish for a silly woman thus', and
rouses Thirsis to an impassioned defence of love as

The noblest portion of humanity,
The worthiest peece of nature set in man,   (ll. 1261–2)

and of woman as 'natures chiefe Viceregent upon earth':

And doe you hold it weaknesse then to love?
And love so excellent a miracle
As is a woman! ah then let mee
Still be so weake, still let me love and pine
In contemplation of that cleane, cleare soule,
That made mine see that nothing in the world
Is so supreamely beautifull as it.
Thinke not it was those colours white and red
Laid but on flesh, that could affect me so.
But something else, which thought holds under locke
And hath no key of words to open it.
They are the smallest peeces of the minde
That passe this narrow organ of the voyce.
The great remaine behinde in that vast orbe
Of th'apprehension, and are never borne.   (ll. 1276–90)

Among the repetition of well-worn ideas there are striking lines
here which extend the whole situation into regions of deeply felt
and complex experience.

The same comment holds good of much of the play, for charming as it is, it is not trivial. Much of it is written in blank verse,
which Daniel thought befitted tragedy, and the movement of the
verse, as Daniel handles it, imparts both beauty and dignity to the
serious sentiments.

Situations always become human and real to Daniel as he works
upon them, whether their background is history, ancient or
modern, or Italianate pastoral drama. He is incapable of the light-
ness of fancy which can sometimes create a fragile and wonderful
magic and his best moments and his worst in his two pastoral
plays derive from the same thing, the essential serious-mindedness

which makes him relate his scenes and his characters to life as he knows it. One result of this is that we may recognise in the fourth song of *Hymens Triumph* a near-quotation from the verse epistle to Southampton:

> ... they that act the worthiest parts,
> Most commonly have worst successes

which compares with:

> Onely the best compos'd, and worthiest harts,
> God sets to act the hard'st and constant'st parts

and the whole tenor of the epistle; and in Lidia's last speech there is a rather sharp reference to the courtly audience which picks up some lines from the epistle to the Countess of Bedford:

> ... you must frame your countenance thereto
> And looke with other faces then your owne.
> As many else do here, who in their parts
> Set shining lookes upon their cloudy hearts

which compares with the lines from the epistle:

> How oft are we forc't on a clowdie hart,
> To set a shining face, and make it cleere.

There are many such cross-references in Daniel's poetry. They indicate some of the settled attitudes and judgements which determine Daniel's outlook on life and their recurrence in all sorts of contexts shows how inevitably he referred new experiences to old and how closely he bound literature to life.

This was a play for the Queen's entertainment and Daniel was hardly likely to indulge in the invective against women which, before and after him, was a common feature of pastoral drama; but he goes beyond mere avoidance of offence in setting the tone of praise and veneration from the beginning when Palaemon offers a conventional criticism and Thirsis at once rejects it (act I, sc. i, ll. 67–74). Daniel was always particularly sympathetic to his women characters and liked to write about them: his delicacy and respect and intuitive sympathy contribute a great deal to the general atmosphere of *Hymens Triumph*, not only in Thirsis's formal defence but in the sweetness of the whole. Thirsis's account, for example, of the growth of love from childhood (Act. I, sc. i, ll.

83–114) is a companion-piece to Amintas's description in Act 1, scene i of Tasso's play. The Italian is much more sophisticated but the deliberate naïveté of Daniel's account is perhaps more touching and one line at least is beautiful:

> ... and thus
> *In that first garden of our simplenesse*
> We spent our childhood ...

Arcadia is naturalised in rural England in the lines which follow about the 'Barley-breake' and the impression of unaffected sincerity, deep but unpretentious feeling, is thereby heightened.

> ... these are onely *Cynthias* recreatives
> Made unto *Phoebus*, and are feminine;
> And therefore must be gentle like to her,
> Whose sweet affections mildely moove and stirre,

Daniel writes in the prologue (ll. 18–21) and this is the keynote of the whole. The tone is perfectly exemplified in 'Clarindo's' words when she finds Thirsis asleep, worn out with his grief:

> ... sleepe thy fill, sweet love,
> Let nothing trouble thee; be calme oh windes,
> Be still you heards, chirp not so loud sweet birds,
> Lest you should wake my love: thou gentle banke
> That thus are blest to beare so deare a weight,
> Be soft unto those dainty lymmes of his;
> Pile tender grasse, and render sweet refresh
> Unto his weary senses, whilst he rests.
>   (Act iv, sc. iii, ll. 1420–7)

The 'tender passions, motions soft, and grave' (Prologue, l. 16) of Daniel's play were to be accompanied with music. There are seven songs interspersed throughout the play ranging from the rough verse of the song for the rural marriage at the end of Act iii (the nearest approach to an anti-masque in the Jonsonian sense that Daniel allowed himself) to the romantic 'Eyes hide my love' of Act iv, scene ii, and the effects of music are several times evoked in the verse. Thus Thirsis calls his boy and bids him sing:

> Record the dolefull'st song, the sighingst notes,
> That musicke hath to entertaine bad thoughts.
> Let it be all at flats my boy, all grave
> The tone that best befits the griefe I have
>   (Act i, sc. i, ll. 186–9)

and at the end (Act v, sc. i, ll. 1770–3) the joyful hour of reunion is to be celebrated by the youths of Arcadia with 'the height of musiques art' so that the rocks and hills may 'Ring with the Eccho of redoubled notes'.

The 'still spectators', then, were to have their eyes feasted with the magnificence of a royal entertainment, their ears delighted with the music of songs and instruments and poetry, and their hearts touched with tender and delicate feeling; but Daniel does not forget that a little sharpness refreshes the appetite for sweets. The social criticism which was much more in evidence in *The Queenes Arcadia* appears briefly in Act II, scene i, and again in Act III, scene ii, being in both places an indictment of the lust for money, but it is by no means a dominant motif in the play. Lidia does rather more to prevent the idyll from becoming cloying. She is like Techne in that she is outside Arcadian standards of behaviour but though she has a sharp tongue and is unscrupulously resourceful, she is much less corrupt than Techne as befits the quieter and more homogeneous colouring of the whole play. To her belongs the tone of the song of the first chorus with its casual cynicism. The song has an off-hand grace and charm which are rare in Daniel and it is worth quoting:

> Love is a sicknesse full of woes,
> All remedies refusing:
> A plant that with most cutting growes,
> Most barren with best using.
> Why so?

> More we enjoy it, more it dyes,
> If not enjoy'd, it sighing cries,
> Hey ho.

> Love is a torment of the minde,
> A tempest everlasting;
> And Jove hath made it of a kinde,
> Not well, nor full nor fasting.
> Why so?

> More we enjoy it, more it dies
> If not enjoyd, it sighing cries,
> Hey ho.

Hymens Triumph was the last of Daniel's poetry to be published in his lifetime. There was only the 1618 edition of the *History* to follow, and few facts remain to be recorded about his life. In 1615, the year of the publication of *Hymens Triumph*, his name appears in connection with the establishing of a company of child actors at Bristol, under the patronage of Queen Anne. Though the grant of the patent for the company was evidently made through the Queen's influence on behalf of Daniel, the actual patent is made out to John Daniel, his brother.[34] All that can be deduced from the transaction on the available evidence is that Daniel was in Anne's favour at this time, that he was well-disposed to his brother, and that he was evidently comfortably enough off himself to be able to afford to make some of the fruits of the Queen's patronage over to someone else.

In 1619 Queen Anne died and Daniel received an allowance of nine yards of mourning and took part with other members of her household in the funeral procession.[35] Although the Queen died in March, the funeral did not take place until May 13th, 'for want of money to buy the blacks' according to a correspondent,[36] but blacks were copious enough on the day. Chamberlain reported that it was 'but a drawling, tedious sight' and though there were great numbers of mourners, 'they made but a poor show; which perhaps, was because they were apparelled all alike, or that they came loggering all along, even tired with the length of the way and the weight of their cloaks, every lady having twelve yards of broad cloth about her, and the countesses sixteen.'[37]

Daniel's presence as a member of the Household in the funeral procession discredits an earlier report, dated June 16th, 1618, that he 'and Sir George Reynolds were discharged the queen's service, and banished the court, only for having visited Sir Robert Floud in this his disgrace, or else for having formerly entertained amity with him.'[38] This Sir Robert Floud (or Floyd) had been high in the Queen's favour but in February 1618 it was reported that the Queen was 'justly implacable against Sir Robert Floyd, who got from her a lease of the royalties of all her lands; those about her

34. Chambers, ii, pp. 68–9.
35. *The President of the Funerall of ye late Soveraigne Lady Queene Anne*, P.R.O., L.C., 2. 5.
36. *The Court and Times of James I*, compiled by T. Birch (London, 1848), ii, p. 153.
37. Ibid., p. 162.
   Ibid., p. 77.

166

feed her anger, for Floyd had slandered them all to her, when he was highest in her favour; he rose from a serving man to an estate of 800*l.* a year, and is likely to fall as suddenly'.[39] The full story of these events has not come to light but it seems to have been connected with the campaign of 1617–18 for economy and reorganisation in the Royal household. If Daniel was temporarily implicated in Floyd's disgrace, he must have been restored to his position about Anne before her death as his official presence in the funeral procession shows. There is also a book of the names of the Queen's officers and servants, compiled in 1619 after her death, which records the time they had served her, the amount of their yearly wages, and the rewards they had received, and Daniel's name figures on this list. He had served, it says, five years (Anne died on March 2nd which by the old style calendar was still 1618: five years would thus go back to 1613 when he became a Gentleman Extraordinary of the Queen's Privy Chamber: he had, of course, been in Court service since 1607), received no rewards and his annual wages were £60.[40]

In October 1619 Daniel himself died and was buried on the 14th of the month. The 'Mrs. Daniell' whose burial is recorded in the Beckington register on March 25th, 1619, may have been his wife for Fuller says he had one and that her name was Justina. Jonson is on record as saying that he had no children which presumably implies that he was married. If so, her death is the only notice so far found of the lady. In his will,[41] dated September 4th, 1619, Daniel made bequests to his sister, Susan Bowre, and her family, and appointed his publisher and 'loving ffriend', Simon Waterson, and his brother-in-law, John Phillipps, to be overseers of his will. His reference to 'my house at Ridge' does not, as Grosart and others assume, imply that his house was called Ridge Farm, but means simply that his home at Beckington was in the hamlet now known as Rudge. Parts of it may stand to this day, incorporated into a seventeenth-century house now standing on the site of an Elizabethan farmhouse on high ground overlooking the handful of houses and farms in deep country some three miles from Beckington.

39. *Calendar of State Papers (Dom.) James I, 1611–18*, p. 522.
40. State Papers 14/107, no. 93 (*C.S.P. Dom., 1619–23*, p. 31).
41. Printed by Sellers, *Oxford Bibliographical Society Proceedings and Papers*, 11, p. 54, and Grosart i, pp. xxvi–vii.

Daniel's last poem was written in 1618, probably in June, for
James Montague, Bishop of Winchester, Dean of the Chapel, and
a member of the Privy Council.[42] Its ostensible object is to console
the Bishop in his sickness (he died in July of jaundice and dropsy)
but as it happens it provides some very appropriate last words for
Daniel himself. Daniel begins by acknowledging that the Bishop's
priestly calling provides him with

> The best munition that may fortifie
> A Noble heart . . .
> Against the batteries of mortality,

but he presumes to offer comfortable words to fortify the Bishop
against 'this close vanquishing, And secret wasting sicknesse' (he
is presumably referring to the jaundice: see the reference to 'yellow
hue' at l. 56) because he is a fellow sufferer and may offer consolations drawn from experience:

> . . . my selfe have struggled with it too,
> And know the worst of all that it can do.

Chief among these consolations is the fact that, unlike some other
fatal illnesses, this sickness steals gradually upon its victim leaving
him time to reconcile himself to his suffering and the issue of it:

> This fairely kills, they fowly murther us,
> Trippe up our heeles before we can discerne;
> This gives us time of treaty to discus
> Our suffring, and the cause thereof to learne.

It is a slow illness and there are intermissions lasting sometimes
for months, sometimes for years, and though the body weakens
the faculties remain unimpaired. There is ample time to put one's
affairs in order:

> So that we cannot say we were thrust out,
> But we depart from hence in quiet sort:
> The foe with whom we have the battaile fought,
> Hath not subdu'd us but got our Fort . . .

No 'gentler passage' can be imagined

> Unto that port wherein we shall be free
> From all the stormes of worldly misery

42. Grosart i, pp. 294–6.

SAMUEL DANIEL.

From an original Picture in the Collection of the Right Honorable the Earl of Thanet.

and though the looking-glass offers daily evidence of the withering of the 'fading leafe' this cannot disturb one who has well considered man's mortality and who has, above all

> ... all comforts vertue can beget,
> And most the conscience of well acted dayes.

The attitudes which Daniel proposes here for the Bishop's consideration are eminently characteristic. There are no heroics, no histrionic gestures. He is glad not to be hustled out of life because that would be undignified and he is especially glad that though the body wilts the mind remains unimpaired and 'the use Of Study' can still be enjoyed. He compliments the Bishop on his Christian faith at the beginning but his poem has no religious aura of its own. Daniel respected religion and its claims to reverence – 'Sacred Religion, mother of forme and feare' – but he does not make poetry of religious experience nor even pay conventional service to Christian doctrines. He is essentially a student of the human scene and religion has meaning for him only, it would seem, at the points where it confirms what his experience of the world has taught him: in its preaching of both dignity and humility, the grace of life and the vanity, the necessity of charity and also of self-criticism – it is, in fact, only another name for the wisdom of the ages.[43] Montague has shown great and praiseworthy care in restoring and adding to the buildings of the Church but, Daniel writes:

> ... you have not only built up walls
> But also (worthier edifices) men;
> By whom you shall have the memorialls
> And everlasting honor of the pen
> That whensoever you shall come to make
> Your Exit from this Scene wherein you have
> Perform'd so noble parts, you then shall take
> Your leave with honor, have a glorious grave.

There speaks the humanist, the same when he contemplates death as he has been all his life, concerned with men and with fame and with the honourable playing of a part on the stage of this world.

---

43. Fuller has a curious note: 'Some tax him to smack of the *Old Cask*, as resenting of the *Romish Religion*', and adds very justly, 'but they have a quicker Palate than I, who can make any such discovery'. There is no suggestion of Romanism in Daniel's work.

The language and the rhythms, the whole tone of the poem, are also specially and distinctively Daniel's. It is quiet. It assumes the manner of courteous but not formal address. What is said issues from experience and thought and is uttered with an unostentatious confidence that it is worth saying. Nothing about the poem is exciting. It takes off on no flights of imagination: the experience of sickness is compared to a struggle with an enemy – death is likened to a passage to a haven sheltered from the storms of the world: the images serve him well to express what he wants to say but touch no secret springs in the reader's mind. We are content when we have finished. We have reached a point of sober equilibrium, our emotions balanced by the persuasive rhythm of these discreetly eloquent periods, and for the moment it seems that there is nothing else to say.

Yet sooner or later we may remember another poem on death, also written in 1618:

> Even such is tyme which takes in trust
> Our yowth, our Joyes, and all we have,
> And payes us butt with age and dust:
> Who in the darke and silent grave
> When we have wandred all our wayes
> Shutts up the storye of our dayes.
> And from which earth and grave and dust
> The Lord shall rayse me up I trust.[44]

The things which Daniel does *not* do spring sharply to mind after reading that, but it seems pointless to argue whether such writing as the verses to Bishop Montague is properly poetry at all. The spectre of prose has always been suspected to haunt Daniel's work, but even Coleridge, when he tried to define the prosaic element in his poetry, succeeded merely in restating the point at issue. 'The sense shall be good and weighty, the language correct and dignified, the subject interesting and treated with feeling; and yet the style shall, notwithstanding all these merits, be justly blamable as prosaic, and solely because the words and the order of the words would find their appropriate place in prose, but are not suitable to metrical composition'.[45] One can only

44. Raleigh's poem traditionally supposed to have been written the night before he died. Most of it, in fact, appears to have been composed earlier.
45. *Biographia Literaria* (Everyman), p. 204.

affirm that the lines to the Bishop of Winchester are a kind of poetry, a poetry which, in the sum of all its parts – language, rhythm, metaphor and substance – presents a *persona*, an image of its writer. Skill and sensitivity have gone into the polishing of the diction and the manipulation of the form in order to remove obscurities and eccentricities so that the poem may slip easily into the mind, but it is the image of the writer alone which, if anything is, is capable of touching the imagination. In this as in other ways, the poem appropriately epitomises some essential features of Daniel's poetry as a whole.

VIII

Conclusion

Daniel was an intelligent and thoughtful poet and thought and intelligence reinforced by eloquence and imagination produce some of his finest poetry – for example, the epistles to the Countesses of Cumberland and Bedford. He was also a conscientious artist, a craftsman who laboured his verses seeking always to perfect them according to the best lights he knew and his untiring zeal in revision deserves in many respects the noble and dignified expression he gives it in his address *To the Reader* of 1607,[1] one of the most revealing personal statements in all his work:

> I may pull downe, raise, and reedifie
> It is the building of my life, the fee
> Of Nature, all th'inheritance that I
> Shall leave to those which must come after me . . .

But there is the reverse side of his virtues. Sometimes he allowed the thinking process to absorb him to the exclusion of all else, as in the epistle to Sir Thomas Egerton, and then, though the quality of the thought may be admirable, the verse itself offers scarcely any pleasures. And the passion for revision is not an unqualified good. With some gains there are also losses, as the examination of *Delia*, for example, showed.

Indeed, when one considers Daniel's work as a whole, the unremitting work of correction suggests some general doubts. Diffidence and sensitivity to criticism have been noticeable traits of Daniel's character from *Paulus Jovius* onwards. They reflect, no doubt, an amiable modesty, but is there not also in Daniel a fundamental insecurity, a hesitation, a failure of confidence at a crucial point? Self-criticism and susceptibility to hostile comment become a kind of neurosis, a restless, compulsive urge leaving, as he says, no 'saboath of the minde', an inescapable, irritable activity:

1. Sprague, pp. 3–5.

As if the thing in doing were more deere
Then being done, and nothing likes thats past.

The young man whom N. W. encouraged at Oxford was by nature reluctant to force himself upon the world, and many passages in his career indicate that he met rebuffs and frustrations severe enough to make their mark on a thicker skin than his. The 'building' of his work becomes a refuge, and his incessant care to perfect it becomes a release for frustrated energies and at the same time imposes its own burden of nervous strain.

The consideration of Daniel's hesitations and uncertainties may lead us a long way into his characteristic attitudes. He was, above all, a man incapable of a single view: he saw his subjects from many angles. Sometimes this leads to weakness, a deflated poetry very depressing to the imagination. On the other hand it can issue in a rich reflectiveness. He is aware, always, of the infinite fallibility of men's endeavours, and literature, like other things, owns the universal flaw:

> . . . who so looks
> T'have all thinges in perfection, and in frame
> In mens inventions, never must read books.

Dogmatism is alien to his character because he is so much aware of the vanity of human assertiveness; and because he is aware, too, of the complexity of things, the unwisdom and the uncharity of conclusive judgements:

> . . . For man is a tree
> That hath his fruite late ripe, and it is long
> Before he come t'his taste, there doth belong
> So much t'experience, and so infinite
> The faces of things are, as hardly we
> Discerne which lookes the likest unto right.

Aesthetic pleasure in the composition of verse as decorous as he can make it, his own individuality, and his vivid awareness of the moral issues involved in the subjects he treats, all these are woven together in the characteristic texture of Daniel's poetry. Because the aesthetic pleasure came to be in some sense an escape, he also came to distrust it even while he continued to indulge it:

Authoritie of powerfull censure may
Prejudicate the forme wherein we mould
This matter of our spirite, but if it pay
The eare with substance, we have what wee wold
For that is all which must our credit hold.
The rest (how ever gay, or seeming rich
It be in fashion, wise men will not wey)
The stamp will not allow it, but the touch.

Substance mattered more than form, he asserted again and again in later years. He is, he writes in 1609, 'indifferent to the weapon of utterance . . . so it may make good my mind, I care not'.

Daniel has been accused, together with Greville, of creating a kind of anti-poetry, of 'introducing a philosophy which made poetry futile', and when one considers his insistence on substance, his contempt for 'gay wordes' as 'but the garnish of a nice time', the charge seems to have some validity. But in fact the poetic instinct was deeply rooted in Daniel's nature. The young man who pored over emblem literature and derived so much satisfaction from the symbolism of imprese was not anti-poetic, nor was the young poet of *Delia* and *Rosamond*. He responded to the ancient themes of time and love and beauty with his own music and welcomed the new stimulus of Italy and France, the new possibilities of poetic expression they had made available. The 1592 *Delia* ends with a lyric, graceful, honey-sweet, and melodious, an excellent example of the new poetry whose influence England received late but gladly.[2] Yet of course the embryo scholar is present in the translation of *Paulus Jovius* as well as the potential lyric poet. Deeper notes sound even in the lyric harmonies of *Delia* and the beauties of *Rosamond* contain an unmistakable core of serious moral judgement. Daniel was serious-minded and the thoughtful questioning and the scholarly scepticism implicit in his character were reinforced by troubles and insecurity in his personal fortunes. He came under the influence of the strongly Puritan household at Wilton and he became the friend of the Calvinist Greville. Under the Pembroke influence he wrote *Cleopatra* and with that the first and decisive stage of his literary development was complete. A thoughtful and deeply serious intelligence had been brought fully into play in his poetry and from then on it is a matter of deeper and wider exploration of the vein of mature reflectiveness. Yet

2. Ibid., p. 36.

though his early lyricism was disturbed and troubled, the lyric poet in him was not dead. He continued to write lyrics up to the time of *Hymens Triumph* and once or twice he managed to combine lyric form with the high seriousness which is so distinguishing a note of his mature verse. An outstanding example is *Ulisses ana the Syren* (1605),[3] one of his treatments of the relative claims of the active and the non-active life, which presents a beautifully controlled and supple lyric surface beneath which subtle thoughts and fine shades of meaning move and interweave.

In his earlier life Daniel shared the Elizabethan interests in pageantry, in poetry, and in patriotism. The Pembroke influence matured him as a poet and roused him to exert his intellect more fully in his poetry, and in so doing and in causing him to dig more deeply into himself, it brought into prominence ideas only partly realised before. Behind great names and great shows are thinking and feeling human beings and behind kings and nobles are the common people, their fortunes bound up with the lives and conduct of the great; behind poetry is life with its moral problems, its difficulty and complexity; behind patriotism is the truth of history – to glorify one's native land may not be a simple project but one must come to think of universal human nature, not of an age or a dynasty. The more elements in a situation he perceives the greater a truly great poet becomes: a man with a more fragile talent may find himself sorely tried by the many-sidedness of truth. Daniel is not a great enough poet to make a new synthesis. He could record, but not create. He allowed too much for the critical intelligence and generated too little imaginative impetus. The research he undertook for *The Civil Wars* destroyed his faith in poetic myths and his studies of human nature in his surroundings and in books undercut conventional belief in progress and qualified his enthusiasm for ideas and achievements. As his experience widened and his intellect deepened he moved inevitably from poetry to history but yet not without many backward glances and never completely surrendering his poet's art. In the last analysis it is his gift of language and also and especially the range and the

---

3. Sprague, pp. 161–3. This is the poem of which Housman wrote: 'Diction and movement alike, it is perfect. It is made out of the most ordinary words, yet it is pure from the least alloy of prose; and however much nearer heaven the art of poetry may have mounted, it has never flown on a surer or a lighter wing." (A. E. Housman *The Name and Nature of Poetry*, Cambridge University Press, 1933, pp. 10–11).

intelligence of his sensitivity and responsiveness, the very fact of the ambivalence of his attitudes which make him 'something' among poets, 'though', as he well knew, 'not the best'. The duality of his apprehensions goes without false simplification into his work, the faith in poetry and the doubt, the love of England and the historian's scepticism, the love of beauty and the distrust for the outside of things. Though he is unable, except occasionally, to create a new vision, he gives us the image of himself, humane, intelligent, thoughtful, sympathetic, and the poetry composed in this image, as he hoped and expected, is certainly 'Worthy the reading, and the worlds delight'.

Select Bibliography

1 *Works of Samuel Daniel*

Sellers, H. 'A Bibliography of the Works of Samuel Daniel', *Oxford Bibliographical Society Proceedings and Papers*, 2, 1927–30, pp. 29–54.

Tannenbaum, S. A. *A Concise Bibliography*, New York, 1942.

(For editions used in this book, see p. xi.)

2 *Biography*

Aubrey, J. *Brief Lives*, ed. A. Clark, Oxford, 1898.

Biographica Britannica, 1750

Birch, T. compiler *The Court and Times of James I*, London, 1848.

Bloxam, J. R. *Register of the Members of Magdalen College, Oxford*, iv, Oxford, 1853–85.

Brettle, R. E. 'Samuel Daniel and the Children of the Queen's Revels, 1604–5', *R.E.S.* 3, 1927, pp. 162–8.

Calendar of State Papers (Dom.) James I, 1603–10, 1611–18, 1619–23.

Camden, William. *History of England*, ii, ed. Kennet, London, 1719.

Chambers, E. K. *The Elizabethan Stage*, Oxford University Press, 1923.

Chambrun, Longworth. *Giovanni Florio*, Paris, 1921.

Clark, A. ed. *Register of the University of Oxford*, ii, Oxford, 1887–8.

Eccles, Mark. 'Samuel Daniel in France and Italy,' *S.P.* xxxiv, 1937, pp. 148–67.

Foster, J. ed. *Alumni Oxonienses 1500–1714*, Oxford, 1891.

Fuller, T. *History of the Worthies of England*, London, 1662.

Hawkins, John. *History of Music*, ii, London, 1875.

Historical Manuscripts Commission (Hatfield House), part v, and Report for 1888, Rep. II, App. vii.

Hotson, L. 'Marigold of the Poets', *Transactions of the Royal Society of Literature of the U.K.*, n.s. XVII, 1938, pp. 47–68.

Law, E. Introduction to *The Vision of the Twelve Goddesses*, London, 1880.

Naunton, R. *Fragmenta Regalia*, Arber's English Reprints, London, 1870.

Nichols, J. *The Progresses of James I*, ii, London, 1828.

Pevsner, N. *The Buildings of England: Somerset*, Penguin Books, 1951.

Public Record Office. *The President of the Funerall of ye late Soveraigne Lady Queene Anne*, P.R.O., L.C., 2. 5.

Rees, Joan. 'Samuel Daniel and the Earl of Hertford,' *N.Q.*, Sept. 1958, p. 408.

Seronsy, C. C. 'Daniel's *Panegyrike* and the Earl of Hertford', *P.Q.* XXXII, 1953, pp. 342–4.

Whitaker, T. D. *The Histories and Antiquities of the Deanery of Craven*, Leeds and London, 1878.

Williamson, G. C. *Lady Anne Clifford*, Kendal, 1922.

Winwood, R. *Memorials of Affairs of State in the Reigns of Queen Elizabeth and King James I*, ed. Sawyer, London, 1725.

à Wood A. *Athenae Oxonienses*, ii, London, 1815.

Wotton, H. *Reliquiae Wottonianae*, London, 1672.

Yates, Frances A. *John Florio*, Cambridge University Press, 1934.

3 *Criticism*

Anon. Review in *Times Literary Supplement*, 5.6.30.

Bald, R. C. Letter in *Times Literary Supplement*, 20.11.24.

Ball, L. F. 'The Background of the minor English Renaissance Epics', *E.L.H.*, I, 1934, pp. 63–89.

Blissett, W. 'Samuel Daniel's Sense of the Past', *E.S.* XXXVIII, 1957, pp. 49–63.

Brotanek, R. *Die englischen Maskenspiele*, Wien und Leipzig, 1902.

Bush, D. *Mythology and the Renaissance Tradition*, Minneapolis, 1932.

Charlton, H. B. and Kastner, L. E. eds. *The Works of Sir William Alexander*, Edinburgh and London, 1921.

Coleridge, S. T. *Biographia Literaria*, Everyman, 1906.
   Literary Remains, ii, ed. H. N. Coleridge, London, 1836–9.

Dobrée, Bonamy. *Restoration Tragedy* 1660–1720, Clarendon Press, 1929.

Evans, H. A. *English Masques*, London, 1897.

Freeman, Rosemary. *English Emblem Books*, London, 1948.

Gottfried, R. B. 'Samuel Daniel's Method of Writing History', *Studies in the Renaissance*, III, 1956, pp. 157–74.
   'The Authorship of *A Breviary of the History of England*', *S.P.* 53, 1956, pp. 172–90.

Greg, W. W. *Pastoral Poetry and Pastoral Drama*, London, 1906.
   '*Hymens Triumph* and the Drummond MS.', *M.L.Q.* VI, 1903, pp. 59–64.

Housman, A. E. *The Name and Nature of Poetry*, Cambridge University Press, 1933.

Jeffery, V. M. 'Italian and English Pastoral Drama of the Renaissance, III Sources of Daniel's *Queen's Arcadia* and Randolph's *Amyntas*', *M.L.R.* 19, 1924, pp. 435–44.

Kastner, L. E. See Charlton, H. B.

Law, R. A. 'Daniel's *Rosamond* and Shakespeare', *University of Texas Studies in English*, XXVI, 1947, pp. 42–8.

Lever, J. W. *The Elizabethan Love Sonnet*, London, 1956.

Lewis, C. S. *English Literature in the 16th Century (excluding drama)*, Clarendon Press, 1954.

McKisack, May. 'Samuel Daniel as Historian', *R.E.S.* 23, 1947, pp. 226–43.

McManaway, J. G. 'Some Bibliographical Notes on Samuel Daniel's *Civil Wars*', *Studies in Bibliography*, IV, 1951, pp. 31–9.

Michel, L. and Seronsy, C. C. 'Shakespeare's History Plays and Daniel: an assessment,' *S.P.* 52, 1955, pp. 549–77.

Miller, E. H. 'Samuel Daniel's Revisions in *Delia*', *J.E.G.P.* 53, 1954, pp. 58–68.

Norman, A. M. Z. 'Daniel's *The Tragedie of Cleopatra* and *Antony and Cleopatra*', *S.Q.*, IX, 1958, pp. 11–18.
'*The Tragedie of Cleopatra* and the Date of *Antony and Cleopatra*', *M.L.R.*, LIV, 1959, pp. 1–9.

Praz, M. *Studies in Seventeenth Century Imagery*, London, 1939.

Redgrave, G. R. 'Daniel and the Emblem Literature', *Transactions of the Bibliographical Society*, XI, 1909–11, pp. 39–58.

Rees, Joan. 'Samuel Daniel's *Cleopatra* and Two French Plays', *M.L.R.* XLVII, 1952, pp. 1–10.
'Wordsworth and Samuel Daniel', *N. Q.* Jan. 1959, pp. 26–7.
'Shakespeare's Use of Daniel', *M.L.R.*, LV, 1960, pp. 79–82.
'An Eye-Witness Account of *Antony and Cleopatra?*' *Shakespeare Survey*, VI, 1953, pp. 91–3.
Letter in *R.E.S.*, 9, 1958, pp. 294–5.

Rollins, H. ed. *Poems* and *Sonnets* in the *Variorum Shakespeare*, Philadelphia and London, 1938 and 1944.

Schaar, C. *An Elizabethan Sonnet Problem*, Lund, 1960.

Schanzer, E. 'Daniel's Revision of his *Cleopatra*', *R.E.S.*, 7–8, 1956–7, pp. 375–81.

Schütze, J. 'Daniels *Cleopatra* und Shakespeare', *Englische Studien*, 71, 1936–7, pp. 58–72.

Scott, Janet. G. *Les Sonnets élisabethains*, Paris, 1929.

Sellers, H. 'Samuel Daniel: Additions to the Text', *M.L.R.*, XI, 1916, pp. 28–32.

Seronsy, C. C. 'Wordsworth's Annotations in Daniel's *Poetical Works*', *M.L.N.*, 1953, pp. 403–6.
'Daniel's Manuscript *Civil Wars* with some previously unpublished stanzas', *J.E.G.P.*, LII, 1953, pp. 153–60.
'The Doctrine of Cyclical Recurrence and some related Ideas in the Works of Samuel Daniel', *S.P.* 54, 1957, pp. 387–407.

'Well-languaged Daniel: a reconsideration', *M.L.R.*, LII, 1957, pp. 481–97.

See also Michel, L.

Shackford, Martha H. 'Samuel Daniel's Poetical *Epistles*, especially that to the Countess of Cumberland', *S.P.*, 45, 1948, pp. 180–95.

Sullivan, Mary. *Court Masques of James I* (New York and London, 1913).

Tillyard, E. M. W. *Shakespeare's History Plays*, London, 1944.

 The English Epic and its Background, London, 1954.

Welsford, Enid. *The Court Masque*, Cambridge University Press, 1927.

Wilkes, G. A. "Daniel's *Philotas* and the Essex Case", *M.L.Q.* XXIII, Sept. 1962, pp. 233–42.

Wilson, J. D. ed. *Richard II*, Cambridge University Press, 1939.

Witherspoon, A. M. *The Influence of Robert Garnier on Elizabethan Drama*, Yale University Press, 1924.

4 Literary Background

Bacon, F. *Of the Advancement of Learning*, Oxford University Press, 1906.

Brandon, S. *The Tragicomoedye of the Vertuous Octavia*, Malone Society Reprints, 1909.

Campbell, L. B. ed. *The Mirror for Magistrates*, Cambridge University Press, 1938.

 Parts added to The Mirror for Magistrates, Cambridge University Press, 1946.

Campion, T. *Observations in the Art of English Poesie*, in *Elizabethan Critical Essays*, ed. G. Smith, Oxford, 1904.

Churchyard, T. *The Tragedie of Shore's Wife Much augmented with divers new Additions*, Collier's Reprints, Green Series, ii, London, 1866.

Desportes, P. *Oeuvres*, ed. Michiels, Paris, 1858.

Drayton, M. *Works*, ed. Hebel, Tillotson and Newdigate, Oxford, 1931–41.

Du Bellay, J. *Oeuvres poètiques*, ed. Chamard, Paris, 1908–31.

Florio, J. *First Fruits*, ed. A. del Re, Japan, 1936.

Garnier, R. *Oeuvres complètes*, ed. Pinvert, Paris, 1923.

Giovio, Paolo. *Dialogo dell'Imprese Militari et Amorose*.

Greville, F. *Poems and Dramas*, ed. Bullough, Edinburgh and London, 1938.

 Life of Sir Philip Sidney, ed. Nowell Smith, Oxford, 1907.

Groto, Luigi. *Il Pentimento Amoroso*.

Guarini, B. *Il Pastor Fido*.

Herbert, Mary, Countess of Pembroke. *Antonie*, ed. Luce, Weimar, 1897, *Litterarhistorische Forschungen*, III.

Jodelle, E. *Cléopâtre Captive*, ed. Ellis, Philadelphia, 1946.

SELECT BIBLIOGRAPHY

Jonson, Ben. *Works*, ed. Herford and Simpson, Oxford, 1925–52.
Kyd, T. *Works*, ed. Boas, Oxford, 1901.
Petrarca, F. *Rime*.
Plutarch, *Lives*, trans. North, London, 1896.
Raleigh, Sir Walter. *Poems*.
Sackville, T. and Norton, T. *Gorboduc*.
Shakespeare, W. *Poems*   *Henry IV*
                Sonnets   *Henry V*
                Romeo and Juliet   *Julius Caesar*
                Richard II   *Antony and Cleopatra*
Sidney, P. *An Apologie for Poetry*.
  The Poems, ed. W. A. Ringler, Clarendon Press, 1962.
Spenser, E. *Poetical Works*.
Tasso, T. *Amyntas*.
Three Parnassus Plays, 1598–1601, ed. Leishman, London, 1949.

Index